The Good Language Learner

MODERN LANGUAGES in PRACTICE

Series Editor
Michael Grenfell, *School of Education, University of Southampton*

Editorial Board
Do Coyle, *School of Education, University of Nottingham*
Simon Green, *Trinity & All Saints College, Leeds*

Editorial Consultant
Christopher Brumfit, *Centre for Language in Education, University of Southampton*

Other Books in the Series
Inspiring Innovations in Language Teaching
    JUDITH HAMILTON
Le ou La? The Gender of French Nouns
    MARIE SURRIDGE
Validation in Language Testing
    A. CUMMING and R. BERWICK (eds)

Other Books of Interest
The Age Factor in Second Language Acquistion
    D. SINGLETON and Z. LENGYEL (eds)
Approaches to Second Language Acquisition
    R. TOWELL and R. HAWKINS
Distance Education for Language Teachers
    RON HOWARD and IAN McGRATH (eds)
Foundations of Bilingual Education and Bilingualism
    COLIN BAKER
French for Communication 1979-1990
    ROY DUNNING
The Guided Construction of Knowledge
    NEIL MERCER
A Parents' and Teachers' Guide to Bilingualism
    COLIN BAKER
Quantifying Language
    PHIL SCHOLFIELD
Reflections on Language Learning
    L. BARBARA and M. SCOTT (eds)
Second Language Practice
    GEORGES DUQUETTE (ed.)
Teaching-and-Learning Language-and-Culture
    MICHAEL BYRAM, CAROL MORGAN and colleagues

Please contact us for the latest book information:
Multilingual Matters Ltd, Frankfurt Lodge, Clevedon Hall,
Victoria Road, Clevedon, Avon, England BS21 7SJ

MODERN LANGUAGES IN PRACTICE 4
Series Editor: Michael Grenfell

The Good Language Learner

N. Naiman, M. Fröhlich, H.H. Stern and A. Todesco

Foreword by Christopher Brumfit

96- 642

MULTILINGUAL MATTERS LTD
Clevedon • Philadelphia • Adelaide

Library of Congress Cataloging in Publication Data

The Good Language Learner/N. Naiman *et al.*; Foreword by Christopher Brumfit.
Modern Languages in Practice: 4.
Originally published: Toronto: Ontario Institute for Studies in Education, 1978
(Research in Education Series No. 7). With new Foreword.
Includes bibliographical references.
1. Language and languages–Study and teaching. I. Naiman, N. II. Series.
P51.G65   1995
418'007–dc20   95-25384

British Library Cataloguing in Publication Data

A CIP catalogue record for this book is available from the British Library.

ISBN 1-85359-313-3 (pbk)

Multilingual Matters Ltd

UK: Frankfurt Lodge, Clevedon Hall, Victoria Road, Clevedon, Avon BS21 7SJ.
USA: 1900 Frost Road, Suite 101, Bristol, PA 19007, USA.
Australia: P.O. Box 6025, 83 Gilles Street, Adelaide, SA 5000, Australia.

Typeset by Wayside Books, Clevedon.
Printed and bound in Great Britain by WBC Book Manufacturers Ltd.

Contents

Introduction to the New Edition

The *Modern Languages in Practice* series attempts to offer a range of useful books to cater for all types of serious interest in modern language teaching. One way of realising this intention will be to offer from time to time reprints of classic and significant studies that are directly relevant to foreign language classroom practice. The first of these is the Canadian study of *The Good Language Learner*, first published in 1978, but still of great relevance.

The 1970s saw a substantially increased interest in the behaviour of language learners, and in the language they produce. This was partly the result of work in language development in the mother tongue. Studies throughout the 1960s and 1970s indicated how children acquiring first languages passed through a series of roughly predictable stages as they moved from baby talk to adult-like control of the language system. Second language researchers began to ask, therefore, whether their learners (who were of course older than first language learners) might share the same characteristic. Researchers referred to learners' 'approximate systems' that showed signs of a 'transitional competence' or of 'interlanguage' – the last term, deriving from Larry Selinker's work in 1972, becoming the one that stuck. Essentially, learners were seen as moving from their understanding of their first language through a gradual restructuring of their grammatical system towards that of the target language, making a series of steadily changing systematic errors on the way. And following these hypotheses, Second Language Acquisition (SLA) research developed, particularly in the United States, into a thriving academic field, with its own conferences and journals.

But scientific studies of second language learning can take many shapes. Some researchers felt that too strong a concern for the language system distracted attention from other equally important aspects of the language learning process. They turned to description of classrooms or of teaching processes, to investigations of learner behaviour, or to the attitudes of successful learners, for their explanation of the learning process. In practice, of course, the process of language acquisition is so complex that only an account deriving from all these and many other types of research will enable us to understand language teaching and learning satisfactorily. At the same time, the impact of interlanguage studies had pushed discussion of teaching and learning towards a greater concern for evidence, and away from reliance simply on the 'effective' experience of teachers.

However, while research was moving in this direction and embarking on a long-term project of empirical investigation and theorising, teaching and teacher education had to continue offering the best advice available. Much SLA work remained abstract, or only distantly relevant to the day-to-day practice of foreign language teachers. When rumours began to reach teacher educators of a substantial empirical study that was directly based on the experiences of good language learners, it was not surprising that their ears pricked up. Before long, copies of *The Good Language Learner* were circulating, usually battered and stuck together with sticky tape, clandestinely marked on the pages that people had quoted in their essays and dissertations. But as the years went by, copies became harder and harder to obtain – hence this reprint.

Why was this study so popular? First, because it genuinely attempts to address key problems for teachers: What strategies do successful learners adopt? What attitudes do they show to the language they are learning? What have been their most successful experiences of learning? Second, because it is a modest study that does not attempt to over-sell its results. It acknowledges that it is only a beginning, but for teachers it is a highly relevant beginning. Third, because it is written clearly: even though there are technical sections that are addressed primarily to researchers, most of the book will be directly interesting to any serious and thinking language teacher. Fourth, because the study provides evidence for being cautious about the more extravagant claims being made for versions of communicative language teaching, or of natural, Krashenite methods. Successful language learners, it finds, are often committed to monitoring their own performance quite consciously; they often want to understand the language system. Along with the determination to be active learners and to communicate effectively there co-exist specific accuracy-based strategies which many learners find helpful. And finally, good language learners can cope with the unavoidable stresses of trying to operate in a foreign language. Even though they appear less knowledgeable and intelligent than they feel they are in their first language, they are not completely thrown by feeling foolish, or by the inevitable frustrations of what is always a demanding task.

Thus teachers could come away from this study with some helpful advice on what must be provided:

(a) activities that will help learners to participate fully and enthusiastically;

(b) opportunities for realistic communication whenever possible;
(c) a chance for individuals to self-correct and to respond to feedback on their own performance, so that they are aware that they *can* make mistakes;
(d) a sense of the language system, so that they can generalise usefully and have a sense of language knowledge to refer to;
(e) a supportive and non-threatening environment to help everyone to cope with the task – an environment in which you do not lose face if you struggle and make mistakes with a genuine desire to succeed.

A classroom that offers all these possibilities will probably maximise the options for all learners.

In the years since 1978 there have been a number of further studies of successful language learners. These can be found summarised in greater detail in such books as O'Malley & Chamot (1990) and Ellis (1994). It is probably a fair generalisation that the position outlined above has stood up well to subsequent research. Other researchers have found all the above features important, and the only really significant addition is the view that good language learners are flexible and vary their learning strategies; they are not tied to one particular set of options. This suggests, of course, that teachers should try to offer a wide range of possible approaches to learners – the notion (sometimes argued) that learners each have their own preferred strategies and that these should not be disturbed is pretty non-sensical. Teachers have a responsibility to extend the repertoire of individuals' learning styles, for individuals are not fixed entities. They change, and will want to change their learning approaches according to whether they are tired, or bored, or enthusiastic at the time. There is probably no-one who will lose by trying out all possible techniques, from rote learning to the most humanistic creativity: we will all find all of them helpful in some moods, at some time.

We should note the warning in the conclusion, though. As the authors remark:

The study as a whole suggests that *the* successful or good language learner, with predetermined overall characteristics, does not exist. There are many individual ways of learning a language successfully. The study has shown that some of the existing stereotypes do not apply. For example, some people believe that a good language learner has to be musical, or have a high language aptitude or an exceptionally good memory. The Adult Interview Study indicated that these qualities may not be essential.

This is a study, then, which illustrates well researchers' contributions to the practice of teaching. It is also honest about its successes and failures. Above, all, it enables us to see how less successful learners may benefit from the experience of more successful ones. A major contribution that teachers can make to learning is to convey such understainding into the classroom.

Christopher Brumfit
Centre for Language in Education,
University of Southamption

References

1. Ellis, R. (1994) *The Study of Second Language Acquisition.* Oxford: Oxford University Press.
2. O'Malley, J. and Chamot, A. (1990) *Learning Strategies in Second Language Acquisition.* Cambridge: Cambridge University Press.

The Authors

Neil Naiman is an Associate Professor in the English Department of Glendon College, York University, Toronto, Canada. In addition to research in the area of language learning strategies, Professor Naiman has conducted extensive research, made numerous presentations and written scholarly publications in the areas of bilingual education, second language acquisition, the teaching of pronunciation, second-language writing, learner-centred curriculum and computer-assisted language learning. He has undertaken teacher training at home and abroad. He is currently Director of the English as a Second Language Program at Glendon College, York University.

Maria Fröhlich has been interested in second language learning/teaching and research for many years. She was a research officer at the Ontario Institute for Studies in Education in Toronto for ten years where she was involved in several classroom-centred research studies. During the past eleven years she has been teaching German for general and special purposes at secondary and adult level and has given courses on second language acquisition at the TESL Centre at Concordia University/Montreal.

H. H. Stern was the head of the Modern Language Centre at the Ontario Institute for Studies in Education from 1968–1981. He directed the National Core-French Study and authored hundreds of articles and several major books in the field of second language teaching. He continued as Professor Emeritus in the Curriculum Department of the Ontario Institute for Studies in Education until his death in 1987.

Angie Todesco is a testing and evaluation expert with Language Training Canada, the centre of expertise for language training for the Federal Government of Canada. She oversees the design and development of achievement, placement and proficiency tests for Federal public servants who are being trained in their second official language. In addition, she designs and develops evaluation tools for the assessment of student satisfaction with courses.

Preface to the First Edition

What makes good language learners tick? What do they do that poor learners don't do? Could we help the poor learners by teaching them some of the good learners' tricks? To forestall disappointment, let it be said at the beginning that this study does not provide definite answers to these very legitimate questions. Nevertheless, we believe it has been worth undertaking. The nature of second language learning is extremely complex and a great deal of research is needed to improve our understanding of it. In spite of much theorizing, very little has been done to study its processes directly and empirically. This study constitutes a beginning.

We set out to discover the strategies of good language learners; they proved hard to identify. But along the way we discovered other things which may help us to understand second language learning processes better. We therefore hope our study will be useful as a basis of further investigation. We also hope our observations will be useful not only to researchers, but also to teachers and to those who make language teaching policy.

A study of this kind is not undertaken with language teaching policy and practice specifically in mind; it focusses on the learner, not the teacher; but we realize that its final justification is its influence on the quality of second language teaching and learning. We urge the reader not to expect immediately applicable results. Language pedagogy needs resolution of some of the more basic issues. This study is a first approach to one such issue, the nature of second language learning.

Certain parts of this study are frankly technical and are intended for readers interested in research on learning and, more specifically, in research on second language learning. But the rest, we hope, will be accessible and useful to teachers, student teachers, teacher trainers, and administrators interested in the topic.

Good language teachers have, of course, an intuitive understanding of language learning. What is lacking is a *systematic* understanding. We hope, therefore, that experienced practitioners and student teachers alike will find these explorations thought-provoking and helpful.

An investigation of this scope is necessarily a joint effort, involving more people than it is possible to mention. The project team has been helped by other staff and students of the Modern Language Centre and of other sections of the Ontario Institute for Studies in Education, where the study was carried out. We are particularly grateful to Merrill Swain, who has contributed many ideas and helpful reactions, to Leslie McLean, for advice on research and research design, and to Christine Currie, who has assisted with bibliographical research, review of the literature, and parts of some chapters.

The project is indebted to the Ontario Modern Language Teachers' Association for its active interest in the study and its help in the distribution of a questionnaire among its members.

We are grateful to Dr R. C. Gardner and the Language Research Group at the University of Western Ontario for permission to use the National Attitude Battery and for help with scoring. Members of this group have also made helpful comments on the prepublication version of this study.

We are also grateful to the school boards, teachers, students, and adult interviewees involved for their help, patience, and goodwill; without them this project would not have been possible. According to our agreement with each of the participants they must remain anonymous, but we want them to know how much we appreciate their help.

Above all, our thanks are extended to the Department of the Secretary of State for the financial support which made this study possible. Members of the staff of the Language Programs Branch of the Department of the Secretary of State have given the project moral support by their personal interest in the substance of this project.

December 1976

PART I
Introduction

All forms of language teaching could be greatly improved if we had a better understanding of the language learner and of the language learning process itself. What is happening to learners in language classes? Why is it that some are successful and others fail?

Some years ago, J. B. Carroll, the American psychologist and psycholinguist, suggested that biographies of individuals speaking more than one language might contain clues to the conditions of successful language acquisition (Carroll, 1967). From such suggestions the idea of studying good language learners gradually developed among us in the early seventies. The research described here was carried out in 1974 and 1975.

The Study of the L2 Learner and L2 Learning[1]

Interest in the learner and learning as such is not new. Teaching implies a theory of both. But one of the weaknesses of language learning theory in the past has been the paucity of any direct investigation. Instead, theorists interpreted second language learning in terms of general learning theory without verifying whether, or to what extent, this theory really applied. In the late sixties, it became increasingly clear that a more direct understanding of the language learner and learning process was needed to improve teaching methods. Considerable work has been done in the last few years, as a number of recent writings (e.g. Jakobovits, 1970; Oller and Richards, 1973; Brown, 1976) and issues of such publications as *ACTFL Annual Review, Language Learning, TESOL Quarterly,* and *Working Papers on Bilingualism* will quickly confirm.

Concepts of language learning
A brief résumé of some of the main concepts in language learning may be helpful. Following Gardner (1975), Hatch and Wagner-Gough (1976), and Schumann (1976), six principal concepts can be identified:

(1) Context
(2) Learner
(3) L2 Teaching

1

(4) L2 Environment
(5) Learning
(6) Outcome

Figure 1 illustrates these six concepts in relation to one another. Investigators are interested in establishing the important variables within each, and their relationships to one another and eventually to the learning outcome. We shall discuss these concepts in reverse order.

Learning outcome

If the ultimate objective is better language teaching, our main concern must be the learning outcome. The problem which everyone interested in these questions faces – whether teacher, student, parent, administrator or researcher – is inadequate knowledge and frequent failure after years of language study. Success in language learning is not the rule. Moreover, failure is accompanied by dissatisfaction, awareness of one's own inadequacy, and sometimes annoyance, disappointment, frustration, and even anger at the colossal waste of time. These feelings may then spill over into negative attitudes to the L2 and its speakers.

Teaching and learning aim at what Figure 1 calls 'L2 competence', or 'L2 proficiency'. This ranges, among different learners at different stages of learning, from zero to native-like fluency. Complete competence is hardly ever reached, and its widely acknowledged among teachers and theorists that in most cases it is wasteful and perhaps even undesirable to attempt it. Nevertheless, it forms an ideal goal to work towards. Native-like proficiency can be defined in terms of four characteristics:

(1) the intuitive mastery of the forms of a language
(2) the intuitive mastery of the linguistic, cognitive, affective and socio-cultural meanings expressed by the language forms
(3) the capacity to use the language with maximum attention to meaning and minimum attention to form
(4) creativity of language use

The stages between zero and native-like competence which present the learner with a 'massive learning problem' (Stern, 1975: 307) have been referred to as language systems in their own right, or 'interlanguages' (Selinker, 1972). Such interlanguages must be constantly revised, or else the learner is arrested at a low level of language command. Each interlanguage has its characteristic error patterns, 'fossilizations' and other features. Because they give clues to how different people tackle language learning, they deserve careful investigation. Much of the research done hitherto has focussed on the analysis of errors and on interlanguage (Corder, 1967; Selinker, 1972; Richards, 1974; Brown 1976). (An error analysis is included in Part III, Chapter 4.)

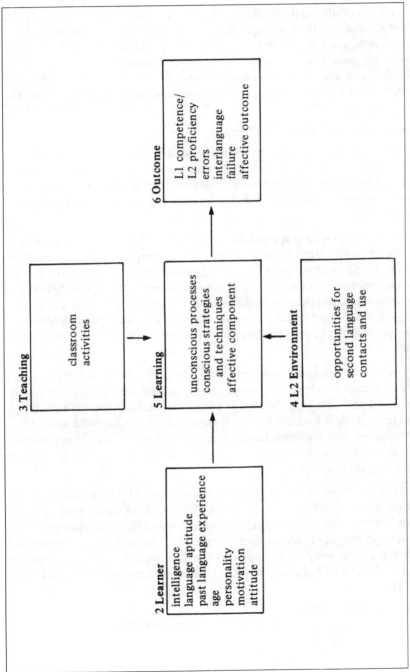

Figure 1 Model of the second language learner and language learning

However, the major focus here is on the analysis of some characteristics of the learner and the learning behavior. *The study set out from the fact that some learners are more successful than others. The question was therefore raised: do good learners tackle the language learning task diferently from poor learners, and do learners have certain characteristics which predispose them to good or poor learning?* In other words, what can be learned from the good language learner?

Learning behavior (Box 5 in Figure 1)

We began this investigation by focussing, first of all, on 'learning strategies' and learning techniques'. Although there is obviously more to language learning than learners consciously recognize, their insights were considered a useful starting point for identifying the conscious strategies and techniques they employ.

Investigators have applied the concept of strategy in various ways (e.g. Jakobovits, 1970; Reibel, 1971; Selinker, 1972; Sampson and Richards, 1973; Rubin, 1975). We have used Stern's definition (1974). Stern has argued that the beginner faces three major problems. The first is 'the disparity between the inevitable and deep-seated presence of the first language (and other languages previously learned) as a reference system and the inadequate . . . development of the new language as a new reference system' (Stern; 1975: 310).

Second is the 'code-communication dilemma'. The learner has to find a way of dealing with both the linguistic forms and the message to be conveyed. The third problem is the 'choice between rational and intuitive learning'. The learner must find the more advantageous. In coping with these three problems, certain *strategies,* i.e. general, more or less deliberate approaches, and more specific *techniques,* i.e. observable forms of language learning behavior, are employed.

On the basis of these considerations Stern (1975) has drawn up a list of 10 strategies of good learners, derived from three main sources: Stern's interpretation of language competence and the three main problems of second language acquisition referred to above; his experience as a teacher and learner; his reading of the literature of language learning (e.g. Nida, 1957; Gudschinsky, 1967; Larson and Smalley, 1972; and Rubin, 1975):

(1) **Planning Strategy**
    A personal learning style or positive learning strategy.
(2) **Active Strategy**
    An active approach to the learning task.

(3) **Empathic Strategy**
   A tolerant and outcoging approach to the target language and its speakers.
(4) **Formal Strategy**
   Technical know-how of how to tackle a language.
(5) **Experimental Strategy**
   A methodical but flexible approach, developing the new language into an ordered system and constantly revising it.
(6) **Semantic Strategy**
   Constant searching for meaning.
(7) **Practice Strategy**
   Willingness to practise.
(8) **Communication Strategy**
   Willingness to use the language in real communication.
(9) **Monitoring Strategy**
   Self-monitoring and critical sensitivity to language use.
(10) **Internalization Strategy**
   Developing L2 more and more as a separate reference system and learning to think in it.

Stern has described this list as 'highly speculative' and in need of confirmation, modification, or rebuttal.

Among other researchers, Rubin (1975) has emphasized the need for such research and the obvious benefits to be reaped from it. However, her definition of strategy is slightly different from Stern's. She does not make the distinction between general strategies and specific techniques, but defines strategies as 'the techniques or devices which a learner may use to acquire knowledge' (Rubin, 1975: 43). Rubin also suggests a list of several strategies, compiled after observing students in classrooms, talking to good language learners and second language teachers, and taking note of her own behavior (see Appendix I). In order to define her list of strategies more precisely, Rubin has been undertaking a study in which second language learners are asked to report their language learning experiences every day. Rubin's ongoing studies, therefore, should lend themselves well to a comparison with the studies to be reported here.

For any degree of mastery of a language, the learner must go through certain mental processes besides the conscious strategies and techniques. These are the 'intake' of new language items, to use Corder's phrase, and acts of perceiving, analysing, classifying, relating, storing, retrieving, and constructing a language output. Such a psycholinguistic analysis of second language learning is needed, but to our knowledge has hardly begun. The present investigation does not claim to study these mental processes systematically.

The learning environment: teaching

Other factors besides strategies and mental processes are important. The first to consider (Box 3) is the input received from the teacher and the class-room. Needless to say, not all language learning occurs in classrooms, but since classroom language learning is in particular need of improvement, our main study concentrates on it, specifically on French classes at grades 8, 10 and 12.

Schools as learning environments are not all alike; some are 'open' and 'free', others are more 'traditional' and 'structured'. Teachers have different goals and use different techniques and materials. If the effect of the environment on the learning process is to be interpreted, the characteristics peculiar to each class will have to be identified.

A classroom shared by good and poor learners alike does not constitute the same learning environment for both. The observer must ask what kind of interaction occurs between teacher and good student, and teacher and poor student. How do different students perceive the goals of classroom instruction, and how do they react to classroom activities? Despite our major focus on the learner and learning, in this study we had to examine some aspects of teaching and also the interaction of teacher and learner.

L2 environment (Box 4)

When Anglophone students in an Anglophone Canadian school study French, the conditions of learning are different for them than for, say, immigrants to Anglophone Canada who attend an English class. For the latter, the class is only one input to language learning in an English-speaking environment. The former must travel to a Francophone environment or deliberately seek Francophone contacts to supplement classroom learning.

In class the learner is usually taught the language as a code: it is the forms of the language that are learned. In the L2 environment the learner communicates with native speakers in a natural context: the language is learned by functional use. It is of great importance to find out to what extent good learners benefit in the long run from the informal or free learning in the L2 environment, in which language use is functional, and to what extent they benefit from formal classroom learning. Some recent studies (e.g. Reibel, 1971; Macnamara, 1973) have questioned the value of formal instruction, because it is 'non-functional'.[2]

The learner (Box 2)

Most language teachers and indeed most language learners are no doubt aware that a student's personal characteristics have a bearing on how and what he learns. Thus, a student may comment on her own lack of a 'gift for languages' or on his own good or bad memory. Certain variables have been the subject of earlier investigations. The student's sex (Burstall *et al.*, 1974), age (e.g. Burstall *et al.*, 1974; Stern and Weinrib, 1977), educational background, and previous language learning experience are all important factors.

Among cognitive characteristics, language learning aptitude was studied by Carroll in the fifies. Two aptitude tests, one for adults, the Modern Language Aptitude Test (Carroll and Sapon, 1959) and the other for children, the Elementary Modern Language Aptitude Test (Carroll and Sapon, 1967) and a similar test at the high school level by Pimsleur, the Language Aptitude Battery (1966), were the result. But beyond general verbal intelligence and language aptitude, it is believed that the learner approaches any learning task with his own individual cognitive or learning style. At the same time, it is often argued that certain personality characteristics, such as empathy, or extroversion–introversion, could affect learning strategies and outcomes. Teachers are often urged to adjust their teaching methods to differences in the learning styles and personality characteristics of their students, yet we hardly know what these differences are or the extent of their influence.

The factors of attitude and motivation have been investigated more thoroughly. Gardner and Lambert (1972) demonstrated their influence in a prolonged series of studies begun in the fifties at McGill University. Gardner has continued these investigations with his language research group at the University of Western Ontario, where he developed the National Attitude Battery, used in the present study. While Gardner in his earlier work paid particular attention to the attitudes and motives that the learner brings to the learning task, more recently he, as well as other investigators (e.g. Burstall *et al.*, 1974; Brown, 1973; and Schumann, 1975) has recognized other affective variables, and acknowledged that the learning process itself can change attitudes.

Context (e.g. Box 1)

Teachers and observers of language teaching know intuitively that the social, political, and linguistic context of teaching and learning has a major influence on the learner, particularly on his attitudes and motivations. Most teachers, for example, know the value to their classes of parental support. Canadian teachers of French or English as a second language know how much their students' attitudes are influenced by political attitudes in the community. The British Pilot Scheme for the teaching of French in primary schools (Burstall *et al.*, 1974) has offered several examples of such environmental influences: children from higher socio-economic backgrounds consistently reached higher levels of proficiency; children in the south of England – nearer to France, with more opportunities to visit – did better than children in the more distant north; children in schools in which the principal believed in the teaching of French reached a higher level than children in schools with an unsupporting principal. In the present study we are aware of these contextual factors, although they have not been the suject of detailed and separate inquiry.

Conclusion

To sum up, in this study we have adopted a certain model of language learning. This model is intended to make explicit the interaction of various concepts and of variables within them that may be assumed to contribute to the successful learning of a language or that might account for the failure to learn. As Figure 1 indicated, learners find themselves in a certain socio-linguistic *context*. The *learner characteristics* that are likely to affect language learning, besides age and previous language learning experience, include (a) cognitive factors, such as intelligence and language aptitude, (b) personality factors and cognitive style, and (c) attitudes and motivation. The learning process is stimulated either deliberately by formal *teaching* in a language class or naturally by the informal *L2 environment* and sometimes by both. The *learning process* consists of consciously employed strategies and techniques, and unconscious mental processes. These lead to a *learning outcome,* a certain level of proficiency, or a characteristic language competence or interlanguage. The main question is, what can best promote a high level of proficiency in an L2, or conversely, how can learning inadequacy or failure be prevent?

The principal concerns of the present study are two aspects that have hitherto not been studied and that may well be considered significant: (1) the strategies and techniques the learner consciously develops and employs, and (2) certain learner characteristics, in particular personality and cognitive style factors, which are likely to influence the use of strategies and techniques and thereby, indirectly, learning outcome. If we can identify differences in both among good and poor learners, we might at a later stage try to help learners with learning difficulties to develop ways of overcoming these difficulties, in other words, to teach learners how to learn.

The present inquiry was undertaken in two stages; they will be discussed in turn in the following chapters. The first stage was the Adult Interview Study and the second the Main Classroom Study.

Notes

1. The term 'L2' will be used as equivalent to 'foreign language', 'target language' or 'second language'. The term 'L1' is used to designate 'first language', 'native language' or 'language of origin'.
2. For a brief discussion of these issues see Stern *et al.,* 1976.

PART II
The Adult Interview Study

1. Introduction

As indicated in Part I, few attempts have hitherto been made to identify characteristics, strategies, and techniques of successful language learners through actual observation or interview (cf. Rubin, 1975; Stern, 1975; Wesche, 1975).

In this part of the study the aim was to interview good and poor language learners in detail. It was hoped that these interviews would provide necessary information about successful and unsuccessful language learning and confirm, modify, or disprove existing hypotheses and hunches about language learning, including such strategy inventories as had been proposed by Rubin and Stern.

2. Description of Instrument

An interview questionnaire was devised, consisting of a semi-directed and a directed part (see Appendix 2). In the first part, the interviewee was asked to describe his second language learning experiences, including the kind or number of languages learned or attempted, the age at which the learning took place, the educational and socio-cultural context in which the language was acquired and the strategies or techniques used or developed.

In the second, more directed part of the interview the interviewee was asked to put himself into a hypothetical language learning situation, in the hope that his response would be determined by a combination of previous experiences and insights and present views and intuitions about language learning. The two parts overlapped to a certain extent, since some interviewees in reflecting on their language learning experiences (Part I) offered information which was specifically asked for in Part II.

3. Method

3.1 Subjects

Thirty-four interviewees were selected, personal acquaintances of the interviewers or recommended to them as highly proficient. No attempt was made to select subjects systematically from a given population, and no proficiency tests were administered. Instead, in the course of the interview subjects were presented with a chart (Table 1) describing various proficiency levels and asked to rate their second language competence accordingly.

9

Table 1 Proficiency levels

	Elementary proficiency	Working knowledge	Advanced (native-like Knowledge
Understanding	I can make essential sound discriminations; understand simple statements & questions on topics very familiar to me (meals, purchases, etc.); I can only understand utterances spoken at a slower rate than normal speech.	I can understand most casual conversations on familiar topics, related to my family, work, daily events, etc. I can get the gist of plays, films, radio, talks, etc.	I am able to follow conversations of native speakers (at normal speed); I can fully understand lectures, professional discussions, radio talks, plays, jokes, different language styles & dialects.
Speaking	I can mimic most of the essential sounds characteristic of the language with fair accuracy; I can express elementary needs, e.g., order a meal, ask for directions; I make many errors but I am understood by native speakers who are used to dealing with foreign language speakers.	I can express myself on matters of concern to me with sufficient fluency and accuracy. To be understood by native speakers I may use circumlocutions; I can talk about daily events, my work, family, hobbies, etc.	I have a broad vocabulary; make few grammatical errors; I can participate in *any* conversation or discussion with high degree of fluency approximating native accent; I can express myself in different social situations (on different levels – colloquial & educated).

Table 1 Proficiency levels *continued*

	Elementary proficiency	Working knowledge	Advanced (native-like Knowledge)
Reading	I am able to read the script; I can read a simple text aloud correctly; I can read simple directions, common public signs, menus, elementary stories especially constructed for beginners, titles of books and captions, with or without a dictionary.	I can read writings of professional interest, familiar news items, magazine stories, popular modern fiction, e.g., detective stories (with occasional use of dictionary).	I am able to read almost as easily as in native language material of considerable difficulty; literary writings, professional literature; I can read with almost no difficulty research articles and background readings in my field or profession (with occasional reference to dictionary).
Writing	I can write the script and copy simple sentences with ease; can compose simple sentences e.g., as demanded in elementary text-books.	I can write a simple "free" composition, such as a personal letter; can write memos, take messages or notes in my field.	I can write on subjects of concern to myself; e.g., reports on professional matters; I am able to deal with all personal and professional correspondence.

The general background information on the subjects included sex, age, educational level, and occupation. Of the interviewees 59% were male, 41% female. The majority were in the age group 26–35 (68%); 15% were between 19 and 25; the rest were evenly distributed between the two age groups of 36–50 and 51–65. The vast majority were born in English-speaking parts of North America.

All of the interviewees but one had university degrees. Most came from our immediate university circles, from departments such as curriculum, anthropology, linguistics, and modern languages. A few were, or had recently been, high school or post-secondary language teachers.

We had intended to interview a substantial number of unsuccessful learners too, but in the end included only two, both female. For the most part a separate analysis of the information they offered was not necessary. Special reference will be made to them where applicable.

3.2 Procedure

The first step was to send the potential interviewees a letter asking if they would like to assist the project by volunteering for an interview. They were told that their personal language learning experience and their intuitions about second language learning would prove extremely helpful, that the interview involved no testing and that the names of the participants would not be disclosed.

Two research officers conducted the 34 interviews during the period from the end of February to the middle of May 1974. The subjects were interviewed very informally, at a place convenient to them, for one to two hours. With the subjects' permission the interviews were all recorded on tape and later transcribed.

4. Results

4.1 Part I of the interview

The results will be presented separately for each part of the interview. Any given percentages refer to the *total* sample of 34 interviewees unless otherwise indicated.

Questions 2–4[1]

Since an individual's environment, the nuclear family as well as larger social groups, has potential influence on language acquisition, we inquired about the family and neighborhood in which the interviewee grew up.

A total of 79% had a monolingual family background. Only 21% were brought up in bi- or multilingual families. For 76% of the subjects the languages spoken in the family were either totally identical with those spoken in the neighborhood or, if other languages were spoken, the interviewees had only very limited contact with their speakers. In most other cases the subjects' native language was one of many different languages spoken in a multilingual neighborhood.

Questions 5, 8, 9, and 10
We also wanted to know *which* languages the interviewees had learned, the *number* and the *proficiency levels* they had reached (see Table 2) and maintained.

The foreign/second language[2] most frequently mentioned was French (29 times), closely followed by German and Spanish. Eighteen interviewees indicated that they had learned Latin. Among the other languages mentioned were, in descending order of frequency: Italian; English; Russian; Greek; Polish; Hebrew; Japanese; and Swedish. A few subjects had learned a variety of others not commonly taught, such as Cree, Mohawk, Icelandic, Thai, Tagalog, and Arabic. (See, for example, case study three, Chapter 5.)

Before presenting Table 2, some explanatory remarks on the analysis of the data are necessary.

Regarding the *number* of languages learned (see Table 2), it has to be pointed out that the term 'language learning' is applied very generally. It does not necessarily mean, for example, a systematic occupation with a language in a formal school setting; the interviewee may have been exposed to the language and absorbed some aspects of it while travelling or living in the L2 country. Furthermore, the duration of the language learning process was not considered when the table was calculated. Therefore, languages to which the interviewees had only brief exposure were counted as well.

With respect to the question of 'maintenance' or 'retention' of the languages learned, the interviewees were presented with a chart describing the four skills of understanding, speaking, reading, and writing on three levels of proficiency, namely 'Elementary Proficiency', 'Working Knowledge', and 'Advanced or Native-like Knowledge' (see Table 1). (These definitions were adapted from Clark [1972].) The subjects were invited to rate their own proficiency in each of the languages they had contact with. Although we had originally intended to give the interviewees the opportunity to indicate their present level of proficiency, in other words, the maintenance level, as well as to ask them the level they had reached at the time of learning, several inconsistencies occurred in the actual interviews. Unfortunately this inaccuracy

Table 2³ Number of languages learned and number of languages in which a high proficiency level had been reached

No. of languages learned by each S.	● 1	2	2	3	3	3	3	3	●4	4	4	4	4	4	4
No. of languages with high profic. level	0	1	½ (1)	½	1	1	1	2	1	0	1	1	1	1 (1)	1 ½ ½	2

No. of languages learned by each S.	4	5	B 5	5	A 5	5	5	6	7	7	10	11	C 19	32
No. of languages with high profic. level	(1)	3	½	1	½	3	3	3	3	½	4 ½	3 ½ ½ ½ ½	2	4	6

Legend

½ = only two skills were indicated under "working knowledge"

● = the unsuccessful language learner

( ) = language learning was actively in progress at time of interview and a high proficiency level had already been reached

A, B, etc. = letters indicate the subjects whose case studies are presented in detail in section 5.

cannot be remedied now. Table 2 will therefore refer only the the proficiency level reached and not to the maintenance level.

For the purposes of the analysis, an interviewee was considered to have reached a *high proficiency level* in a given language when he reported that he had an 'advanced knowledge' or a 'working knowledge' in at least three of the four skills mentioned. Where only two skills under 'working knowledge' were indicated, a special symbol (½) was introduced. As the subjects were not given any proficiency tests but evaluated their own knowledge in terms of the chart, Table 2 offers the interviewees' self-reported language competence.

The question of whether the subjects' ratings of their proficiency levels were absolutely accurate or not[4] was considered to be of minor significance, since the major purpose of the study was to investigate the conditions under which successful language learning took place and what kind of strategies and techniques were developed and employed to achieve this goal.

Table 2 gives an overall picture of the interviewees' language learning attempts and their success rates. As shown in Table 2, most of the interviewees had learned between three to five languages, 21% had learned three, 29% had learned four, and 21% had learned five. Most of the subjects had reached at least a 'working knowledge' or better in one or two languages.

Question 6

In view of the current discussions about the optimal starting age for second language learning (see Burstall *et al.*, 1974; Stern, 1976), the interviewees were asked when they had started to learn their first foreign language and for how long they had studied it.

The starting ages ranged from seven to 15, the most frequently reported being 12 (32%) and 14 (26%).

These data, however, do not indicate whether the languages started at that age level were learned successfully, i.e. whether at least a 'working knowledge' had been achieved. Of the total number of languages in which a high proficiency level (see Table 2) had been reached, 41% were begun later than the normal high school age level. Starting young may not be essential to success in language learning (see also Burstall *et al.*, 1974).

As length of exposure to a foreign language is thought to be one of the principal variables affecting achievement (e.g. Carroll, 1975: 276f.), we compared the time each subject reported he had spent on the different languages he had learned. These periods ranged from six months or less to more than seven years. After seven years most subjects had achieved high proficiency.

But in quite a number of cases a high proficiency level had been reached in a relatively short time. On the basis of the interviews, then, it can be argued that length of exposure alone does not determine achievement. The factors the interviewees attributed their success to will be reported later.

Question 7

Another influence on achievement in a foreign language appears to be the learning environment, defined as formal or informal. For purposes of analysis, a *formal setting* is a school, or university. A language may have been started at school and continued at university, or begun at university.

Besides the two formal settings, four further environments were distinguished. An *informal non-school situation* refers to immersion[5] into the target language, which in most cases meant being in the L2 country itself. *Independent study*, although formal learning of a kind, differs from the two major settings in that the learner has much more control over what is studied, and for how long. Independent study was frequently combined with learning in an informal situation.

Another possible combination is a *formal setting within an immersion situation,* for example, a course taken in the country of the target language. Finally, some learning took place in formal settings other than those mentioned above, mainly in adult education, such as evening courses at culture institutes representing foreign countries, courses at military academies, classes for civil servants, or private tuition.

Most language learning was initiated in a formal school setting: The majority of the subjects continued studying at least one or two languages at university, and were also exposed to an informal situation at some point in their language learning careers.

An individual might not acquire all his languages in the same sequence of settings. Furthermore, he might 're-visit' previous learning settings. One interviewee interrupted his university studies several times in order to take a language course in the target country.

It is impossible to judge which setting, formal or informal, produced greater achievement. There is some evidence in the interviews that those subjects who learned a language in the country where it is spoken usually did so successfully. However, in a few cases interviewees did not do well in an informal situation. These exceptions were generally attributed to a lack of interest and motivation or to too brief a period of exposure to the language.

As the majority of the interviewees had been taught with the traditional emphasis on grammar and translation, many of them (38%) commented on the fact that at the end of high school they lacked oral skills. Several interviewees who had won high marks in school language courses attached little significance to them in retrospect, since they spoke the language badly or not at all.

A few subjects did benefit greatly from the formal learning situation in high school and/or university. Nevertheless, a greater number had experienced a 'linguistic breakthrough' in an immersion situation after discouraging attempts in a formal one. No matter how successful or unsuccessful the interviewees had been in formal learning situations, in most cases their oral/aural competence increased considerably when they found themselves in immersion situations, i.e. in contact with native speakers.

The exceptions were the unsuccessful language learners. They did not profit from an immersion situation; one of them, who attended a course in the L2 environment, was dissatisfied with the teachers, the teaching, and the lack of contact with native speakers. The other did not seek opportunities to improve her foreign language competence when visiting the L2 country, but accepted her low level of proficiency.

Question 11

The subjects were asked whether they were satisfied with their achievement levels in the different languages.

Most, including the two unsuccessful language learners, indicated that they would like to increase their knowledge in at least one language, sometimes the language in which they were already fairly competent and sometimes one in which that had not reached a satisfactory level. Two interviewees wanted a concrete reason for improving, not being interested in language *per se*: 'I'm so sick of snobbish polyglottism.'

Question 12

Another factor supposedly operating in second language learning is aptitude. Though the interviewees were not given any aptitude test, we did seek out their estimation of their 'gift' for languages. Forty-four per cent regarded themselves as 'strong' in languages; 21% 'average'; 29% denied having a 'gift' for languages; 6% did not know. One interviewee, who had learned a considerable number of languages, remarked that he had no 'gift' for languages, but that he had acquired a skill in learning them. Another thought that the crucial factor in language learning was not aptitude, but personal determination, willingness to apply oneself, and, above all, strong motivation. Of the two poor learners, one considered herself weak in languages, the other average.

The interviewees were then asked about certain principal features of aptitude, as identified for example by Carroll and Sapon (1959), such as auditory discrimination, rote memory and inductive learning ability.

Sixty-nine per cent[*6] felt that they had a good ear for languages; 19% did not. Three subjects did not know and one felt that 'his "good ear" was only average'. Fifty per cent stated that they had a good memory; 16% a bad one. The rest qualified their answers by specifying the aspects of language learning in which their memories were good or bad. Four subjects, for example, reported that they could remember sounds but not words. When asked if they liked analyzing languages, 66% responded positively, 28% negatively; 6% were undecided.

Question 13

To discover the factors the subjects themselves regarded as most influential in language learning, we asked them if, in retrospect, they attributed their success to the teachers or to the way of teaching, to the school or the environment, to some special study habits which they might have developed, or to some particular personality characteristics.

All subjects mentioned a combination of factors. One, for example, believed that his bilingual upbringing gave him insight into the nature of language, and a general mental flexibility. He did not feel confused or disturbed by the 'oddity' of a foreign language, as his own native languages (French and Arabic) were extremely different. He felt he had acquired a positive attitude towards languages. After this general open-mindedness he regarded the immersion situation as the most influential factor in the learning of his first foreign language.

Among those factors most frequently reported were motivation (47%) and immersion into the target language (44%). Motivation was occasionally specified by indicating an 'integrative orientation' (Gardner and Lambert, 1972: 14), for example, an interest in the culture of the target language (9%), or an 'instrumental orientation', for example, professional advancement (9%). Another variable frequently referred to was a positive attitude towards languages in general or towards one in particular (34%).

Other factors mentioned were positive parental influence, insight into the nature of languages, bilingual upbringing, multilingual and multicultural environments, effective study habits, and approaches to language learning appropriate to the individuals' learning styles.

Among personality characteristics, sociability was regarded as important (31%). Several interviewees (22%) thought extroversion a help, especially in acquiring oral skills. Lack of self-confidence and inhibition (self-consciousness) were named as hindrances. Three subjects experienced an interesting phenomenon which could be called 'social sensitivity'. They were afraid of imposing themselves upon native speakers. As one put it:

> I am not a very forceful person . . . I don't impose myself too much . . . they have to listen to my idiotic attempts to say 'Where's the bathroom?'

The two unsuccessful language learners attributed some of their failure to poor teaching. One of them said further that she had convinced herself she had little language learning aptitude, as she always had great difficulty in pronunciation and comprehension.

4.2 Part II of the interview

The second part of the interview was more directed than the first in that the subjects were generally expected to restrict their responses to the questions asked. A number of specific questions had been developed, but additional questions were formulated if the interviewer thought it appropriate. As indicated earlier, we asked the subjects to put themselves into a hypothetical language learning situation so that they could combine their recollections of past language learning experiences with their present insights (see Appendix 2, Questionnaire Part II).

Question I[7]

Recent research has investigated the role of attitude in second language acquisition (see Gardner and Lambert, 1972) and demonstrated a relationship. In order to investigate the subjects' attitudes towards the (hypothetical) prospect of learning another language, the following question was asked:

> Imagine that you had the opportunity and time to learn another language now. What would you be inclined to say at the thought of learning a new language?
>
> (1) I hate the thought of it.
> (2) It scares me.
> (3) I don't mind doing it.
> (4) I would look forward to doing it.
> (5) I am very excited at the idea of it.

The great majority of the 34 interviewees had a very positive attitude towards the idea of learning another language – 38% looked forward to it and 44% were indeed very excited. Two interviewees stated that they were not interested in learning another language because they preferred to improve their knowledge of a language already begun, an indication of their abiding interest in language learning.

A great variety of reasons influenced the choice of a particular language for this hypothetical learning situation. A few had a general or specific linguistic or personal interest in the language chosen: one woman was interested in learning an African language because her ancestors had come from Africa. For some, the language had an aesthetic or exotic appeal. One subject felt attracted by the different ways of perceiving reality through a foreign language. Several indicated a political reason; for example, learning French in Canada was felt to be essential because it is a bilingual country. A few revealed an 'instrumental orientation', in that they felt that learning a second language allowed one to get a better job; whereas several subjects showed an 'integrative orientation' (Gardner and Lambert, 1972: 14), in that they were interested in the target country and its people. Several others displayed a positive attitude towards language learning *per se*, with no particular reasons for choosing one language over another.

When asked which language they would like to learn, many subjects also mentioned specific goals. The majority wanted to emphasize aural/oral skills (speaking and understanding the foreign language).

Question II

Language teaching theorists and practitioners frequently discuss which language learning setting is more effective, the classroom or the L2 environment. Opinions vary. Some maintain that language learning should be taken out of the classroom altogether (see Macnamara, 1973), others believe in a combination of formal and informal learning environments (see Stern, 1970 & 1973). Research has provided some evidence that formal instruction enhances the level of achievement reached in the foreign language (see Krashen and Seliger, 1975; Krashen, 1976). Teaching the foreign language via other subjects, as do some Canadian 'immersion' programs, is another possible way of providing opportunities for genuine communication (see Swain, 1974; Stern *et al.*, 1976).

In view of these discussions, we asked the subjects what they considered the ideal conditions for learning the new language. They were presented with the following question:

What would you like to do *first* of all?
(1) Travel to the country and simply immerse yourself in the language?
(2) Travel to the country and take a language course there?
(3) Buy a course and study by yourself?

(4) Go to a teacher or a language school for private lessons?
(5) Join a language class?
(6) A combination of these?
(7) Other?

Thirty-nine per cent[8] chose to go to the L2 country and take a language course there, i.e. a combination of a formal and informal setting. On the other hand, 39% preferred some kind of instruction to start with, whether self-instruction, private lessons, or a language class. All of the subjects who had opted for initial formal instruction want to immerse themselves in the target language afterwards. A few wanted to work in the new language.

Question II.1

Is it more effective to study a language intensively, e.g. several hours a day, or gradually, e.g. 30 minutes a day? Research has so far not produced conclusive results to this question (see Carroll, 1975; Stern *et al.*, 1976). We asked the following question:

> If time were no consideration, would you prefer to learn the language in a concentrated effort (e.g. an intensive course for 4 weeks) or gradually (e.g. 2 hours a week and homework)?

On the basis of their experience, 85%* of the subjects felt that initially a concentrated effort and intensive study would be most beneficial. 'Intensive', however, meant anything from all-day courses to different combinations of courses, homework, and informal, unstructured exposure to the language and culture, going to the theatre or meeting native speakers, for example.

Question IV

There is some discussion over whether language learners should initially be allowed to be 'receptive' participants in the classroom, in order to become attuned to the new language, or whether they should be compelled to produce the language, i.e. to be 'active' participants, from the very beginning of their language learning.

Although listening and understanding are no longer regarded as 'purely "receptive" or "passive" processes' – the individual selects what he listens to – the 'relative order of listening and understanding preceding the productive use of language' was, until recently, widely accepted as a 'natural' order (Stern, 1970: 61).

In order to elicit the interviewees' opinions, which would presumably be based upon their language learning experience, the following question was asked:

Some of the ways of learning a language seem to involve you as a learner more *actively* (for example, in some cases you are made to speak right from the start), others allow you to be more *passive* (for example, you just listen to the teacher or you read widely).

Generally speaking, would you prefer to be relatively passive or rather active in the early stages of language learning?

Of the interviewees, 82% considered it best to be active right from the beginning, regardless of certain personality characteristics they might have, such as shyness, that would tend to make them follow a more passive approach. As one interviewee put it:

I would try to get involved as much as possible. . . . Language is a skill you've got to use all the time. The best way of learning a skill is by using it, doing it, by practising it. . . . Participation seems really essential. . . . What the heck, you might as well just get up and make a fool of yourself.

However, in one interviewee's opinion, representative of those of a few others, the option for activity did not have to exclude passive moments totally:

If you're studying a language for a long time, a bit of passivity at the beginning is not bad, because you have time to think and form hypotheses.

Question III

The next question touched the problem of 'stages' in language learning. There exist many definitions of achievement levels, referring to the ultimate language command (see Clark, 1972; Ontario Ministry of Education, 1974). Very few attempts, however, have been made to describe stages in language learning (see Wilkins, 1972; van Ek, 1975).

The question of whether the language learner himself experiences different stages in his learning has never been investigated. The interviewees were therefore asked how they would interpret the notion of stages, based upon their personal language learning experience. A total of 67%* agree that they could actually differentiate between several stages in their language learning process. However, when asked to describe them, they expressed a great diversity of views.

Some interviewees, for example, referred to a change in competence, motivation, or in their personal perception of difficulty and progress. Others regarded the differences between stages as those of learning content. One interviewee felt that differences were externally imposed, through the program (course), the setting, and the way of teaching.

Many language learners immediately rejected the idea of *three* stages; 41%* seemed to have experienced two stages rather than three (19%*). For example, the initial stage was characterized by a great effort to establish 'a basis in vocabulary and grammar'. Passing through the second stage meant building 'on this platform'. One interviewee described her experience as follows:

It was very difficult up to a major hurdle, and then it became easier, there was more familiar material, the ratio of familiarity grew as I advanced.

Where a third stage was mentioned, it was usually defined in terms of refinement. One interviewee described this stage as 'a matter of gaining fluency, of bringing sophistication to your linguistic skills'. One might use the descriptive headings offered by one subject as an illustration of how several of the interviewees viewed the concept of 'three stages' in language learning. These were:

Stage 1. Assimilation of new linguistic material

Stage 2. Implementation and practice of these aspects

Stage 3. Refinement

Those who rejected the idea of stages argued that one's personal approach remained basically the same at all times: 'It's only a question of degree, . . . the same things are involved – pronunciation, . . . grammar, and finally the usage.' The language learning process was further described by five interviewees as a 'continuum', without any sharply divided stages. Another subject described her language learning process as going in 'leaps and plateaus'.

Question III.1

Material developers and language teachers are constantly confronted with the problem of content of their language courses. In the early stages of instruction, most teaching materials emphasize the spoken language and everyday topics. However, the question of what should be introduced *first* to make language learning more effective has not been resolved.

The interviewees were therefore presented with several choices of initial content. All but one opted for a combination. Seventy-one per cent said that in the early stages they would choose to learn mainly pronunciation; 68% checked off simple conversational phrases. The third and fourth most frequent choices were learning to understand the spoken language (65%) and getting an overview of the grammar (62%). One interviewee expressed the desire to be immersed in a 'speeded-up natural process', learning the language 'like a child'. He did not choose any of the possibilities offered.

Question III.2

Considering that most of the subjects had successfully acquired one or more foreign languages, it was felt to be of interest to discover if they preferred 'to be firmly guided' by a teacher or a course or to be left to their 'own devices' and learn the language in their own way.

Eighty-two per cent of the interviewees regarded it as necessary to be guided at the beginning by a teacher, who would advise and motivate them, and organize the material. There were differing opinions, however, regarding the intensity and firmness of the teacher's guidance. Some wanted total guidance while others merely wanted the teacher present as a resource person if needed. However, 59%, the majority, tended to want fairly firm guidance by the teacher.

Question V

To discover if the emphasis would shift to different language aspects with time, the interviewees were further asked what they wanted to learn at intermediate and advanced levels.

Many subjects indicated that they wanted to emphasize reading and writing, to expand their vocabulary (including more idioms and different registers), and to improve their communicative competence in different social situations. Generally speaking, they wanted to immerse themselves into the target language and culture.

Question VI

As Stern pointed out, the learner has the choice between 'rational and intuitive learning'. He has to decide whether he 'should treat the language learning task intellectually, conceptually, and systematically as a mental problem, or whether he should avoid thinking about the language and absorb the language more intuitively' (Stern, 1975: 310–11). Stern suggests that the good language learner handles this dilemma to his advantage.

The issue was presented in the following manner:

Some people say that you *cannot* make a *conscious* effort in learning a foreign language. They hate to study grammar; they say you must simply allow the language to sink in gradually.

Others argue that language learning is a *conscious and systematic* process. You set about it by studying, by constantly asking for explanations and rules. In short, by actively thinking about it.

Which of these ideas would more represent your point of view?

The vast majority of the interviewees (94%) considered their language learning either a highly conscious and systematic process (68%) or one comprising both conscious and unconscious elements (26%). One interviewee commented:

> You have to simply sit down and work out a way that you can do it and spend a lot of time at it and expect not to get very far for a while and expect to have a lot of setbacks and to get boring work to do a lot of times, but it just depends how badly you want it.

One interviewee regarded it as possible to learn through 'osmosis . . . if you have got unlimited time and an optimum situation'.

But as very few learners learn under those ideal conditions, the reality of language learning is quite different. As another interviewee pointed out, 'There is an unconscious process of absorption going on all the time. . . . But there has to be practice, questioning. . . ; just absorbing the language doesn't get you very far.' It may be significant that the two subjects who regarded language learning as a totally unconscious process were the unsuccessful learners.

Question VII

Another problem the learner has to face when learning a second language is that of the 'discrepancy between L1 and L2' (Stern, 1975: 310). The presence of the first language (and possibly other languages) is 'inevitable and deep-seated'. The learner has to decide whether to consciously attempt to suppress L1 references – as far as this is possible – or to make use of them.

In order to find out how the interviewees had coped with this problem, they were asked the following question:

> Some people find that in learning a new language you must completely forget your native language. Others say you cannot and should not.

> To what extent do you find that comparing your native language with the foreign language helps you in learning a new language?

In general, it was seen as both inevitable and useful to compare the new language with the mother tongue, but more so at the initial phases of language learning than at the later ones. The following two comments illustrate this point of view:

> Instead of approaching the language like a blank wall . . . try to find everything that you can that is related to what you already know, especially in lexical items.

Initially, one's native language is useful; but after you've reached a certain level of proficiency one tends to completely forget one's own language . . . I become one of them and I completely exclude English.

The interviewees were also questioned about their attitudes towards the usefulness of translating into the native language (see Question VII.1). Only 26%* considered this useless or a hindrance in the assimilation of the new language. The rest generally regarded translating as useful to a certain extent. Some interviewees felt that translation could be used as a 'checking tool' for comprehension, especially at the beginner's level in a formal learning situation.

As learners are very often advised to use monolingual rather than bilingual dictionaries, the interviewees were asked their preference (see Question VII.2). The majority preferred to work with a bilingual dictionary. Many subjects modified their response by stating that a bilingual dictionary was necessary initially, but that a monolingual dictionary should be used later. Only six subjects opted for monolingual dictionaries right from the beginning.

Question IX

As most of the interviewees had learned more than one foreign language, their perception of a possible negative or positive influence on the learning process of each individual language was considered to be of general interest. They were therefore presented with the following question:

If you have learned a third or fourth language, to what extent did you find that your learning was influenced by your previous language learning experience?

In general, would you say that knowing another foreign language helped you or hindered you in learning a new language?

Of the interviewees, 73%* had experienced a definite influence: 'The compartments in the mind are not completely watertight.' Only 9%* denied that their learning of another language was influenced by their previous language learning experience.

For 78% of the 27 respondents who commented on this influence, it had been positive. 'As I learned languages, I learned how to learn them.' Not only were personal strategies and suitable techniques developed, but, as another subject expressed it, one's mind became flexible to the idea that there were completely different ways of conceptualizing. Another influencing factor was mentioned by two other subjects. Thye felt a positive reinforcement through success and each further language was approached with a more relaxed and confident attitude.

Four interviewees pointed out that the influence of one language on the other could be both positive and negative. Within linguistic families cross-lingual comparisons facilitated comprehension and production, but also produced some confusion, especially at the early stages.

Each language learned makes the next one easier, because you are more detached from your native language, you have more knowledge about structure, about meta-language. However, there is also some interference, for example, in the area of vocabulary.

Only two interviewees regarded the influence as negative, in that feelings of inadequacy and failure, experienced previously were transferred to the new language learning situation.

Question VIII

As Stern pointed out, the ideal end-point of second language learning is native-like competence, which is characterized by the 'intuitive mastery of the linguistic, cognitive, affective and sociocultural meanings expressed by language forms' (Stern, 1974: 16). The layman usually refers to this level of competence by saying that the learner has learned to 'think' in the foreign language. In order to elicit the subjects' views and experiences in this matter, the following questions were asked:

Do you feel that one can actually learn to *think* in a foreign language?

How do you think one might achieve that?

How important do you think it is?

Of the interviewees, 79% agreed that it was possible to learn to think in a foreign language. For 10 subjects learning to think in a foreign language was an unconscious process. They felt that it could be equated with a certain degree of competence that came with the facility developed in the foreign language: 'It just clicks one day after you've had enough.' 'It just happens or it doesn't.'

The majority of our interviewees, however, achieved thinking in the foreign language by conscious practice and use of the language; for example, by soliloquizing in the foreign language, or if the opportunity arose, by immersing themselves in the foreign language environment.

Question XI[9]

Psycholinguists and language teaching theorists have frequently discussed affective variables in second language acquisition (see Brown, 1973; Rubin, 1975; Schumann, 1975; Stern, 1975). At the end of the interview, the interviewees were asked about certain feelings involved in their language learning experiences.

The first question referred to the discouragement, frustration, impatience, and/or confusion caused by the language learning task.

Eighty-five per cent had experienced some or all of these feelings, especially frustration. Discouragement (8 subjects) and confusion (3 subjects) had been experienced more at the beginning of their language learning careers than later. Five interviewees stressed the fact that these negative feelings were not continuous, but intermittent. Many of the interviewees pointed out that they accepted these feelings as somehow inevitable, occasionally even helpful, in that they motivated them to learn more in order to overcome them. Persistence appeared as a key word in the process of coping with these affective demands.

> Persist! There's lots of plateaus . . . just keep on going . . . try more, until it happens.

> Be realistic! Take them (the feelings of frustration and impatience, etc.) with a pinch of salt and learn a little more of the language.

In his paper Stern (1975) stated:

> While first-language competence is compelling, and self-evident, many features of the new language . . . appear, to begin with, as arbitrary, unnatural and sometimes as finicky, fussy, and often plainly ridiculous.

The question of emotional reactions towards the language itself was put to the interviewees. For the most part, they said that the foreign language did not sound strange to them. One interviewee, however, mentioned that all the languages (about 12) he had learned sounded 'absurd', but that it did not bother him: 'It's part of their charm.'

Occasionally, the sound of the language provided an amusing element at the beginning of language learning. A few interviewees regarded the language as interesting or aesthetically pleasing. Two subjects learned a language despite considering it aesthetically displeasing. It was felt, however, that to belittle the language would be an expression of disrespect for its native speakers. One interviewee felt very strongly about this:

> Nothing is peculiar. . . . When learning a foreign language, one thing never to do is to say, 'Why do we have to do it that way?' Humility in the most extreme variety is required – no matter what they do it is right if they do it.

The last subquestion attempted to uncover emotions such as inhibition and helplessness, which might be factors in communication. A few learners (6) commented on the fact that they did feel ridiculous actually expressing themselves in the foreign language, but that usually this feeling was only temporary.

One interesting comment came from one subject who remarked that although she did not feel ridiculous speaking the language, she did feel 'phony', as if her personality had changed into something 'artificial'. Another interviewee reported that once native speakers of the foreign language responded positively to his attempts to communicate, he no longer felt ridiculous.

Inhibition or embarrassment were experienced by about half of our interviewees. Eight learners had felt helpless from time to time when they had to communicate in the foreign language. Some learners indicated that they were less inhibited among fellow students than among native speakers. Making a friend of a native speaker was often recommended (see Part II, section 2.3), because communication in such a situation would provoke less anxiety.

Again, it was felt to be of particular interest to investigate the kind of coping mechanisms the interviewees had developed over the years.

Many subjects emphasized action. It was essential to increase one's efforts and, generally speaking, to persist. Several subjects overcame their inhibitions by consciously seeking out situations where there was no choice but to talk in the foreign language:

> What hindered me a great deal was my reticence, awkwardness, shyness. . . . I really had to force myself. . . . I would go through the cafeteria [at Kiel University, West Germany] and all the tables would be taken. I'd try to find somebody, preferably alone, in order to start a conversation. I found it very difficult and I don't know if I would find it any easier now, but it certainly helped my German.

Others consciously accepted those feelings, deciding not to let it upset them when they made mistakes and people laughed at them. Two subjects advocated maintaining a sense of humor:

> I am not particularly extroverted; but when it comes to learning a language I think you've got to have a sense of humour, you've got to be able to laugh at your own mistakes, you cannot take yourself seriously.

Or, as the other interviewee commented:

> In order to learn you must make mistakes. People with whom you speak are not going to be surprised if you make mistakes – it's not going to

upset them. People are delighted if you can speak their language, and they don't care how well you speak it.

4.3 Strategies and techniques

A major purpose in analyzing the interviews was the identification of language learning strategies and techniques. As previously mentioned, Stern's list of strategies provided an initial frame of reference (pages 4 and 5). The list of strategies was modified and extended according to the statements and views expressed by interviewees.

Strategies

The analysis focussed on the most salient features of the interviews. The strategies identified are presented below. The five major strategies describe the overall approach to language learning and appear to be essential to successful language acquisition. The minor strategies subsumed under the major ones are not necessarily applicable to all successful language learners. The two sets of strategies form a composite picture of good language learning, as suggested by the interviewees' reports.

Strategies of Good Language Learners (GLLs)

(The statements or actual quotations following the strategies are selected from the interviews for illustrative purposes.)

STRATEGY 1: ACTIVE TASK APPROACH

GLLs actively involve themselves in the language learning task:

(a) by responding positively to the given learning opportunities or by identifying and seeking preferred learning environments and exploiting them.

(Subject No. 12 accepted the rigid way of teaching in high school, as this method provided him with the foundations for different languages; the method demanded rote learning and memorizing.)

(Subject No. 23 knows – through her previous language learning experience – that she needs structure and organization, especially at the beginning, and both formal and informal settings to learn a foreign language. Before immersing herself into the target language, she would, for example, take a crash course; in addition to the informal learning situation in the country itself, she would continue with formal instruction.)

(b) by adding related language learning activities to the regular program and/or intensifying their efforts.

(In addition to courses Subject No. 20 read a lot, though he did not look up unknown words: 'one must read something – in the foreign language – continually, every day.')

(Subject No. 13 actively pursued the learning of French outside the classroom; he listened to linguaphone records and tapes in the car, read French novels, etc.)

(c) by engaging in a number of practice activities.

(In order to practise correct pronunciation, Subject No. 24 tried to 'isolate behaviorally certain sounds'; 'she would look at people's mouth' and 'then repeat it over and over again'.)

(In order to learn vocabulary, Subject No. 5 memorized words and wrote down as an aid to memory.)

(Other practice techniques are given in the list of techniques presented in the following section. The importance of practice was emphasized by several interviewees. Subject No. 13, for example, considered practice to be the most useful part of the *conscious* effort one can make in learning a language.)

(d) by identifying individual problems connected with their language learning and actively dealing with them.

(As the foreign language was mainly an 'oral language' for her, Subject No. 23 found that she had difficulties in reading: 'I had to read out loud in order to hear the sound of it, in order to figure out what was said.')

(e) by changing the usual purpose of an activity in order to focus on L2 learning.

(Subject No. 24 went to movies every day – though she knew most of them – because they were dubbed into the foreign language she was learning.)

(Subject No. 28 worked as a truck driver in the foreign country: 'I was using the day more as a language course.')

STRATEGY 2: REALIZATION OF LANGUAGE AS A SYSTEM

GLLs develop or exploit an awareness of language as a system. In dealing with language as a system, GLLs:

(a) refer back to their native language(s) judiciously (translate into L1) and make effective cross-lingual comparisons at different stages of language learning.

(Subject No. 24 tried to find cognates: '. . . instead of approaching it – the new language – like a blank wall . . . try to find everything you can that is related to what you already know, especially in lexical items.'

(b) analyze the target language and make inferences about it; they guess by using clues.

(Subject No. 35, for example, made inferences about the surface structure of Thai by using rules and generating 'all mathematically possible sentences'.)

(c) develop learning techniques which make use of the fact that language is a system.

(Subject No. 5, for example, when looking new words up in a dictionary, tried to 'associate them in a field'.)

STRATEGY 3: REALIZATION OF LANGUAGE AS A MEANS OF COMMUNI-CATION AND INTERACTION

GLLs develop and exploit an awareness of language as a means of communi-cation (i.e. conveying and receiving messages) and interaction (i.e. behaving in a culturally appropriate manner).

(a) In the earlier stages of language learning GLLs may emphasize fluency over accuracy. They may concentrate on speech flow rather than error-free production.

(Subject No. 31 did not hesitate to speak; if necessary, he simplified and attempted to use circumlocutions.)

(Subject No. 28: '. . . the main thing is that you overcome the inertia and *use* the word and not if you use it absolutely correctly.')

(b) GLLs seek out situations in which they can communicate with members of the target language and/or increase their communicative skills in the language.

(Subject No. 14 used French (L2) to communicate whenever possible: in class with discussion groups; in the foreign country with native speakers.)

(Subject No. 35 attempted to establish close personal contact with native speakers of the languages he was learning.)

(Subject No. 15 found that writing to pen-pals increased his motiva-tion and urge to communicate.)

(c) GLLs display critical sensitivity to language use, for example, by attempting to find out sociocultural meanings (even before first contact with native speakers).

(Subject No. 28 memorized courtesies and conversational phrases before he went to the foreign country.)

(Subject No. 4 would like to learn more about 'verbal behavior' in different social situations.)

STRATEGY 4: MANAGEMENT OF AFFECTIVE DEMANDS

GLLs realize initially or with time that they must cope with the affective demands made upon them by language learning and succeed in doing so.

(Subject No. 4 overcame her inhibition to speak 'just by doing it', by getting herself into situations where she had to use L2.)

(Subject No. 15: when learning a language, 'You've got to be able to laugh at your own mistakes, you've got to have a sense of humor.')

(Subject No. 28: 'You have to simply sit down and work out a way that you can do it and spend a lot of time at it and expect not to get very far for a while and expect to have lots of setbacks and get boring work a lot of times.')

STRATEGY 5: MONITORING OF L2 PERFORMANCE

GLLs constantly revise their L2 systems. They monitor the language they are acquiring by testing their inferences (guesses); by looking for needed adjustments as they learn new material or by asking native informants when they think corrections are needed.

(Subject No. 23: 'I was on the look-out for clues'; 'I generated sentences . . . If they weren't correct people around me told me how to say it.')

(Subject No. 34 emphasized the importance of being constantly corrected, because 'learning your mistakes is fatal'.)

Techniques

In addition to the general strategies, the interviews yielded a large number of more specific techniques. A list of all techniques had been mentioned during the informal part of the interview, in the directed part the interviewees had been asked explicitly whether they had developed any 'language study habits, techniques or gimmicks' useful in acquiring the sound system, the grammar, the vocabulary, and oral/aural, reading, and writing skills in the foreign language concerned (see Questionnaire Part II, Question X).

The following list of techniques enumerates the different items in order of frequency. The numbers in brackets indicate the number of subjects who reported this particular technique or study habit. It became apparent that not every subject had developed special study habits in every area. The greatest number of techniques appeared in the area of vocabulary acquisition. It will further be noticed that some techniques are described in very general terms only.

Language Learning Techniques

I. SOUND ACQUISITION

(1) repeating aloud after teacher and/or native speaker (16)

(2) repeating after tapes, for example, in a language laboratory (8)

(3) reading aloud (6)
(4) using phonetic symbols, for example, transcribing spoken texts pho-
netically (5)
(5) listening carefully (4)
(6) repeating silently (3)
(7) talking aloud, including role-playing (3)
(8) acquiring a general knowledge in phonetics, i.e. how one's mouth
functions, where one has to put one's tongue, etc., in order to know
what a sound *feels* like; or looking at people's mouths, in order 'to isolate
behaviorally certain sounds', and then imitating them (3)
(9) doing special exercises for sounds not existing in the learner's native
language (1)
(10) practising different sounds, first in isolation and then in the context of
words (1)
(11) listening carefully to errors, for example, in pronunciation and/or
intonation, made by speakers of the target language when they themselves speak the learner's native language; from their errors one can
infer certain key sounds or structures (1)
(12) practising 'mock talk', which means imitating the foreign language, for
example, sounds or intonation, by using words of one's own language (1)

II. GRAMMAR

(1) following the rules as given in grammar books or text (12)
(2) trying to *use* grammar without thinking about rules all the time (4), for
example, using the grammar book only as reference when problems come
up during conversations, or waiting for corrections and then integrating
them.
(3) inferring grammar rules from texts (3)
(4) memorizing structures and using them as often as possible (2)
(5) guessing (e.g. the endings of words); having hunches and building 'abstract
patterns in your mind' (2)
(6) comparing L1 and L2 (1)
(7) learning from paradigms (1)
(8) changing the word order of an English sentence into the word order of
the foreign language, e.g. 'horses the grass will eat' (Japanese) or writing down sentences in English and deleting one word after the other,
replacing it by L2 items (1)

III. VOCABULARY

(1) making up vocabulary charts in L2/L1 and memorizing them (this was
regarded as especially useful for beginners) (14); writing vocabulary
down (3) in different situations, e.g. when watching TV; making index

cards (1); going over vocabulary lists at regular intervals; making new lists of the words one doesn't know yet (1)

(2) learning words in context (textual, situational) (8); (at an advanced level one must learn the whole concept of a word, usage, accent, etc.)

(3) putting words into different structures and drilling oneself (4)

(4) learning words that are associated in a field (4) (same subject area, the same lexical and semantic fields)

(5) reading alound and/or silently (4) (looking up words either after one has finished reading or when one is reading, putting a number over the word one doesn't know, making a list at the top of the page of the words unknown and then reading the paragraph again to check if one remembers the words)

(6) using a dictionary when necessary (4) (underlining the words one has looked up so that one can check later if one remembers them)

(7) reading a dictionary (3)

(8) listening to conversations or the radio (e.g. songs – trying to break the sound stream into words) (3)

(9) (a) carrying a notebook around and writing down items, if possible in context (1)

   (b) writing down words one hears in phonetic transcriptions (if one doesn't know the spelling) (1)

(10) using new words in phrases or in a practical context (1)

(11) games (1)

   (a) trying to think of words which have the same ending – even with the help of a dictionary (checking later if one remembers them)

   (b) giving a French (L2) word and four choices for translations (only one is correct)

   (c) 'French baseball' (team-pitcher asks batter a word – if he knows the word, batter goes to first base, if he doesn't know it but the catcher does, he is out)

(12) repeating words (1)

(13) switching on tape-recorder with vocabulary – when one feels relaxed (subconscious learning) (1)

IV. LISTENING COMPREHENSION

(1) listening to radio, records, TV, movies, commercials (21) ('Kill two birds with one stone: listen to something you would be interested in in your native tongue.')

(2) listening to *what* people say and *how* they are saying it (exposing oneself to different accents, registers) (12)

(3) listening to tapes (e.g. while one is driving or in a language lab) (8)

(4) listening to news broadcasts first in L1, then in L2 (2)

(5) teacher builds a *model* with cars, street, etc. . . . . each student gets a car and has to obey instructions; thus the students are practising their comprehension (1)

V. LEARNING TO TALK

(1) basic principle: 'don't be afraid of making mistakes'
(2) having contact with *native speakers* (23)
    (a) who are your *friends* (6)
    (b) talk to older people because they are more patient (1)
    (c) talk to anybody (e.g. teacher) (5)
    (d) talk to variety of native speakers (2); it trains your ear
    (e) participate in class (1)
(3) soliloquizing aloud (7) or silently (3)
(4) asking for corrections and integrating them (4)
(5) learning by heart, e.g. dialogues (3)
(6) subvocalizing when reading (1)
(7) cf. *model* (5.) mentioned under 'listening Comprehension' (1) – this time the students have to give instructions and the teacher corrects their pronunciation

VI. LEARNING TO WRITE

(1) having pen-pals (8)
(2) writing anything (exercises in class, business letters, etc.) (7) (keep business letters you receive and copy formulas of greeting, introduction, etc.)
(3) spelling games (1)
(4) reading a lot of whatever you want to be able to write (1) 'It's got to go in before it comes out.'

VII. LEARNING TO READ

(1) reading anything: magazines, newspapers, professional articles, comics (e.g. *Reader's Digest* because it offers a wide variety of texts in the second language) (18)
    (a) reading something that interests you (4)
    (b) reading something that is familiar (1) – especially at the beginner's level
    (c) reading headlines, receipts, labels, menus and translating them into L2 (big letters appeal to one's eye and may facilitate reading) (1)
    (d) reading bilingual texts at the beginner's level (1)
    (e) making it one's principle to read *something every day* (1)
(2) trying to figure out meaning from the context without consulting a dictionary (2) (don't interrupt your reading, underline the most important words and look them up later)

(3) subvocalizing when reading (1)
(4) reading a paragraph in L2, translating words and expressions one doesn't know into L1 (check with dictionary); studying them; reading the paragraph again; silently translating it into L1; then reading out loud in L1 until one is sure that one knows it in L1; going back and reading it in L2: 'It's a real drudgery, but it works.'

4.4 Discussion of research instrument and results

Research instrument

The interview proved to be a useful research technique, though with certain shortcomings. For the most part, the combination of semi-directed and directed interviews was successful. The first, semi-directed part allowed the interviewees to examine their past language experiences without feeling restricted by a series of specific questions. Since a great part of the learners' reported experiences had taken place long before the interviews, some information could be elicited only through free recollection.

Some interviewees tended to digress. On the other hand, a few who did not volunteer a great deal of information had to be prompted. In doing so, however, the interviewers had to be careful in the wording of their questions, so as not to influence responses.

The semi-directed interviews also created a problem in statistical evaluation. Not all interviewees provided specific information on identical topics. The calculated percentages can therefore be regarded only as indications of what a certain number of interviewees mentioned without having been asked directly. This difficulty generally did not present itself in the directed or structured second part of the interview, altough a question was occasionally overlooked.

Since the primary purpose of the interviews was to gather information about the interviewees' past language learning experiences, it was appropriate to have the semi-directed part of the interview precede the more directed section, which attempted to induce the interviewees to combine their past insights and present views about language learning. As it turned out, the main disadvantage of this sequenciang was that a number of questions had already partly been asnwered in the first part of the interview, for example, questions about specific learning techniques developed and affective demands upon the learners. In retrospect, it might have been better to incorporate some of the questions contained in the second part into the first part of the interview.

Another aspect to be considered was the duration of interviews. They lasted much longer than originally anticipated. In order to avoid impatience or fatigue on the part of the interviewees, it would have been advisable to limit each interview to approximately one hour. Such a restriction, however, would have meant eliminating those questions that referred strictly to the hypothetical language learning situation, and it was not desirable to lose this information.

Apart from critical remarks on the format of the interview, the study gave rise to two fundamental questions:

(1) How valid are the statements made in the interviews, considering that the subjects, in the first part of the interview, talked about their actual learning experiences *in retrospect* and, in the second part, expressed views related to a *hypothetical* language learning situation? How many insights were lost due to the time gap between the language learning experiences and the interview?

(2) Is language learning mainly a conscious or an unconscious process; if the latter, can an interview uncover the unconscious aspects?

Although these reservations must be borne in mind, we feel that interviews are a valid research technique in that they provide interesting insights and ideas about language learning which observation, for example, could not yield.

Two other possible criticisms may be made of this part of the investigation. First, the number of interveiwees was relatively small and the spectrum of educational backgrounds and present occupations fairly narrow. If the sample had been larger and had included members of more distinct professional groups, such as language teachers, businessmen, interpreters, and translators, a greater variety of strategies and techniques might have been identified.

Second, in view of the fact that not all the interviewees had reached an advanced level of proficiency in the language(s) learned, more rigorous selection criteria should be applied if a similar study is conducted again. Homeogeneity of achievement levels and heterogeneity of social and educational background and professions would provide a more clearly defined sample than did the present investigation. The question arises, of course, whether self-evaluations of language competence are reliable. In cases of doubt, achievement tests might have to be administered.

These criticisms do not invalidate our finds, since all interviewees have shown a great potential in language learning, whether they have achieved advanced proficiency or just a working knowledge in the language concerned. Futhermore, it has to be kept in mind that the major purposes of the present study were, first, to test interviews as a research tool in the investigation of language learning; second, to identify strategies and techniques developed and employed by good language learners; third, to gather information about other factors which influence successful language learning.

Results

Generally speaking, the interviews demonstrated the uniqueness of each language learning career, but at the same time identified many common experiences and characteristics. The more general shared attributes are reflected in the strategies presented in the preceding section. In general, the good language learner is someone who actively involves himself in the language learning process, either right from the beginning or later; he also finds ways to overcome obstacles, whether linguistic, affective or environmental; he monitors his own performance; he studies, practises, and involves himself in communication.

The good language learner was not necessarily the one who had equal success in all the languages he attempted to learn. He may have selected one particular language for intensive study for a variety of reasons, professional, personal, or an interest in languages *per se*. It could be hypothesized that the last type of language learner would succeed in many different language learning situations since he does not need motivation other than the language itself.

In each individual language learning career, the complexity of the interplay of variables that led to success becomes apparent. Thus, personality characteristics, learning environments, attitudinal aspects, learning strategies, and accidental circumstances appear to be influential to varying degrees and in different combinations for success in language learning.

Furthermore, it is worthy of note that language learning aptitude, early starting age, and length of exposure appear to be less significant for success in language learning than a strong motivation and positive attitude towards the learning task, favorable learning circumstances (e.g. immersion into the target language environment), certain personality characteristics, such as sociability and persistence, and the development of learning techniques suitable to the learner's personal needs.

The following three detailed case studies illustrate some of the statements made above. These case studies represent some of those interviews which, from the point of view of understanding language learning, are particularly interesting.

5. Case Studies of Selected Language Learners

Out of the 34 interviews conducted, three interviews were selected to illustrate unique learning approaches and experiences. They represent different kinds of successful language learners and their strategies and techniques, and illustrate the following situations:

(1) limited success in a formal language learning setting, success in an informal setting, consciously developing and applying interesting techniques; (Ms. A.)

(2) success in learning a *new* language in an informal learning situation, in which language becomes the means for fulfilling other functions; (Ms. B.)

(3) successful systematic approach to foreign languages; (Mr. C.)

5.1 Case Study One

The following case study illustrates the development and application of learning techniques appropriate to the subject's needs, in an immersion situation which led to the successful acquisition of the foreign language concerned. The initial language learning experiences, in a formal setting, had been of limited success.

NAME: Ms. A.

AGE GROUP: 26–35

OCCUPATION: MA student in applied linguistics

LANGUAGES LEARNED AND MAINTAINED: Latin, German, Polish, French**, Swedish (½) [10]

Ms. A. was born in Virginia (USA) and spent most of her life in different cities and countries: Windsor (Ontario), Detroit, Burma, France, Edmonton, Montreal, Poland, Sweden, Germany, and now Toronto.

She comes from a unilingual English-speaking family background; as a child she was occasionally exposed to German, as she played with German-speaking children in Detroit and went to German movies with them. When living in Burma for two years (at the age of 13), she heard Burmese being spoken in her neighborhood, but did not acquire any.

The first foreign language she took at school was Latin, for two years. During her first year at university she took German; in her second year she studied French.

German was taught in a very traditional way; they did translations and drills, read a little, memorized dialogues, and learned some grammar. After one year of German, she was able to speak the language a little.

The French teacher used an audio-lingual approach. Despite the emphasis on oral production, Ms. A.'s oral skills remained extremely limited. She now believes that one of the reasons for her poor performance was a personality clash with the teacher. In addition, she also had a very negative attitude towards the French sounds and grammar. She was put off by French grammar – it struck her 'as odd', the nasals 'sounded sort of ridiculous'. She also did not make any cross-lingual comparisons, which she had found very useful for understanding and retaining German vocabulary. In general, she found German much easier than French – 'it was so much like English' (perhaps this was also attributable to her contacts with German children).

At the age of 21 Ms. A. went to France with the expectation and intention of never returning to North America, as she hated life there. She later realized that she could neither identify with France nor with North America. Her first weeks in France were very difficult: 'When I got to France, I couldn't say a thing in French, but there was no linguistic shock, there was a cultural shock.' She felt threatened by the throngs of people 'always talking, always moving around'.

I was afraid of these people; when you're sitting in a café in North America, somebody isn't sitting almost on top of you. . . . as to the French language itself – when I got into the French environment, I really liked it. I found it was beautiful. I liked the mentality of the people.

In order to improve her near zero-competence in French, Ms. A. went to see one or two French movies *every day*. Most of the movies were American ones, dubbed into French, and she had already seen quite a few of them. 'I was relating what I heard to what was going on.' After three months she was able to follow and understand·French movies without too many problems.

The second day in Paris, Ms A. met her future husband, a linguist, who was bilingual in French and German. At first, German was their only language of communication. However, she wanted to improve her French quickly. 'So I decided to do the same things with French that I had intuitively done with German: finding cognates – lexical items which are the same in both languages,' and to a certain extent, also comparing the grammar, for example, word order:

. . . so instead of approaching [the language] like a blank wall . . . try to find everything that you can that is related to what you already know, especially in lexical items.

She also started reading in French. This reading consisted for the most part of newspapers or magazines and American comic books. She consulted a dictionary whenever necessary. All these activities increased her comprehension fairly rapidly. However, she still had difficulties in actually using the language. 'I was a little timid about speaking . . . I didn't find French people very tolerant', especially not towards North Americans. Another reason why her oral skills did not improve at the same rate as her comprehension was that she and her husband began to communicate in English. English was his fourth or fifth language. 'He was used to learning languages.'

Ms. A.'s husband was learning English much faster than she was learning French. As a linguist he suggested a few ways of tackling the language learning task. He suggested, for example, that she should use the Latin she had learned and English, her native language, and 'francicize' words. For example, knowing that the English sound /ei/ used in 'table' usually becomes /a/ in French, she would apply this rule in all cases. The English word 'cave' /keiv/ thus became /ka:v/. However, she was not aware of the possibility of a semantic change; for example, *la cave* means 'cellar' in French, not 'cave'. Therefore, this method very often resulted in confusion on her part and in laughter on the part of the French:

> . . . and I got myself into very funny problems in understanding, because I would have the meaning in English but I would 'francicize' the work; I was feeling sorry for those poor devils who had to get out of their houses and live in caves during the war.

People laughed at her, and she 'began to find it funny, too'. But as much as she used this method of applying French pronunciation rules to English words these experiences made her 'decide to be active and find out what it really means in French and gradually to do away with English altogether'.

She began to study history at the Sorbonne and was able to talk with many French students. At the end of her first year in France her comprehension still far outweighed her fluency in the spoken language. It was not until the second year that she began to gain fluency. She learned a good deal but also acquired a lot of student jargon, occasionally misapplying it; for example, she used *Je m'en fous* ('I don't give a damn'), when speaking to a professor.

Ms. A. constantly and consciously monitored her French:

> I would listen in on people's conversations . . . I would repeat to myself, that's when I started really talking to myself . . . I would start repeating things I had noticed that I was doing wrong, e.g. pronouns, articles, etc.

She always tried out whatever she heard in order to get some feedback and to correct herself. She was also very interested in perfecting her pronunciation of French. She tried looking at people's mouths:

I wanted to sound *so* French that someone would say, 'Well, are you French? – no, there is something funny about the way you speak – [hesitation] – but are you French?' I wanted to speak like a native speaker.

After three years in France, Ms. A. and her husband returned to North America; but they went back to Europe every summer, mostly to France and sometimes to Sweden and Germany.

When living in Quebec, they started speaking French at home. Her main language of communication outside her home was French as well, as she refused to speak English:

I finally came to a phase where I felt fluent enough *not to worry* about French anymore though I still made mistakes. And I had to circumscribe occasionally.

After a couple of years, Ms. A. left North America and went to Poland for one year. She had no intention of staying in Poland, and therefore did not want to learn Polish. She was, however, able to follow simple conversations.

The tentative strategies and techniques Ms. A. had adopted in France were reinforced and consciously reapplied when she learned Swedish. She spent a total of three years in Sweden, though not consecutively. Again she went to Swedish movies, listened carefully, and made many cross-lingual comparisons – a technique that was particularly useful, as Swedish is very similar to English and German. She also taught English to Swedish students, using them at the same time as teachers of Swedish for herself by listening carefully whenever they spoke Swedish.

Though comprehension was still her primary objective in learning Swedish at the initial stages, a more active approach towards learning to speak was adopted. Any feeling of timidity and inhibition had disappeared and had been replaced by confidence. 'I had learned how to learn languages.'

The following quotations indicate strategies and techniques used by Ms. A.:

. . . I would soak myself in the environment and try to understand all that is going on . . . first listen, comprehension, comprehension!

She had also developed a trial and error technique:

. . . whatever you pick up, whether it's one word or two words . . . *use* it . . . even if it is wrong, try it out, it doesn't matter.

She would further pretend not to understand English in order to increase her opportunity to use the language. As mentioned before, she would make cross-lingual comparisons wherever it was possible and appropriate. In addition, she would set aside days on which she would try to think only in the foreign language.

According to Ms. A., she has maintained French and Swedish up to the present: French on an advanced level, Swedish on an intermediate level, and German on an elementary level.

Regarding her language learning aptitude, Ms. A. felt that she had a good ear for languages, which in her view might be due to her muscial training. She also had a very good memory for sounds though not words, unless she could relate them to a meaningful context. She did not like analyzing languages grammatically; however, she had her 'hunches' about regularities and irregularities and always tried them out.

Commenting on the reasons for her success in learning languages, she felt that it was mainly due to the immersion situation and to her strong motivation to learn the languages, especially French. Regarding certain personality characteristiocs which might facilitate or hinder acquiring a language, Ms. A commented that learning to speak would be much more difficult for an introverted person than for an extroverted person: 'One good characteristic is to be outgoing, to be willing to take risks.' In order to make it easier for the learner she recommended: 'One of the best ways to learn to talk in a foreign language is to have a friend.'

5.2 Case Study Two

The following case study illustrates the successful acquisition of a new foreign language with which the subject had not had earlier contact. The learning took place in an informal situation in which language became the means for fulfilling other functions. Formal and informal learning settings were, at least at times, combined. Previous attempts at learning other languages had been of limited success.

NAME: Ms. B.

AGE GROUP: 26–35

OCCUPATION: PhD student of Special Education

LANGUAGES LEARNED AND MAINTAINED: Hebrew, French, Latin, German, Italian½

Ms. B. was born in Nova Scotia and brought up in a bilingual family. The languages spoken in her home were English and Yiddish.

Ms. B. had no recollection of her early childhood competence in Yiddish. She was told that she spoke it fluently until the age of seven. Yiddish was the only language in which she could communicate with her grandparents, who at that time lived in her parents' home. Ms. B. reported that at present she understood only a little Yiddish, but that she could use the language actively and generate words and sentences. Despite her bilingual family background she regarded English alone as her native language.

Ms. B. did not come into any contact with other languages until she was sent to Hebrew school at the age of about 10 or 11 for a period of five to six years. The focus of instruction was reading the Hebrew script, without attention to meaning. As she did not understand the content of what she had to read, Ms. B. regarded this exercise as completely useless.

The second foreign language Ms. B. attempted to learn was French, which she started in grade 7 of the regular high school. She recalled that the students followed a text-book, learned grammar, did some reading, and memorized a few dialogues. In general, oral production was extremely rare, despite the teacher being a native speaker of French.

Ms. B. continued studying French until the second year of university. The teaching of French at university did not differ greatly from the way French was taught in high school. The focus was on language as a system, and not on language perceived as a means of oral communication. Summing up her achievement in French, Ms. B. reported: 'I discovered later that I could read scientfic articles quite well, but I have never been able to speak French.'

During her high school and university years, Ms. B. went through two other similar language learning experiences. She learned Latin from grade 9 to 11 and took German at university for three years. She felt that her achievement in both languages was again very limited, as the emphasis was on grammar and not on communication.

Her experience with language learning, which had previously meant occupying herself with a lifeless academic discipline, was completely revolutionized when she decided to go to Italy for a year and train as a Montessori teacher. From a professional point of view, she could also have been trained in Britain. However, she still regarded learning another language as 'a valuable experience', and therefore chose to take a training course in a small town in the north of Italy, deciding to try to learn the language at the same time. The course was to be conducted in both Italian and English.

Ms. B.'s linguistic adventure proved to be extremely successful. Starting from zero competence, she developed more than adequate comprehension and oral production within one year.

Summarizing the outcome of her learning efforts in a self-imposed immersion situation, she explained:

The travelling I did . . . was . . . to go to Italy knowing absolutely none of the language and coming back a year later able to carry on a conversation with five or six different people simultaneously, not completely idiomatically, but at least, knowing enough about generating words to get myself around a difficult situation.

When asked to elaborate upon the way she approached the new language learning task, Ms. B. revealed many strategies and techniques and showed a great deal of insight into the affective demands made upon her in this unfamiliar situation. In her recollection the first 10 days of her stay were rather traumatic. She lived with an Italian family. The other English-speaking students had not yet arrived. 'I felt completely cut off . . . I had nobody to talk to. It was an incredible experience.' She tried to make herself understood by looking up every word in a dictionary, which she regarded as an 'extremely exasperating' way of communicating. Once the other students had arrived, the feeling of being completely isolated decreased.

By following the daily lectures, Ms. B. was amazed to find how much she 'picked up' in terms of words, word arrangements, and intonation during the first couple of weeks. As the lecture itself was accompanied by practical demonstrations, she was able to relate language to meaning. 'Since you could see what was happening – along with the language – it made a lot of sense.' In addition, Ms. B. made lists of useful words by looking them up in the dictionary.

Ms. B. attributed a gread deal of her initial progress in Italian to *Signora,* the lady she was living with:

I found that *Signora* was a very fine language teacher. . . . She was teaching me the way you would teach a younger child to speak the language. She'd be giving me words when I'd stumble. She'd say them for me, I would try and repeat it; it wouldn't be quite right, she'd say it again. She had tremendous patience.

Ms. B. learned a lot of phrases by carefully listening to *Signora*:

If I knew the words, or at least some of the words in a phrase, when it was used in a practical situation, I'd sort of say 'Click, click, that's how you say it' . . . As I had heard, I would imitate.

However, after a while, Ms. B. realized that she was very restricted in the kinds of sentences she could construct. Together with other students, she approached the teachers in the 'English Centre' of the town, where English was taught as a second language, and asked them if they would be willing to teach them Italian. One teacher agreed and Ms. B. attended classes twice a week for a period of three hours each time. The content of instruction was grammar as well as conversation, based upon practical situations. It was fairly easy to learn certain grammar aspects, such as tenses, as she heard them actually being used outside the classroom. Ms. B. emphasized that it was only through formal instruction that she got an insight into the structure of the Italian language. She realized that both formal instruction and an informal immersion situation were essential for her progress in language learning:

> I needed that first few weeks . . . not worrying about grammar, hearing the intonation, where it really made very little sense and where I was exasperated most of the time, because if I tried to say anything, I would, maybe, get out one or two words. I could begin to understand them, but I couldn't make them. I had to learn the grammar in order to do that.

When she compared her own competence in Italian with that of her roommate, her belief in the necessity of formal instruction was confirmed. Her friend never reached a high level of grammatical sophistication. She also had more difficulty in expressing her ideas in Italian.

After three and a half months Ms. B. went on a trip with two Italians and one American. It was during this vacation that she experienced her 'linguistic breakthrough'. As she was the only one who spoke English as well as Italian she became the bridge between the two languages. She was forced to overcome her inhibition and a certain uneasiness with the foreign language as she had to translate constantly. By the time she came back, she had suddenly become fluent in Italian. She had gained confidence in her ability to cope with the foreign language. She tried to speak as much as possible and monitored her language through the feedback she got from native speakers:

> I wasn't afraid anymore, I generated sentences . . . if they weren't correct, people around me told me how to say it. I was on the look-out for clues . . . I don't suppose there was a lot of correction that I didn't pick up on fairly immediately and put into the language I was building.

Ms. B's attempts at communicating as much as possible very often made native speakers laugh, because of the ambiguity of some of her statements. It was mainly *Signora* who explained to her the double meaning of what she had said. However, it was done in such a way that Ms. B. never felt ridiculed but was able to share the joke.

Ms. B. found that for a long time her comprehension remained 'person-specific', in other words, when listening to somebody for the first time her comprehension level dropped. By the end of the year, however, she was able to understand speakers with different accents talking to each other or to her.

Ms. B. attempted not only to learn the language, but also to integrate into the Italian community as much as possible. She would have extended her stay if she had been able to find an acceptable position.

When presented with the chart describing the different proficiency levels and asked to indicate the level of proficiency she had reached within a year, Ms. B. explained that her ability to comprehend and produce was slightly above working knowledge, but that she had never concentrated on reading and writing skills:

It was always an aural language. Anything that was writing I had to read it out loud, unless it was on a very simple level, in order to hear the sound of it, in order to figure out what was said.

With regard to her present knowledge of Italian, Ms. B. indicated that her competence in comprehension and oral production had decreased due to lack of usage.

When questioned if she was satisfied with her achievement in Italian, Ms. B. stated that she was pleased with her progress during her stay in Italy, but that at present there was no need for her to be fluent. She felt very confident, however, that she could re-activate not only Italian but also French if the circumstances required it. On a few more recent occasions, when it would have been desirable to have re-activated her latent French, she discovered that Italian interfered greatly. Similarly, she had experienced some French interference at the beginning of her Italian immersion and had had to suppress French consciously.

In reply to the question of whether she thought she had a gift for languages, Ms. B. emphasized that even though she had to work at learning Italian she nevertheless felt that she had a reasonably good ear for languages as well as a good memory. She also enjoyed analyzing Italian and looking at language as a system.

After having described her main language learning experience in detail, Ms. B. was asked to indicate which factors she would regard as the most influential on her success and her failure in language learning. Ms. B. emphasized that the immersion into an Italian environment, and therefore the motivation for having to learn to speak the language, were the most significant factors at first. In order to develop her language competence further, she had to take recourse to formal instruction. Commenting on her very limited achievement in French and German, she pointed out that she lacked motivation because the languages were learned in a vacuum, without applicability outside the language classroom. She indicated further that she would not hesitate to learn another language and that she felt competent to do so, if, for example, she went to live in another country. 'My feeling about learning another language is that it has to be immediately useful.'

5.3 Case Study Three

The following case study is an example of language learning made a life-long occupation. The interviewer found it difficult to establish the exact sequence of language learning events. Mr. C.'s experience was so rich that the conversation triggered off a multitude of associations and general comments on language learning.

NAME: Mr. C.

AGE GROUP: 26–35

OCCUPATION: Professor of Anthropology

LANGUAGES LEARNED AND MAINTAINED: German**, French**, Rumanian**, Icelandic**, Italian, Spanish, Albanian, Greek (classical and modern), Russian, Polish, Serbo-Croatian, Latin, Mohawk, Swahili, Gaelic, Hungarian, Hittite, Japanese, Lithuanian

Mr. C. was a native-born American from Massachusetts. He was brought up in a predominantly English-speaking environment, in his home as well as the immediate neighborhood. There were only two exceptions: his paternal grandmother spoke Canadian French and he recalled that French was sometimes used as a 'secret language', which aroused his curiosity, but he never learned any French from his grandmother. The other language he heard in his childhood was Swedish: a friend of his mother's taught him to count to 10 in Swedish before he could count in English. He was aware of the fact that other languages existed and, with amusement, he recalled that he had a theory how they were related to each other:

> I imagined that if you took the alphabet and changed the order around you'd get another language; so all I had to learn eventually . . . was in which order I had to put the letters in order to get the other language.

Mr. C. had to abandon this theory when he actually started to learn another language, namely Latin, in grade 9. For the following four years, he continued with Latin. It was taught by the grammar-translation method. His first teacher supplemented the course with Latin songs and the Lord's Prayer. He was told that Latin was a 'more logical language' than English and that learning Latin was 'good training for the mind'. Mr. C. emphasized that this view was 'no more true of Latin than of any other language', but at that time he believed his teacher. He enjoyed Latin so much that he continued studying it at university. He indicated that he was still in the process of learning Latin.

When asked how he studied Latin, Mr. C. mentioned that he had to make 'a conscious effort to memorize vocabulary' and that he did not succeed too well: 'When words came to me it was . . . out of some context . . . language vocabulary I have never enjoyed memorizing and it doesn't come that easily.' In order to facilitate remembering the meaning of words, he would write translations between the lines of the foreign text. 'I would remember words by the passage or at least the part of the page they were on.'

During high school, Mr. C. also began studying Greek on his own, with the help of books his Latin teacher had given to him. He did not learn a lot of Greek, the reason being: 'When I learn languages myself, I tend not to study them systematically. Even now I sort of enjoy looking up things that I am interested in – structures, vocabulary, etc. . . .' He indicated that he often preferred reading reference grammars to reading textbooks, since grammar books were very organized and he knew what to expect.

Mr. C. encountered his next formal language learning experience in his first year at Harvard. He wanted to learn Russian and recalled that he prepared himself for the course in advance. The language had aroused his curiosity several years before. He had looked up the Russian alphabet in Webster's Dictionary, which listed all the letters with their equivalents, 'including the occasional misunderstanding'. For example, the definition of 'palatalization' as explanation for the Russian 'soft sign' (b) was incomprehensible and he believed it was like an 'h'. This misunderstanding led, of course, to a very strange pronunciation of Russian words, which, however, was easily remedied when he attended the language course. The course offered grammar sections as well as conversation classes. He attended both 'religiously', quite in contrast to other academic subjects, because he enjoyed them. His grammar teacher was so interesting that Mr. C. regularly stayed after class to discuss various problems with him, especially Indo-European origins of Russian words. He found Russian grammar generally 'easy and enjoyable'. The conversation class, which was attended by two students, met twice a week. In addition, Mr. C. had conversation exercises with a White Russian priest. It took him a while to figure out that the differences between the pronunciations he heard at university and from the priest were due to the fact that the priest spoke a different dialect of Russian.

Asked about his study habits, Mr. C. reported that he did 'the minimum possible at home'. However, he read a fair amount on grammar, since grammar was of particular interest to him, and above all he talked to himself. He also remembered that he practised aloud for several months trilling the Russian 'r', again following the written instruction 'of beating the tip of [your] tongue against the roof of [your] mouth' which he found very hard to do. One 'miraculous' day he realized that this sound was not any different from the noise he used to make as a little boy when playing airplane, 'so I just had to learn making an airplane noise in the middle of words'.

Since Mr. C. failed his first term examinations in math and science, two subjects he wanted to major in (he had fallen asleep during the examinations), his advisor suggested that he concentrate on subjects he liked, which apparently were languages. Mr. C. was by no means in agreement. He felt it had just been bad luck that he had failed those two subjects. He did not give up math and science, but to follow his advisor's suggestion he also took the only two languages which he could begin in the second semester, namely Rumanian and Hittite.

When learning Hittite Mr. C. came into contact with German, because the Hittite textbook the professor recommended and used was written in German, and he also had to refer to a Hittite/German dictionary. Thus he learned not only Hittite but also a great deal of German. The translation process was rather complicated: Mr. C. had to translate from Hittite into German and back into English, and as expected, errors in translation would occur, e.g. Hittite *taku* ('if'), German *wenn*, English 'when'. Since the Hittite course was a graduate class, it was taken for granted that the students knew French and German. The professor was very surprised to find after several weeks that Mr. C. knew no German at all: 'Nobody had bothered to ask.' Despite these 'handicaps' Mr. C. enjoyed this class very much and 'it turned [me] on to linguistics thoroughly. . . . And I learned a lot about language learning from linguistics'.

Asked to elaborate on his approach to language learning, Mr. C. first commented on one problem in language learning: retention. Looking back on all the languages he had studied for a fairly brief period of time, such as Greek and Italian, Mr. C. reported that he only remembered things he had memorized, such as songs, poems, etc. He concluded that rote memorization served a good purpose, although he had hated it earlier in his language learning: 'One has to have in one's head a certain minimum corpus thoroughly memorized, that one is . . . able to put out mechanically.' The only exception had been his learning experience with modern Greek. During his stay in Rumania (which will be reported on later), Mr. C. went to Greece for six weeks, concentrating on similarities between Rumanian and Greek and studying grammar all the time he was there; however, he did *not* memorize vocabulary, songs, etc.

I studied the grammar in the context of speaking it. . . . As a result, my Greek sticks with me today much better without even any conscious practice. . . . I was forced to speak, living with Greek students who quite unashamedly corrected me, which was essential.

In addition, he always checked what he heard against what was written in grammar books.

Mr. C. emphasized once more the importance of being corrected when learning a language. When encountering a language learner he would always interject corrections. Similarly, he always asked native speakers to do the same to him. 'If you don't get corrected on the spot, you'll learn your mistakes and learning your mistakes is fatal.'

After his first year of university, Mr. C. attended a French course at summer school. He indicated that he has continued learning French until the present, which makes French one of his 'main languages'. Asked about his approach to learning French, Mr. C. enumerated two 'essentials':

I used to ride around with my pocket dictionary . . . I also had a French-speaking girlfriend – these, I think, are two essentials.

He remembered that when he was riding along on his bicycle, if a word suddenly came to his mind he would stop and look it up:

And . . . the only way that I learned vocabulary I found was by looking it up when I was curious and not at other times and then it worked very well. I was astoundingly successful that summer.

To continue with the history of his language learning, Mr. C. reported that one summer, before returning to college, he travelled along the Mexican border and learned some Spanish in a very informal way: 'I just listened to what somebody said or asked him how you said this . . . it was just a pure lark.' He did not write down any words. Although he had earlier been of the opinion that one had to write words, etc., down in order to remember them, he began to find that the things he learned best were those he did *not* write down. He admitted that he had a visual memory to a certain extent, as had been evidenced in his learning of Latin. However, Mr. C. indicated that he could remember words very well if he was 'aware of the segmentation'. 'This is why the analysis of sounds is pretty essential.'

Back at university he audited or enrolled in a number of language classes, usually for about a year. He continued with Rumanian and started classical and modern Greek, Swahali, Gaelic, Albanian, and Serbo-Croation, as well as Japanese in a field course. The Serbo-Croatian teacher taught grammar very traditionally, with lots of exercises. Since he knew the language well, he was able to give many illustrative examples. Mr. C. enjoyed the course and developed 'a friendly feeling' towards the language. The teacher provided 'a rough overview of the language', which Mr. C. felt was 'essential at the beginning'. Details could always be filled in later.

Commenting on his learning approach in general, Mr. C. pointed out that although there may be a few essential techniques for learning a language, he had learned each language differently due to his personal 'evaluation'. He considered it an advantage to have good scientific materials available. The Greek grammar he was using, for example, had everything transcribed into the International Phonetic Alphabet, which made accurate prounuciation easier. It was also very traditionally arranged, 'so that you could find things'. Mr. C. pointed out that languages for which no materials were available were naturally much more difficult to learn. Later in his life, he had to learn about and apply techniques of field work and field analysis (which will be reported on later).

Apart from good textbooks, the teacher himself had a certain degree of influence on Mr. C.'s achievement in learning languages. 'When I have a teacher who turns me off I don't tend to learn as much.' He happened to have a very 'stimulating' teacher of Italian and a very nice Viennese teacher in German conversation class, two languages he learned outside university when he interrupted his university studies for a year. As in the case of Russian he was exposed to different dialects of German. Mr. C. developed a 'strong attachment' to his Viennese teacher and learned *Wienerisch*. Mr. C. indicated that his teachers had an influence on his motivation, which he considered to be a more important factor than the teaching methods:

> The methods have changed from time to time, but when the motivation changes the amount of what I learn changes. This is an important thing and I think it is much more important than pedagogical methods in the long run.

Regarding different methods of teaching and learning languages, e.g. the traditional versus the aural/oral approach, Mr. C. mentioned that he preferred a 'modernized' traditional method. He would not support the technique of reciting paradigms. The one aspect of the traditional method he emphasized most was 'the necessity of learning rules – externalizing rules, making them explicit rather than simply memorizing things as the behaviorists would have us do'. He suggested the term 'rational grammar' or 'rule-based grammar'.

Mr. C. further recommended that the rules be worked out by linguists and not by traditional grammarians. He also mentioned that he did not mind having rules presented to him and not having to deduce them. If he had to deduce the rules from a given text, he would like to be able to check his deductions against written versions in order to test his hypotheses efficiently; i.e. he does not want have to spend too much time on their verifications and he would also like to guard himself against internalizing wrong rules, which would be extremely difficult to unlearn.

A change in his approach to language learning came with his stay in Rumania. Before leaving for a summer course there, Mr. C. memorized sentences in a phrase book, but did not remember them very well when he arrived. He had a very 'lopsided' knowledge of the language. He had been taught old and modern Rumanian simultaneously and could remember its history but very little of the language itself. The summer course proved to be rather uninteresting. The emphasis was on 'reciting rules, a lot of rote work, which treats learners as children, and when learners are not children, they don't like being treated as children'. Very few teachers attempted to add some 'fun' to the courses, which decreased his own motivation to learn. The only class he faithfully attended was one in which the teacher taught songs.

Generally speaking, he profited very little from the course. What he did learn that summer, however, was Polish, because 'the Polish students were equally bored . . . and also did not feel like attending classes. So we just took off . . . and they taught me Polish'. Mr. C. also had a Polish girlfriend. In this context, he mentioned that he had a girlfriend in just about every language he had learned:

> The language has to be the language of somebody. Until I know somebody in that language and care for them, I don't give a hoot about the learning of the language.

Although Mr. C. modified this last statement – he had studied Lithuanian out of his linguistic interest in Indo-Eurpoean languages – he nevertheless emphasized the importance of personal involvement with speakers of the target language as a motivational stimulus. The way he learned Polish was fairly unstructured. He 'did a little bit of linguistic thinking' about the language but did not really analyze it, nor did he put down on paper what he was learning.

One unfortunate incident, which occurred during the first few weeks of his stay in Rumania, turned out to be good luck. Due to food poisoning, Mr. C. had to spend one month in a Rumanian hospital. He did not have his books with him, which proved to be an important factor, since he had already started to learn 'stilted' Rumanian of the 'it is I-type' at the summer school, as well as from his books. In hospital, he found that 'the more colloquial you speak, the more people are going to treat you with less formality, and consequently, the more easily they are going to correct you. . . . By learning it [Rumanian] the way people use it and not the way they ought to use it, you join in with them'.

The change in approach to language learning made through his hospital stay, was 'simply talking to people, not writing things down' (although he did some writing down later). In Mr. C.'s opinion there are essentially two approaches to language learning, depending on the amount of exposure:

> When your exposure is less than every day or less than continual, then you have to be analyzing; . . . where you have plenty of time on your hands, as I had in Rumania . . . you don't have to spend the time analyzing the forms because gradually you'll be seeing the analysis of them; this is taking for granted that you *can* analyze them.

Mr. C. pointed out the importance of first breaking down one's inhibitions and learning to talk freely to people before beginning to analyze the language. He described these initial phases of learning Rumanian as follows:

> You have to get an overview of the language, then you have to pick up enough conversational vocabulary that you know how to use, and then you take the two things together and start building sentences and have people correct you.

Being a 'naturally talkative person', Mr. C. was desperate to communicate in the hospital. He therefore indulged in this game of 'making up things' in order to communicate and he would receive confirmation or correction from the native speakers.

Mr. C. stayed in Rumania for a total of two years, working at the Centre for Dialectology. With respect to his level of achievement, he indicated that he had frequently been mistaken for a native Rumanian. Since he learned the language from native speakers, he could not be identified as a foreigner through 'oddities of construction' or the 'so-to-speak correctness of speech'. He knew different stylistic levels, for example, forms appropriate to express polite social distance; however, he was not interested in acquiring constructions 'which simply show your breeding'.

Another language Mr. C. came into contact with in Rumania was Albanian. He had studied Albanian for several years at Harvard, but only as a written language. He had written an undergraduate honors thesis on Albanian. It was in Rumania that he heard Albanian spoken for the first time. He was amazed at how much Albanian he could actually understand and produce. Since he learned Albanian via German and Rumanian, he always recalled those two languages when searching for the meaning of an Albanian word.

This new focus on language as it was actually spoken, and this ability of 'being able to talk with other people naturally' meant something like a 'watershed' for Mr. C. and influenced his later language learning experiences. For example, the only German he had previously learned had been 'a very correct *Hochdeutsch*'. When spending two months in Germany, partly with a friend whom he had met in Rumania, he learned slang; he also learned about possible abbreviations, such as *ne* for *eine*. He got accustomed to different dialects of German by staying in different areas. He improved his German mostly by listening and did no analysis of the language: 'I had to hear something, I would ask for it again and again, until I was sure of what I was hearing.'

The third type of approach to language learning which Mr. C. experienced was field work in Mohawk. For the first time there existed no references, no ready answers for his questions. There was no reliable research, so he had to analyze the language, phonology as well as morphology, himself. He was very motivated to learn Mohawk, because he discovered from his grandmother that he was part Mohawk: 'That was a sufficient romantic attachment to make it [the study of Mohawk] quite real.' Mr. C. used native informants but he did not like imposing upon their time too much. He indicated that by now he knew a large enough corpus to read Mohawk but not to use it.

One of the languages Mr. C. knew best was Icelandic. He learned Icelandic from his first wife, together with his baby daughter. He would listen to his wife, trying to pick up the sounds – 'Of course, you form an hypothesis and it's for practical purposes, you use the word and eventually it gets fixed.' Unfortunately, his wife never corrected him. He indicated that he was still coming across words he had learned incorrectly but 'thoroughly'.

His problems in communicating were enormous, especially during his first visit to Iceland. ('It almost broke up my marriage five years earlier.'). His wife ignored him and did not even relate the gist of the conversations to him. He was getting rather frustrated at not being able to understand anything. His wife's five-year-old sister finally began to teach him. He was not aware at first that he was learning 'Baby-Icelandic', which led to a few humorous and slightly embarrassing situations. For example, he asked a policeman, 'Excuse me, Mr. Copper-wopper, where . . . ?' The policeman enjoyed the incident, and so did he.

Mr. C.'s progress was fairly slow at the beginning. Icelandic morphology and phonology did not come easily to him. He did not remember words very easily, although finding cognates helped to a certain extent. It was mainly through constant exposure to Icelandic in his home, and above all during one summer in Iceland, that he acquired the language. It was his mother-in-law who provided the necessary constant correction, after she had found out that he wanted to be corrected: 'She virtually corrected everything that I said wrong.'

Mr. C. emphasized the importance of overcoming one's shyness and attempting to talk. 'You have to talk. If you sit around and are quiet, you don't learn as much.' Since he did not push himself much during his first visit, he did not improve his Icelandic much. The complexity of the language also made it very hard to pick up words and phrases.

Mr. C.'s most recent language learning experience was in Hungarian. He reported that he regularly talked to the Hungarian janitor of a particular university building, and was learning Hungarian 'by osmosis'.

Despite the multitude of languages Mr. C. has come into contact with, he indicated when queried that he would like to learn some Slavic languages other than Russian, because he head a liking for 'underdog' languages.

When asked if he felt that he had a gift for languages, Mr. C. responded that he was highly motivated but not particularly gifted. He had gradually developed a good ear for languages; he did not consider his memory to be extraordinary; however, he certainly enjoyed analyzing languages – 'That is my life now'. Mr. C. indicated that he had not always liked languages. As a matter of fact, he detested English in high school. The change in attitude came through meeting people who spoke other languages. He realized 'that learning a language is the key to other people's culture and their way of life'.

To conclude his biography, Mr. C. was asked to name the main factors of his success in language learning. The first mentioned was motivation:

Motivation means a lot, whether it is dedication to people you know, or to even an abstract idea – like my Indian ancestors – or whether it is to a teacher you like.

The second was 'techniques'. Mr. C. was convinced that linguistics had helped him with language learning and that language learning had helped him with linguistics. But linguistics gave him a 'phonetic awareness', enabled him 'to analyze what was being said and to arrive at rules'. He further indicated that he had 'an ability to segment forms and to try toform hypotheses'.

5.4 Discussion of case studies

The preceding three case studies illustrate both individuality and similarities in the different language learning careers. One of the common aspects, which becomes apparent in the outcome of these different language learning efforts, is that none of the interviewees, including the three individual cases, achieved a high proficiency level in all the languages they had started to learn. A variety of reasons may account for this phenomenon: (1) too brief an exposure to the language(s); (2) unfavorable learning environments; (3) lack of interest and motivation; (4) circumstantial factors which determine an individual's selection of a certain language.

Since the interviewees had not been explicitly asked to explain why they had selected a particular language for their concentrated efforts, the above-mentioned reasons should be regarded as tentative explanations on the part of the interviewers. However, these remarks can be supported indirectly by some of the statements made in the interviews. For example, Ms. B. consciously chose an Italian training centre in order 'to kill two birds with one stone', i.e. she felt it was worthwhile trying once more to learn a language, since language learning could be combined with her professional development. In the case of Mr. C., who, as one might say, made language learning into a life-long hobby, accidental circumstances, favourable learning environments, and his professional development may have been some of the factors acting as selective determinants; for example, due to his unexpected hospital stay in Rumania, he learned Rumanian as actually spoken by natives. Having been married to speaker of Icelandic may have provided the necessary motivational stimulus to achieve a high proficiency level in Icelandic.

It might have been impossible for the interviewees themselves to explain clearly why they focussed on one language rather than another, perhaps with the exception of those situations involving a professional activity, as in the cases of Ms. B. and, at times, of Mr. C. Whatever the initial selective determinants may have been, it appears that one of the major factors making the learners persist in language learning was the development of an emotional bond to the language. The development of this bond was frequently stimulated by experiences external to the actual language learning process, such as experiencing a fascinating teacher or developing a close personal contact with native speakers. Generally speaking, once the learners' interest in learning a certain language was aroused, they involved themselves actively in the language learning process.

The ways in which the three successful language learners approached their task again demonstrate individuality as well as similarities. The broader context and the individual circumstances are unique; the learners' approaches to the learning task at hand are similar. The experiences reported ty these interviewees validate the different strategies presented earlier. For example, Ms. A and Ms. B. practised pronunciation as well as different structures by using native speakers as linguistic models (Strategy 1c); Ms. A. changed the usual purpose of an activity (Strategy 1e): she went to movies she had already seen because they were dubbed into the foreign language she was learning.

In addition, all three successful language learners developed a sense of language as a system (Strategy 2) and as a means of communication and interaction (Strategy 3). For example, Ms. A. used the technique of cross-lingual comparisons, finding cognates. Mr. C. perfected this technique and extended it to phonology and morphology. The case studies provide ample evidence for Strategy 3; the interviewees deliberately sought out communication situations in order to increase their oral skills (3b).

The affective demands of language learning were also reported by all three interviewees. For example, Ms. B. recalled how she was forced to overcome her inhibition against speaking the foreign language by having to act as an interpreter between an Italian and an American friend. Mr. C.'s initial experience in Iceland confirmed him in his conviction that one had to overcome one's shyness and use the language as much as possible (Strategy 4).

The fifth identified strategy, monitoring of L2 performance, was evidenced in the selected case studies. Ms. B., for example, constantly monitored the language she was producing, being 'on the look-out for clues'; Mr. C. repeated elicited corrections from native speakers for newly generated (hypothesized) constructions.

In sum, the three case studies show that good language learners take advantage of potentially useful learning situations, and if necessary create them. They develop learning techniques and strategies appropriate to their individual needs. They demonstrate that, contrary to popular belief, language success is not so much attributable to an 'innate gift', as to a conscious effort and constant involvement.[11]

Notes

1. Since this part of the interview was only minimally directed, not all the questions were asked systematically. Furthermore, some of the questions are significant only in relation to the individual case history. Therefore, in this part only those results are presented which are of general importance to the total sample.
2. For the purposes of the present study the difference between foreign and second language learning was considered irrelevant. The terms are therefore used interchangeably.
3. The sequence in *all* tables referring to the individual subjects is the same.
4. It appears that self-ratings can be regarded as a fairly accurate measure of language competence. In the Montreal Study, for example, which attempted to measure the degree of bilingualism of grade 6 students, self-ratings were 'found to be powerful predictors of the criterion measures' (Macnamara, 1969: 86).
5. The term 'immersion' does *not* refer to school 'immersion programs' in which L2 is the language of instruction.
6. *Adjusted frequency – data missing.
7. Occasionally, the presentation of the results follows the logical flow of the argument and not the original sequence of the questions.
8. *Adjusted frequencies due to incomplete data designated by an asterisk.
9. Replies to Question X (techniques) will be reported in the following section, subsequent to a list of identified strategies.
10. ** Indicates that the subject ranked his/her competence in the language marked as 'Advanced' (pp. 10–11) in at least three skills.
   (½) Only two skills were ranked as 'Working knowledge' by the interviewee.
11. For more case studies of successful language learners see Fröhlich (1976).

PART III
The Main Classroom Study

Introduction[1]

The interviews with the good adult language learners described in Part II provided many interesting insights and ideas which aided in the planning of a major empirical investigation. It became evident that strategies of successful language learning could not be identified in isolation from other learner characteristics and learning situations. In addition, language learning behavior had to be observed directly, not discussed solely in retrospect or reported by teachers.

Therefore, the purpose of the major empirical investigation became to isolate some of the critical variables among the common charactertistics, personality traits, cognitive styles, strategies, and learning environments of the good language learner in a formal second language learning situation. Consequently, it was necessary to conduct this proposed research within the formal educational system. It was decided that the students to be studied should be selected from various levels of the program in French as a second language, i.e. beginners, intermediate, and advanced students. The grades chosen as appropriate for these levels of proficiency were grade 8, grade 10, and grade 12 respectively.

As criterion measures of linguistic competence, it was considered necessary to have a measure of both receptive and productive competence. A French test of listening comprehension was chosen as a measure of the former, while an imitation task to measure the latter had to be developed.

In order to accomplish the overall aim of the project, objective observation of the good language learner in action in his learning environment was essential. This necessitated the development of an appropriate observation schedule.

In addition, it was hoped that some of the observable learning behaviors of good and poor language learners could be correlated with or accounted for by some of the 'unobservables' underlying them. Therefore, it was necessary to identify testable cognitive styles and personality characteristics relevant to language learning. In addition, it was considered important to find suitable means for assessing the attitude and motivation of the students.

In order to gain as much information as possible about the subjects, a detailed interview of individual students was considered to be worthwhile. The students would be asked about their language learning experiences, including the difficulties they might be having, their likes and dislikes, and their attitudes towards the learning of French.

Furthermore, the individual teachers whose students were to be observed were also to be interviewed. They were to describe, as best they could, the attributes and learning behaviors of the selected students and the reasons why they considered the students successful or not.

The present study was thus to provide access not only to students' and teachers' perceptions of the learning context and individual learning styles, but also to objective measures of the very same phenomena through the use of an observation schedule. In addition, it was hoped that some of the observable learning behaviors and linguistic performances of the students could be accounted for by the identification and quantification of some of the 'unobservables' underlying them.

Note

1. In conjunction with the 1974 spring conference of the Ontario Modern Language Teachers' Association (OMLTA) 700 questionnaires were sent to its members one month prior to the conference. In the questionnaires the teachers were asked to describe two successful and two unsuccessful language learners they were presently teaching. It was suggested in the covering letter, attached to the questionnaires, that the teachers focus on language learning strategies, ways of learning, study habits, and the differences in approach to language learning between successful and unsuccessful language students. Due to the limited return (10%) the results are not reported in this version of the report. They are available in the draft report.

CHAPTER 1

Apparatus

1. Criterion Measures

For the purposes of the present study, means of identifying students as good or poor language learners were necessary. French grades at school were not adequate, nor were they comparable across schools. Using teacher identification alone also presented many problems. It was decided that the most appropriate criteria were objective measures of the linguistic competence of the students. It was felt that measures of receptive as well as of productive competence should be administered to the students. One of the IEA Tests of French Achievement was selected as the measure of linguistic receptive competence, while an imitation task had to be developed as a measure of productive competence.

1.1 IEA Tests of French Achievement

In 1966, the International Association for the Evaluation of Educational Achievement (IEA) appointed an International Committee in French as a Foreign Language with representatives from England, France, Canada, USA, and Iran. Their task was to develop a program for the assessment of proficiency in French as a foreign language of students in several countries around the world, as part of the IEA Eight-Country Survey (Carroll, 1975). Over a period of five years, a set of tests was developed, pilot-tested, and revised; by 1970 final forms of the tests were produced by the IEA Council and distributed to the participating countries.

During the period from February 1971 to January 1972 the tests were given to defined populations of students in eight countries: Chile, England (and Wales), The Netherlands, New Zealand, Scotland, Sweden, Rumania, and the United States. In all, about 30,000 students were tested.

Even though the overall purpose of the IEA study was evaluation and not the development of tests *per se,* it was nevertheless necessary to develop tests that would have the highest possible reliability, validity, and practicality. Four tests were developed for each test administration, in listening, reading, writing, and speaking.

These tests were mainly of the 'global' type, in constrast to the 'discrete-point' type. In other words, the tests were designed so that the student's response to an item was dependent upon a complex function of his total degree of competence in French, not on his knowledge of any particular item of vocabulary, morphology, or syntax.

The tests were also designed for several distinct populations, as specified ages or educational levels. The specific definitions of populations adopted for the study were as follows:

Population I:
All students aged 10 in full-time schooling currently studying French.

Population II:
All students aged 14 in full-time schooling currently studying French.

Population III:
All students in the pre-university year grade in full-time schooling who are currently studying French and have studied it for at least two years before the present academic year.

Population IV:
The subpopulation of Population IV consisting of students who are specializing in French.

For the purposes of the present study, it was decided that Population I would be suitable for grade 8 subjects, Population II for grade 10 subjects, and Population IV for grade 12 subjects. Because of the time constraints involved in 'school-experimentation' only one of the tests was to be given to each of the populations. Of the four tests the listening test was chosen, because it had high intercorrelations with all the other tests and because it measured not only listening skills but also reading skills that were necessary in choosing the correct responses. Nevertheless, the listening test was considered to be, for the most part, a measure of receptive competence.

The test itself consisted of 35 (Population I) or 40 (Population II and IV) items in which the student heard words, sentences, or discussions on the tape recorder, his task being to choose the appropriate responses from a list of four alternatives presented to him. The test items were divided into units based on:

(a) picture recognition
(b) sentence recognition
(c) comprehension of long passages
(d) comprehension of long conversations

The students were to mark their responses on answer cards presented to them. The test is approximately 25 to 35 minutes long.

1.2 Imitation task

Since the IEA Test principally measures aspects of *receptive* competence, it was considered important that another criterion measure of linguistic competence be given which would measure *productive* competence. Some researchers might have felt that a collection of spontaneous speech from these students would have provided the necessary data on productive competence. However, there are several problems inherent in spontaneous speech collection; namely, (1) the quantity of speech data that would have to be collected would be vast, (2) spontaneous speech would provide only a conservative estimate of the learner's productive competence.

In spontaneous speech subjects tend to avoid structures they are in the process of acquiring, occasionally replacing these structures with alternative forms. Therefore, an evaluation of a speaker's productive competence based solely on his spontaneous speech would tend to be conservative and inaccurate.

An alternative method for measuring productive competence was therefore sought. The use of 'elicited imitation' was suggested in research by Naiman (1974) and Swain, Dumas, and Naiman (1974).

In his study Naiman (1974) showed that accurate imitation of the syntactic structures contained in L2 sentences beyond a subject's short-term memory capacity involved first decoding of the structure, followed by encoding according to the child's own productive system. Subjects were not able to repeat accurately structures they did not know, but on the other hand they were often able to repeat structures that they were in the process of acquiring. In other words, imitation was a valid source of information about a subject's productive competence in L2, but a conservative estimate of receptive competence.

Since an imitation task could be administered in a short time, it was considered an ideal instrument for measuring productive competence when time constraints existed, as they did in the present study. It was therefore decided that an imitation task would be developed for use as an additional criterion measure of competence in the second language.

Coinciding with the present study, another research project at the Modern Language Centre (Swain, 1976) was investigating the linguistic competence of young Anglophone children acquiring French in an 'immersion' program. For this study, an imitation task had been developed to measure linguistic competence. The vocabulary and structures included were considered to be fairly representative of some of the basic elements of French grammar and vocabulary.

We felt that it would be interesting to compare the results of the imitation task given to the grade 8, 10, and 12 students of our study to the results of the grade 1, 2, and 3 'immersion' children.

The imitation task used by Swain consisted of 15 sentences, each 15 syllables long.[1] The students were tested individually and each subject heard the same sentences repeated twice on a tape recorder. The students were then asked to repeat, as best they could, what they had heard on the tape recorder.

Procedure in the present study was to be identical. However, it was necessary to adapt the task in several ways. For the grade 12 students, only 10 of the original 15 sentences were used, but it was felt that this reduction would not affect the validity of the task. Subjects were already to receive a considerable number of other tests, therefore the shorter the imitation task could be made, the better.

Originally, the same 10 sentences were to have been given to all the grades. But after a brief period of pilot-testing, it was evident that the sentences were too difficult for the grade 8 and 10 subjects, and would have to be modified.

For the grade 10 students, the 10 sentences were adapted and shortened slightly, so that the resulting 10 sentences were each 13 syllables long, although they contained many of the same structures and vocabulary items. Similarly, the grade 8 sentences were adapted and shortened to 10 sentences, each 9 syllables long. These sentences also consisted of many of the same structures and vocabulary items as the original set of sentences. The final set of imitation sentences for each grade can be found in Table 10.

2. Cognitive Style and Personality Tests

Recognizing the need to study the relationshops of cognitive styles and personanlity characteristics to second language learning, and building on the interviews conducted in the first stage of the project, it was decided to administer several personality and cognitive style tests to the subjects. A description of the tests chosen follows. In addition, hypotheses about the relationships of these measures to language learning are presented.

2.1 Cognitive style tests

The Hidden Figures Test

The Hidden Figures Test (1962) is a test of perception, specifically of an individual's ability to perceive a simple figure within a larger complex figure which serves to obscure and embed the simple figure. Whereas this is the basic purpose of the test, individual differences in perceptual performance appear to relate to more than perceptual functioning – they also signify types of functioning in intellectual activities. In fact, research with the number of different versions of tests of figure embeddedness have shown formal stylistic similarities across many psychological areas – perceptual, cognitive, affective, and psycho-motor.

The perceptual task that the subject faces is to break up an organized visual field and keep a part of it separate from that field. A *field dependent* person perceives all parts of the organized field as a total experience and is dominated by the overall field, while the *field independent* person is able to experience parts of the field as discrete from the organized ground. Tasks involving senses other than sight show similar field dependent or independent responses. Perhaps of particular interest to this study is the field dependent–independent perceptual style displayed in auditory disembedding (White, 1954) when subjects were asked to identify particular tunes while other melodies were played in the background.

The same stylistic tendencies occur in intellectual functioning as well. The subject who has difficulty in performing the perceptual task of identifying simple figures also has difficulty in solving problems which require isolating an essential element from the context in which it is presented and using it in a different context (Goodman, 1971; De Fazio, 1973). Field dependent subjects are very much tied to the context in which they first meet the element while field independent subjects are able to abstract the element from its context, to reorganize a strictly organized field, or even to impose structure on a field with little inherent structure (Witkin *et al.,* 1962, 1971).

In the Hidden Figures Test, the subject is given a booklet containing complex geometric figures, one on each page. On a separate page, he is given a simple geometric figure, with instructions to find this simple figure within the complex one. The task is the same throughout the test; the simple figure to be found in the complex design is always exactly the same in size, proportion, and position as the one found on the separate page. The subject is asked to sketch in the lines of the simple figure he has discovered in the complex one. In the test version used in the present study, four basic geometric designs are used, obscured within 16 complex design (Jackson *et al.,* 1964).

The designs are graded in difficulty, and the simple figure varied to counter-act the effect of practice.

Relation to Second Language Learning. Learning a second language is con-sidered a highly complex affair. The learner has to acquire a new system of communication with a new sound system and a new set of syntactic rules and lexical items. He may be overwhelmed by the initial novelty and complexity. The second language may appear to him to be a confusing disarry of complex verbal stimuli that reach him solely as 'noise'. Language learners will differ in the way they cope with this complexity and uncertainty.

We hypothesize that the more successful language learner is the one who is able to focus on those language stimuli relevant to the language learn-ing task at hand and to disregard the inappropriate ones, whereas the less successful language learner will be distracted by irrelevant cues which produce an overall effect of noise. He is dependent on the entire stimulus field and cannot select the proper cues for attention. If he does choose from the various stimuli, it is the stimulus with the most sensory impact which usually attracts his attention and this may or may not be a correct choice. Alternatively, he may attend to cues he recognizes from past experience. Again, these may or may not be the appropriate ones. If these are cues that have been overlearned in the past, they are likely to be related to aspects of his first language and may occasionally be inappropriate for the second. On the whole, the poor language learner may over-react to the immediate availability of some cues or to their sensory impact, without regard to their appropriateness.

The Stroop Phenomenon.[2] *The Speed of Color Discrimination Test*

The Speed of Color Discrimination Test (Messick and Fritsky, 1963) is one of a number of versions of the Stroop color-word interference test which investigates a subject's responses to a conflict situation created when response to a stimulus sets up competition between two 'habits' of unequal strengths, the stronger habit having to be inhibited in favor of the weaker one. Subjects cope with this task in different ways; some are better able to 'foreground' the weaker habit and to suppress the stronger one than others. The purpose of the test then is to differentiate subjects who are able to suppress the stronger habit from those who have more difficulty in so doing and who, despite the instructions to produce the weaker habit, find that the stronger habit inevitably emerges.

In this version of the interference test, the subject is first faced with a number of pages with samples of patches in four different colors – red, blue, green, and orange. Under stringent time restrictions the subject must print under each sample the first letter of the color's name. In the second part of the test the items consist of the names of the four colors printed in different colored inks. For example, the name 'orange' is printed in either blue, red, green or orange ink. This second part is the conflict situation. A printed word imples a verbal response in our literate culture; moreover, only one particular and dominant response habit is associated with each word, while objects and colors are associated with a variety of response tendencies. This makes the reading response much more dominant than the naming of color response. Yet the conflict task requires the more dissipated color-naming response. When the color word is incongruous with the color of the ink in which it is printed, investigators generally have found that it is almost twice as difficult to name the color of the ink than in cases where the ink is presented merely as a color patch. Those subjects who are able to suppress interference are considered to be low-interference prone while those who are less able to suppress interference are considered to be high-interference prone.

Relation to Second Language Learning. Another feature of effective second language learning is the ability to cope adequately with native language interference. The language learner has to resist the overpowering influence of a firmly entrenched first language system. The first language has, in fact, become a highly overlearned set. A learner must be flexible enough to break away from the first language and the learning set associated with it, and attend to the aspects of the second language independently.

It is hypothesized that the successful language learner will learn to accommodate and develop a new and revised set of language responses that may map over or complement his previously learned set.

Pettigrew's Category-Width Scale – Estimation Questionnaire

The Estimation Questionnaire (Pettigrew, 1958) investigates categorizing consistencies, specifically the width of categories that individuals will assign to a number of events whose ranges could be either very wide or very narrow depending on how thay are perceived. A category average is supplied and the subjects must decide the limits for this average. By giving a category a top and bottom boundary, individuals establish that all that comes between these points will be considered equivalent.

The responses that are given indicate whether subjects are Broad Categorizers, that is, accept a very wide range of events as belonging to a category, or Narrow Categorizers, that is, accept a much more restricted range of events. It is felt that individuals who respond consistently to a questionnaire in the manner described above react similarly in assimilating incoming information from any source. Broad categorizers categorize their world in a loose, all-encompassing fashion, while narrow categorizers categorize their world in a tighter, more constricted fashion.

Categorizing behavior is also felt to include risk-taking. Subjects who risk inclusion of many items that do not fit the category are considered Broad Categorizers. Those who risk exclusion of many possible valid instances in order to minimize the number of negative instances are considered Narrow Categorizers.

An example of the items tested for categorizing style follows. Each question has two parts and the subject is to make a choice from the four numbers shown in (a) and then another choice from the four numbers shown in (b). These choices set the limits for the range for the individual. He is told to choose whatever he feels is most appropriate and is cautioned that there are no right or wrong answers.

(1) It has been estimated that the average width of windows is 34 inches. What do you think?

(a) is the width of the widest window . . .

(1) 363 inches		(3) 48 inches
(2) 341 inches		(4) 81 inches

(b) is the width of the narrowest window . . .

(1) 3 inches		(3) 11 inches
(2) 18 inches		(4) 1 inche

Relation to Second Language Learning. The learner may construct very broad generalizations about the language, under which he subsumes a number of examples that do not really fit or that are only partly related. In a sense, he is overgeneralizing in his inclusion of many inappropriate examples in order to fulfil his tendency towards broad generalization. Alternatively, he may make very fine, precise distinctions, so that every example has its own rule. This approach may not be very efficient either, since some of the examples may actually be subsumed under one more general rule.

Both extremes involve risks, one of exclusion of appropriate examples, one of inclusion of inappropriate examples. The overgeneralizer may make a large number of errors, the overly precise learner may be too overburdened with rules to apply them efficiently. The good language learner may be the middle-of-the-roader who is reasonably precise but risks broadening his rules in order to simplify learning.

2.2 Personality tests

From the results of the interviews in the first stage of the present study, we decided that it was important to examine the relationship between certain personality characteristics and second language learning. Originally we had intended to investigate a large number of features; for example, intolerance of ambiguity, rigidity, tolerance of anxiety, fear of rejection, self-esteem, empathy, inhibition, extroversion, risk-taking, etc. However, since the students could not be submitted to such a massive battery of tests, only four were selected for this research project: intolerance of ambiguity, sensitivity to rejection, empathy, extroversion.

Budner's Intolerance of Ambiguity Scale

This test (Budner, 1962) has a questionnaire format with a 7-point scale and measures the tendency of subjects to perceive and interpret ambiguous situations as sources of threat. Ambiguous situations are those characterized by novelty, complexity, or insolubility, and the responses to such threatening situations are characterized by expressions of dislike, by depression, by attempts to avoid the situation, or by destructive behavior. The 16 items of the scale have ambiguous situations as their central theme, and invite responses indicative of threat, that is, expressions of dislike, desire to avoid the situation, etc. The scale was shown to correlate with other scales of intolerance of ambiguity. Individuals who score highly on the scale are highly intolerant of ambiguity and those who score low are relatively tolerant of ambiguity.

Relation to Second Language Learning. The scale has not been part of any study related to language. Pimsleur did use Walk's Tolerance of Ambiguity Scale in his study of underachievement in second language learning (Pimsleur *et al.*, 1966) but found no relation between this and a number of other personality measures, and language achievement. However, it has been suggested by Stern (1975) and Rubin (1975) that the ability to tolerate ambiguous language situations is a quality that could promote successful second language learning.

Mehrabian's Sensitivity to Rejection Scale

This scale (Mehrabian, 1970) consists of 24 statements with responses to each item coded on a +4 (very strong agreement) to a −4 (very strong disagreement) scale. The statements describe situations that could bring negative feedback from others or that elicit discomfort, e.g. being asked to express desires or feelings that might incur rejection from others. Other statements express a preference for warm, accepting people, a desire to be liked, even by people not well known, and negative feelings associated with the presence of many people. The aim of the test is to identify the individuals who react fearfully to situations where they might feel rejected and excluded by others. No major validation studies have been made.

Relation to Second Language Learning. Although this scale has not been used in studies involving language learning, it was felt that students who are sensitive to rejection would display a number of behaviors and characteristics that might be detrimental to language learning. For example, such students might tend to avoid active participation in class, for fear of volunteering incorrect answers and being subjected to ridicule by classmates. These students might also find the imitation task, a speaking task, particularly trying, again for fear of failure. Sensitivity to rejection might also be revealed in person-to-person interviews with the students. Support for these hypothese comes from Stern (1975) who notes that a second language learner must be willing to risk making mistakes and making a fool of himself if he is to succeed in language learning.

Hogan's Empathy Scale

Hogan's measure of empathy (1969) is a 41-item questionnaire that elicits yes–no responses to statements derived from well known personality inventories such as the California Psychological Inventory and the Minnesota Multiphasic Personality Inventory. The definition of empathy used in the initial stages of the scale construction was conceived as the act of constructing for oneself another person's mental state. The empathic individual considers the effects his actions might have on others and so must be willing to put himself in another person's place, assess how that person would feel and modify his behavior after having exposed himself to another point of view. Individuals judged to be capable of this displacement of the self and individuals judged to have a low capacity for doing this were given a battery of items from the above personality inventories and those items that discriminated well between high- and low-rated empathic individuals were retained for the final scale. The purpose of the scale then is to discriminate between high and low empathic individuals. An empathic individual would have the following characteristics:

(1) Is socially perceptive of a wide range of interpersonal cues.
(2) Seems to be aware of the impressions he makes on others.
(3) Is skilled in social techniques of imaginative play, pretending, and humor.
(4) Has insights into his own motives and behavior.
(5) Evaluates the motivation of others in interpreting situations.

Relation to Second Language Learning. Guiora *et al.* (1972) showed that empathy as measured by a number of empathy tests such as the (1) Micro-momentary Expression Test (where the number of different facial expressions of filmed actors noted by students gives them an empathy measure), (2) the Thematic Apperception Test (where students' interpretations of ambiguous pictures are evaluated for empathic responses by trained judges), and (3) empathic responses to literature passages (again rated by trained judges) was related to good language learning, specifically to good pronunciation.

However, this testing method is quite complex, requiring elaborate, time-consuming procedures and training of judges to score responses. A paper and pencil measure such as Hogan's Empathy Scale was considered a more efficient way of measuring a quality that could be predictive of language learning success.

One of the characteristics of good second language learners, mentioned by Stern (1975), is sensitivity to language use. Whereas the poor learner 'blunders cheerfully', the good learner is 'not crude and insensitive in tackling the new language and culture' (p. 315).

Eysenck's Introversion–Extroversion Scale

This scale consists of 24 yes–no questions that describe situations or feelings where preferences for outgoingness or solitude, self-control or lack of self-control, subjective or objective decision-making, impulsiveness or reflectiveness, predictability in behavior or lack of predictability in behavior, etc. are indicated. The purpose of the scale is to identify subjects who answer consistently to item questions and state tendencies to introversion or extroversion. The scale is widely used and a number of validating studies have been reported (Eysenck and Eysenck, 1963).

Relation to Second Language Learning. Although Eysenck has not reported any study in second language learning involving this scale, studies related to the extroversion dimension and second language learning have been noted. Pritchard (1952) found a correlation between sociability as measured by student activities on the playground and fluency in spoken French. In the Pimsleur *et al.* (1966) study of underachievement one of the many personality measures used was outgoingness, which was defined in bahavioral terms similar to extroversion. Moreover, Rubin (1975) regards lack of inhibition as an asset in language learning, particularly in developing communication skills.

2.3 Attitude Test

Gardner and Smythe (1975b) of the Language Research Group at the University of Western Ontario have developed an attitude battery assessing various motivational characteristics which play an important part in the learning of French as a second language. Among these characteristics are attitudes towards French Canadians and European French, attitudes towards the specific language learning situations, parental encouragement, and general interest in learning foreign languages.

This battery has been validated for students across Canada. In the present study, because of the inherent classroom time constraints, an experimental abbreviated version developed by the Language Research Group was used.

3. Classroom Observation

3.1 Purpose

In view of the critical questions raised when evaluating the interviews with adults, it was felt to be essential to observe good and poor language learners objectively in their actual learning environments. It was hoped that direct observation would supplement this preliminary picture of good and bad language learners. As most young Canadians learn language in the public school system, the regular classroom was chosen as the place for direct observation.

Assuming that language learning comprises both conscious and unconscious aspects and expresses itself in observable and unobservable learning behavior, classroom observation can only contribute to the recording of *overt* learning behavior, of which the learner or may not be conscious.

Since the main purpose of the present study was to identify learning strategies and techniques, it followed that the primary focus of classroom observation had to be on individual students and not on the classroom as a whole. As a detailed review of a large number of existing observation schedules revealed,[3] none of them could easily be adopted for the purposes for the present system. Neither the dyadic interaction coding systems nor those instruments specifically developed for language classroom obversation were considered elaborate enough to record detailed items in the observation of individual language learners.

3.2 History of the development of the observation schedule

The critical evaluation of existing observation schedules as well as the review of literature on language learning strategies and techniques contributed to the development and formulation of observational foci for the main experimental phase of the present study.

In view of the limited number of stategies identified through direct classroom observation up to the present time, several specific questions were raised. It was hoped that the answers to these questions would indicate language learning strategies and techniques (or a lack thereof) on the part of successful and unsuccessful students in a formal learning setting.

(1) (a) Does the hand-raising behavior of good and poor students differ? Do good students volunteer more frequently for certain types of questions, activities, etc., than poor students?

    (b) Do good students initiate interaction with the teacher or another student more frequently than poor students?

(2) (a) Do good students indicate more certainty in responding?

    (b) Do they hesitate less?

    (c) In which circumstances, for example, after what kind of question, do (a) or (b) occur?

(3) Do good students circumlocute more often than poor students?

(4) Do good students insert native language items less frequently than poor students?

(5) (a) Do good and poor students react differently to teacher or student correction; for example, do good students repeat a correction voluntarily?

    (b) Do good students attempt to correct themselves more frequently than poor students do?

It was also considered of interest to investigate whether a teacher treats students whom he perceives as successful differently from students whom he perceives as poor. Several educational psychologists, among them Rosenthal and Jacobson (1968), indicated that teachers form their own expectations regarding students' potential performance, and that these expectations function as long-term self-fulfilling prophecies.

In view of a possible differential treatment of successful and unsuccessful students by the teacher, it was hoped that classroom observation could answer some of the following questions, and perhaps indicate their relative importance:

(1) Does the teacher ask good and poor students different types of questions?

(2) Does he ask good students more questions than he asks poor students?

(3) Does he ask good students more often when they have not indicated that they would like to respond?

(4) Does he react differently to their native language insertions?

(5) Does he react to their responses with more or less feeling?

(6) Does he more often use responses given by good students as correct models for classroom repetition?

(7) Does the teacher interrupt good students less frequently than poor students?

(8) Does he correct good students differently from poor students?

(9) Does he more often ask good students to correct other students?

(10) Does he provide good students more or less frequently with clues, before or during their responses; what kind of clues (intra, inter, or extra-lingual) does he give to good and poor students?

(11) Does he make good students repeat his corrections more or less frequently?

Taking into consideration the questions raised, an observation schedule was required which would allow for the exact coding of dyadic interactions between the teacher and individual students or between the students themselves, integrating behavioral items specific to the language learning situation. As none of the existing instruments could meet these specific demands, it was necessary to develop a new observational system for the purposes of this project.

Pilot phase

For several days two researchers attended small adult language classes and observed the interactions between teacher and individual students. Different aspects of students' verbal responses and reactions and teachers' evaluating procedures were noted. The researchers subsequently compared their impressions, and devised a rough outline of an observation schedule, following the basic sequential nature of teacher–student classroom interaction as observed: presentation, elicitation, response, evaluation.

For several weeks the research team visited eight schools, including classes from grades 7 to 13 inclusive. In the beginning, the lessons were taped to enable the observers to recall the verbal interactions in detail and categorize them appropriately. Each time the preliminary categories were modified or extended, and different aspects were added to allow a more detailed and refined coding of behavior. As the focus was on the learner interacting with his teacher (and vice versa), it was decided to record the length of time teacher and class spent on different activities, and furthermore to mention the material being used for instruction and learning. It was also felt to be useful to observe and record the students' facial expressions and their general behavior.

Towards the end of these preliminary class visits a coding sheet was developed, with columns for the coding of elicitative, responsive, and evaluative behavior. Room was also left for general observations and for frequency counts of students' hand-raising behavior.

The researchers memorized the coding categories, randomly chose two (later three) students and coded their verbal interactions with the teacher. Subsequently, the results were compared and discrepancies discussed. At the end of the pilot phase a high degree of inter-judge reliability had been attained.

3.3 Observational schedule

The observational schedule developed for the present study consists of two separate parts: (1) the coding categories and additional coding symbols, and (2) the coding sheets (see below). The components of each part will be explained in the pages that follow Tables 3, 4, and 5.

Table 3 Coding categories

A. ELICITATIVE
 (1) Elicits specific information (+ clues)
 (2) Elicits general information (+ clues)
 (3) Elicits clarification
 (4) Elicits elaboration
 (5) Elicits repetition of preceding statement (or asking the student to 'speak up')
 (6) Elicits recommencement of previous response
 (7) Elicits confirmation of comprehension (or asking if there are any questions)
 (8) Elicits a complete response
 (9) Elicits correction
(10) Elicits other activities (+ activities)

B. RESPONSIVE
 (1) Gives a complete response
 (2) Gives a partial response
 (3) Gives no response (or says 'I don't know')
 (4) Continues responding
 (5) Questions or comments on preceding statements, responses, etc.

Aspects of Responses
 (a) + repetition (/ partial repetition)
 (b) with self-correction (b with help)
 (c) + clarification
 (d) + elaboration
 (e) with circumlocation
 (f) callouts
 (g) not volunteering a response
 (h) with hesitation (initial, medial)

Table 3 *continued*

C. EVALUATIVE

(1) Accepts response
(2) Partially accepts response
(3) Rejects response
(4) Gives no feedback
(5) Reacts to behavior

Aspects of Evaluation

(a) + repetition (/parital repetition)
(b) + correction
    (1) explicit
    (2) implicit
    (3) localization of incorrectness
    (4) indication of incorrectness
(c) + clarification
(d) + elaboration
(e) + providing the answer (/partially providing)

Table 4 Additional coding systems

CLUES

EM   emphasis clue
GR   grammar clue
IL   intralingual clue
EL   extralingual clue
CR   crosslingual clue

ACTIVITIES

R   reading
WR writing
DR drill
RT   rote
XR exercises
MM memorized material
RO role playing
MC mutual correction
DC declension

Table 4 *continued*

MODE (free-speaking assumed)
Oral
R   reading
TR   tape recorder
Visual
BB   blackboard
PM   printed matter
G   gestures
P   pictorial

SUBJECT MATTER
(1) Phonology
(2) Syntax
(3) Lexicon
(4) Homework, etc.

TONE OF EVALUATION

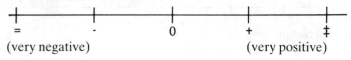

=   -   0   +   ‡
(very negative)   (very positive)

OTHER SYMBOLS   **Meaning**

↑   answering with rising intonation
E   use of English (native language)
↘ E   reaction to an English insertion
→L2   asking for an equivalent in the
                     actual second language
⌐ ⌐   interruption

| ELICITATIVE | RESPONSIVE | EVALUATIVE |

the question has been asked before

the teacher turns to someone else
to ask the same question

=   =   =
1, or 2, 3 etc.   request for the identical information

Table 4 *continued*

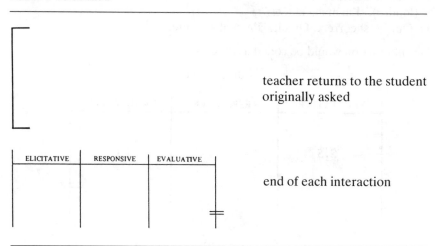

teacher returns to the student
originally asked

end of each interaction

Table 5 Coding sheet

S₁				
S₂				
S₃				
SUBJECT MATTER	ELICITATIVE	RESPONSIVE	EVALUATIVE	GENERAL OBSERVATIONS

Coding categories and some additional coding symbols

The super-ordinate categories (A-Elicitative, B-Responsive, C-Evaluative) represent the three basic steps of an interpersoanl interaction. It is assumed that the teacher initiates the interaction by eliciting information from either the whole class (C) or from a specific student ($S_{1,2,3}$, etc.), that subsequently a student responds and that the teacher, in return, evaluates the answer. Each category under A, B, and C is marked by a number, which is entered into the respective column on the coding sheet. (The coding sheet will be explained later in more detail.) For example, the teacher (T) asks a specific student (S_1) to speak louder and to repeat his answer, the student complies, and the teacher then accepts the response and repeats it for the rest of the class.

T: Plus fort! Répétez votre résponse!
S_1 (louder): J'ai mal à la tête.
T: Oui, c'est correct. On dit, 'J'ai mal à la tête.'

This interaction would be coded as follows:

Coding Sheet

ELICITATIVE	RESPONSIVE	EVALUATIVE
$S_1 5$	1	1 a

Whenever a student elicits information from the teacher or another student and reacts to the response give, the difference from the original assumption (above) has to be indicated specifically on the coding sheet. For example, student (S_1) seeks clarification from the teacher (T); the teacher gives a satisfactory explanation, which the student accepts.

S_1: Pourquoi est-ce qu'on dit, 'Hier, j'ai vu un oiseau' et pas, 'Hier, je voyais un oiseau'?
T: Parce qu'en français on emploie le passé composé pour indiquer une seule action dans le passe.
S_1: Bien, je comprends.

This interaction would be coded in a different way from the previous one:

Coding Sheet

ELICITATIVE	RESPONSIVE	EVALUATIVE
$S_1 \rightarrow T\ 3$	T 1	$S_1 1$

With regard to the different categories under A, B, and C, a few explanations are necessary.

In Part A of Table 3, category 1 refers to narrow questions, to which there is only one correct answer. For example, the answer to the question *Quel est le participe passé du verbe écrire'* can only be *'écrit'*. The second category refers to the elicitation of views, opinions, or general information such as *'Qu'est-ce que tu as fait pendant tes vacances?'* The elicitation of both general and specific information can be accompanied by clues. It was decided to code different types of clues, as some may facilitate responding more than others. It was found convenient to differentiate between five types of clues: emphasis clues, grammar clues, intralingual, extralingual, and crosslingual clues.

An emphasis clue (EM) is preceded by a misunderstanding of the question on the student's part. The teacher usually repeats the same question, or part of it, putting special emphasis on that part of the question which carries the gist of the intended communication. For example:

T: Quelle est la troisième personne du singulier au présent du verbe *finir?*
S: Tu finis.
T: Ecoutez, quelle est la *troisième* personne du singulier?
S: Il finit.

A grammar clue (GR) is related to language as a system and refers to rules without giving a concrete example. For example:

T: Conjuguez le verbe *écouter* au singulier, rappelez-vous que c'est un verbe de la première conjugaison.

An intralingual clue (IL) refers to an actual model which should enable the student to arrive at the right answer by analogy.

T: Quel est le participe passé du verbe *choisir* – c'est comme la forme pour finir qui est *fini?*

Extralingual clues (EL) provide the student with more general background to the question. Rephrasing the question is also regarded as giving the student an extralingual clue.

T: Qu'est-ce que tu fais pendant les mois de juillet et août?
S: Je ne comprends pas.
T: Qu'est-ce que tu fais pendant les grandes vacances, quand tu ne vas pas à l'école?

Crosslingual clues (CR) refer to linguistic examples in a language other than the one studied in the classroom. For example:

T: Devinez le mot français qui indique le frère de mon père!
S: Je ne sais pas.
T: C'est presque comme le mot anglais.

Returning to the categories, 'clarification' (3) refers to the process of arriving at a response and aims at identifying the kind of criteria which were applied to produce a correct answer. For example, the teacher asks the student, *'Pourquoi est-ce que tu as employé le passé composé et pas le présént?'*

In contrast to a 'clarification', an 'elaboration' (4) is defined as an extension of the previous response. For example, the teacher asks the student to give another example of certain irregular plural forms or to rephrase his answer. The elicitation of an elaboration is usually preceded by a total or partial acceptance of the student's response by the teacher. For example:

T: Quel temps fait-il?
S: Le soleil brille.
T: Bien! Est-ce qu'on peut dire autre chose?

The behavior items referred to in categories 5–8 are very explicit and need no further explanation. Category 9, 'Elicits correction' occurs, for example' when the teacher asks one student to correct the response of another.

S_1: Il font beau.
T: Jean (S_2), est-ce que c'est correct?
S_2: Non, il fait beau.

Category 10 has to be supplemented by the actual activities which occur in the classroom, such as reading (R), drill (DR), and exercises (XR). This category can be extended by the observer if the situation requires it.

The first three 'response' categories describe basic possible reactions. The student either responds or remains silent. His answer, however, can be complete or partial. It was considered useful to add and code separately the reaction 'I don't know' (-), as this response may provoke a different reaction from the teacher than mere silence on the student's part.

Category 4 applies to situations where no elicitation by the teacher preceded the student's verbal output. The student may have been interrupted by the teacher or the teacher may have already indicated that he accepts the student's answer, but the student continues responding. Category 5 again describes a non-elicited reaction. In a strictly logical sense, it does not belong to the established categories of responses which follow an elicitation. It was included, however, because it represents a reaction to a preceding statement or response.

In addition to the five major 'response' categories, several 'aspects of response' were added to describe a student's verbal reaction. For example, a student may repeat a preceding statement, usually the teacher's correction.

When a student repeats more than the corrected aspect, it is regarded as a full repetition (a). If he repeats the corrected item alone, it is considered to be a partial repetition (a/). While responding, a student may also attempt to correct himself (b). If he has received any help (clues, or prompts) this is indicated by a circle around the letter ⓑ.

Furthermore, a student may clarify (c) to himself and his fellow students how he produced a linguistically correct statement, or he may add an elaboration to his answer (d). When learning a foreign language, the learner is often searching for a particular word or expression. In this case he may attempt to circumlocute (e), in order to complete his response.

Importance was also attached to the willingness with which a student answers. If a student volunteers an answer by calling out, the letter (f) codes this behavior. Callouts are sometimes taken up by the teacher. He may ask the student who called out to repeat his response (A5) or he may acknowledge and evaluate it (C-categories). In both cases an arrow serves to indicate the sequence of the interaction. For example:

S_1 (calls out): Je mange du pain.
T: Répétez votre réponse!
S_1: Je mange du pain.
T: Oui.

This interaction would be coded as follows:

Coding Sheet

ELICITATIVE	RESPONSIVE	EVALUATIVE
	S_1 (f)	
$S_1 S$	1	1

For ease of coding, voluntary student responding, i.e. hand-raising, is assumed. However, when a student is called upon by the teacher without having indicated his willingness to answer the teacher's question, his involuntary response (B1,2,3) is indicated by the letter (g).

Another aspect of responding is hesitation (h). The student may hesitate at the beginning or during his response. The latter case would be coded as 2h4 – the student begins his response, hesitates, and then continues. Another symbol which was introduced in addition to the letter (h) was an arrow pointing upwards (↑), which indicates that the student answered with rising intonation thus seeking confirmation from the evaluator and indicating self-doubt.

With regard to the third step (part C of Table 3), four basic evaluative reactions have been distinguished. The teacher can entirely (1) or partially (2) accept the response (1: *Oui, ou Bien*; 2: *Oui, mais il y a une meilleure réponse*). The teacher can reject it (3: *Non* or he may shake his head); he can refrain from giving any evaluation at all (4). A blank in the evaluation column on the coding sheet indicates C4.

Several 'aspects of evaluation' were added to allow for a more detailed description of the evaluator's reactions. After accepting a response (1) the teacher may repeat the student's reply entirely (a) or partially (a/). Writing the answer on the blackboard is also regarded as a form of repetition and is coded as (a) followed by an abbreviation for blackboard (a→ BB). Similarly, the repetition of a student's answer by the whole class is coded as (b→ C).

As the teacher's critical evaluation very often includes a correction of the student's response, it was decided to differentiate between four types of corrections (b1–4). The teacher may correct explicitly (b1) or implicitly (b2). The teacher may, for instance, accept the message but not the linguistic form of the utterance. An explicit correction, therefore, can follow a rejection as well as a partial acceptance of the previous response. For example:

T: Où est le livre?
S: Le livre est sur le table.
T: Non, ce n'est pas correct. Le livre est sur *la* table.

When correcting implicitly, the teacher usually accepts the response and repeats it by substituting the error with the correct form, without drawing special attention to the error itself. The students may or may not register the correction. For example:

T: Quel temps fait-il?
S: Il font beau.
T: Oui, il fait beau.

Localization of incorrectness (b3) refers to a way of correcting which makes the student notice *where* the error in his sentence lies. This is usually done by repeating the student's statement, with rising intonation and special stress on the error. For example:

T: Quel temps fait-il?
S: Il font beau.
T: Il *font* beau?

An indication of incorrectness (b4) is the vaguest form of a correction and does not offer any help to the student. It can be verbalized by a question, such as '*Est-ce qu'on dit ça?*' or it may be expressed by gestures (G) conveying doubt, criticism, etc.

The next two aspects, clarification and elaboration (Cc, Cd), need no further explanation as these terms have been defined previously. The final aspect, 'providing the answer', allows the description of situations in which the teacher (or another student) totally or partially provides the expected answer; for example, when the respondent pauses or appears to be confused. It is usually accompanied by at least a partial acceptance of the response, but could also follow an immediate rejection, indicated by the teacher's interrupting the student as soon as he begins responding. For example:

T: Comment vous appelez-vous?
S: Je m'a . . .
T: (nods) Je m'appelle . . . (partially providing the answer) or: Je m'appelle Marie (totally providing the answer).

The last category, 'reacts to behavior', (C5) is entirely different in that it is not initially related to a verbal interaction between the teacher and the students. It was included, however, because a certain percentage of the teacher's time in class, especially in lower grades, is spent on regulating behavior.

In addition to the categories mentioned so far, several symbols were introduced to further describe classroom interactions. In order to indicate the emotional aspect or the tone of an evaluation, a five-point scale was introduced.

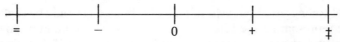

=   –   0   +   ‡

The double negative (=) on the extreme left indicates a very negative (cutting, insulting) emotional reaction. The double plus (+) on the opposite end of the scale signifies outstanding praise. The scale allows for one variation on both sides (+; –). The middle point (0) is defined as indicating the overall prevailing classroom atmosphere. '0' does not have to be coded. The observer is asked to describe explicitly his overall impression of the teacher's responses and criticisms as well as of the general classroom atmosphere at the end of the observation period. On the basis of these impressions, he has to decide whether to index any of the teacher's and students' reactions to indicate a deviation from the mean.

It was further felt to be of interest to be able to code any verbal inter-action in the native language, in this case English. The letter E (for English) can be added to any of the coding categories, if English is used. When a student inserts English to fill a gap in his foreign language utterance, the teacher may or may not react, independently of accepting or rejecting the message. A specific reaction to an English insertion is signified by ↓ E. For example, the teacher accepts the student's response but rejects his use of English. He may then provide the L2 equivalent and ask the student to repeat the response in L2. For example:

T: Qu'est-ce que c'est?
S_1: A book.
T: Oui, mais en français s'il vous plâit. C'est un livre. Répétez!
S_1: C'est un livre.
T: Oui, bien.

The incident would be coded as follows:

ELICITATIVE	RESPONSIVE	EVALUATIVE
S_1 1	1E	1
		↓ E e (L2)
5 ←	1	1

In a real coding situation the symbol L2 (in brackets) would be replaced by a letter representing the foreign language. The arrow pointing towards 5 indicates that the teacher wants the student to repeat the L2 sentences and not his original response, which was in English (L1). If a teacher or a student asks for an equivalent in the target language, an arrow precedes the symbol for L2 (→ F).

Another more or less frequent form of behavior is interruption of the person responding. Interruption is coded as ⌐ in the evaluation column on the coding sheets. If, however, a student (S_n) calls out the answer, thus pre-venting another student (S_1) from even beginning to answer, a blank in the

'Responsive' column followed by the symbols S_n ⌐ f in the next line indicates this. For example:

T asks S_1: Quelle est la date aujourd'hui?
S_n calls out: Le cinq juin.

This incident would be coded as follows:

ELICITATIVE	RESPONSIVE	EVALUATIVE
S_1 1		
	S_n ⌐ f	

Similarly, a teacher may not give the student a chance to respond and provide the answer himself. For example:

T asks S_1: Quelle est la date aujord'hui?
S_1: (hesitates)
T: Le cinq juin.

This would be coded as follows:

ELICITATIVE	RESPONSIVE	EVALUATIVE
S_1 1	h	⌐ e

It may also be important to know if the students under observation respond only to questions which have been asked before. A circle at the margin of the left coding column indicates that the same information has been elicited before. The same symbol at the end of the interaction signifies that the teacher turns to somebody else to ask the same question. If necessary, the request for the identical information can be indicated by a double bar over the number of the type of elicitation, for example $\overline{\overline{1}}$ or $\overline{\overline{4}}$.

When a teacher returns to the student originally asked, for example, in order to make him repeat the answer given in the meantime by someone else, bar brackets are used. For example:

T: Est-ce que tu as faim, Jean?
S_1: Je suis . . .
T: Non. Quelqu'un d'autre?
S_n: Oui, j'ai faim.
T: Jean, répète!
S: Oui, j'ai faim.
T: Bien.

This would be coded in the following way:

ELICITATIVE	RESPONSIVE	EVALUATIVE
$S_1 2$	2	3
$S_1 5$	1	1

The end of each interaction between the teachers and the specific student observed is indicated by a double line (========) on the last column, for example:

ELICITATIVE	RESPONSIVE	EVALUATIVE
$S_1 1$	1	3

With regard to the mode of the classroom interaction, free speech is assumed. Any other type of oral or visual mode can be indicated by special symbols, such as TR for tape recorder, or it can be spelled out and described in the column for general observations.

Explanation of the Coding Sheet

The actual coding sheet is 14 inches long to allow for ease of coding during a long period of observation. The top of the sheet is reserved for the description of the student's hand-raising behavior. It is important to record how often a student raises his hand in each observation period and to establish a frequency pattern. The best indication that a student was not disturbed by the observer's presence is a regular pattern. In addition, the teacher should be asked at the end of the total time observed if he noticed any difference in the student's participation pattern.

In very informal learning environments the students may not have to raise their hands, being allowed to call out the response. In these cases, callouts are equated with hand-raising. If the observer finds it too inconvenient to note down callouts on the top part of the coding sheet, for example in situations where the teacher reacts to the callouts and thus establishes an interaction move, they can be coded under 'Responsive'.

The different columns on the coding sheet reflect the three basic interaction steps: elicitation, response, evaluation. In addition, room is left on both sides to describe the subject matter (left column) and to enter general observations (right column).

The observer is asked to note down the different time units into which each period is divided according to the activities undertaken. For example:

General observations

9:00 T asks general questions about the weekend
9:05 grammar exercises (Present Tense – Present Perfect) Students (S_n) write answers on blackboard
9:20 free conversation, etc.

The entries of different time units and the coding of interactions should correspond on the coding sheet, so that the general background of a student's response can be recalled later, if necessary.

Apart from the time units the observer should note down everything he regards to be of importance: for example, the material used, the behavior of the students, impressions of their personality (shyness, extroversion), etc.

The observer may find that he describes most of the subject matter in the column 'General Observations'. The left column can be used to point out explicitly the content of a particular question, or it can be left blank.

4. Student Interview

The interview with the students observed was to cover a variety of aspects related to the learning environment, learning behavior, characteristics, and attitudes of each student concerned. Nine super-ordinate categories relevant to these issues (a–i) were isolated, for each of which a set of specific questions and subquestions was developed for the students to answer.

Regularity of classroom activities

The first question[4] referred to the degree of representativity and regularity of the instruction learning activities observed in the classroom.

(1) Do you think that what we have seen of your classroom is representative of your classroom activities?
    (a) Was anything missing?
    (b) Was anything different?

A positive answer to question 1 was assumed to confirm the researchers' hypothesis that their presence in the classroom would influence neither the content, the method of instruction, nor the students' behavior to any significant extent.

Students' perception of classroom climate

One of the variables influencing student achievement is considered to be the general classroom climate, including the student's relationship with the teacher and with fellow students. The following questions were formulated.

(1) Do you regard the classroom as formal or informal?
(2) Do you feel comfortable and at ease in this class?
(3) How does the atmosphere in this class compare with that of other classes?
(4) Do you feel that you get along with your teacher and the other students in class?

Students' goals in comparison with teachers' goals

Since the teachers were to be asked to describe their teaching goals, including the kind of skills they considered most important, it was thought to be of interest to inquire about the students' impressions of the teacher's emphasis in teaching and to compare them with the students' expressed personal goals.

(1) Which aspects of French do you think your teacher regards as most important and emphasizes in the classroom?
    (a) Do you think he wants you to be able to *understand* French more than *speak* it, etc.?
(2) What would you like to get out of the French course in the long run?
    (a) Would you like to be able to read French, or rather to speak it fluently, etc.?

Students' attitudes towards classroom activities

It was felt to be important to question the students about their personal preferences in the different learning activities they carried out, voluntarily or not, and, furthermore, to invite their suggestions for change.

(1) Which classroom activities do you most like or dislike?
(2) Which ones do you consider to be the most or the least effective and useful?
(3) If you were asked to change some classroom activities in order to make the learning of French more interesting and useful to you, what would you suggest?

Students' insights into the language learning process

The questions belonging to this category attempt to tap the student's insight into his language learning process.

(1) Could you tell me which aspects of learning French are easy or difficult for you?
(2) Do you have any idea *why* this particular aspect is so easy or difficult for you?
   (a) Do you think that you may have special abilities (or do you lack any) which help (or hinder) you in learning French?
(3) Have you developed any special techniques or study habits which help you to learn how to talk in French, to study the pronunciation, grammar, vocabulary, etc.?

The next question (4) refers to the so-called 'modality preference' in learning. Some students, for example, learn new words better when they see them written down, others when they hear them. It may be imp-ortant for the teacher to be aware of the student's individual preference. The question to be asked is as follows:

(4) When the teacher introduces a new word, do you learn better when you see it written down or when you hear it?

The following questions are more specifically related to the learning situation in the classroom. They attempt to uncover the students' attitudes towards different interactional incidents such as being corrected, and to classroom teaching and learning behaviors. The additional questions are as follows:

Use of native language

(1) Teacher's use of English:
   (1) Do you think that the teacher speaks in French too much or too little?
   (2) When the teacher introduces a new word, would you prefer an English equivalent or an explanation of the meaning in French?
   (3) When you learn new grammar aspects, would you like to be given a rule in English, in French, or no rule at all?

(2) Student's use of English:
   (1) What do you do when you get stuck while responding because you don't know the right word in French?
      (a) Do you insert English, for example, or do you try to find other French words which would somehow express what you intend to say?

Participation behaviour: Attitudes and reactions

(1) Do you feel that you put up your hand often enough?
   (a) Do you know why you don't participate so often?
(2) Do you wait until you are absolutely certain before you put your hand up or do you take a chance and attempt an answer anyway?
(3) Do you mind being called upon by the teacher when you don't have your hand up?
(4) Would you like to be able to call out?
   or: Do you like calling out?
   and/or: Does it bother you if someone calls out?
(5) Do you feel that you are asked sufficiently by the teacher or would you like to be asked more often?
(6) When you haven't understood something, whom do you ask, the teacher or another student?

Attitude and reaction to correction

(1) Do you mind being corrected?
(2) When you make an error, would you prefer to be interrupted right away or would you rather finish your response?
(3) What do you do when you have been corrected? (Do you repeat the correction?)
(4) Do you know what kind of error your teacher corrects most frequently when you give a response?
(5) Do you correct other students when they make an error? Do you do it silently or aloud?

The final question is concerned with affective variables which might influence the students' classroom behavior and achievement. The answers to some of the questions listed above may indicate the existence of anxiety, embarrassment, uncertainty, etc. in the students. However, it was felt to be important to ask the students explicity if they felt embarrassed in speaking the foreign language in front of the class, if they were afraid of making fools of themselves and of being laughed at, etc.

Other affective variables

(1) Are you embarrassed to speak French in class?

(a) Does the language sound strange to you?
(b) Are you afraid of being laughed at by the other students when you try to imitate the French accent?

The researchers are free to ask further questions which they consider to be significant, for example, questions based upon their observations in the classroom.

Notes

1. Naiman (1974) found this length to be beyond the immediate memory span of comparable subjects.
2. For further details see Jensen and Rohwer, 1966; and Dyer, 1973.
3. A description of this review was included in the pre-publication version of this report.
4. The wording of the actual questions was adapted to the students' ages and comprehension levels.

CHAPTER 2

Method

1. Introduction

We originally intended to conduct the experimentation in three schools alone. It was felt later, however, that in order to give more statistical validity to the results of the investigation it was necessary to double the original sample. The study was therefore extended to six schools. Moreover, two of the three additional schools were chosen to represent types of language programs and educational environments alternative to the ones found in the original sample. This was considered to be important for the fuller investigation of relationships between good and poor language learners and various language learning environments.[1] One of the additional high schools chosen offered individualized instruction and the other was an open-plan school. The other four had been chosen randomly. Five schools were lcoated in Metropolitan Toronto, in the boroughs of North York, East York, and Scarborough; the other was in the Halton Board of Education school district.

Three different grades were chosen, 8, 10, and 12. The teachers concerned received an introductory letter briefly describing the major purposes of the study. They were specifically asked not to inform the students of the reasons for the classroom observation, in order not to influence the students' behavior. (They could explain to the students that a survey into the different ways and techniques of the teaching of French in Ontario was being conducted.) Furthermore, the teachers themselves were not specifically made aware of the fact that their own behavior as well as that of certain children was going to be observed. Thus the research team hoped to get as unbiased results as possible.

2. Subjects

As indicated, the research was conducted in three different grands, 8, 10, and 12. These levels were chosen in order to observe language learning at three different stages, at an early though not absolute beginners' stage, an intermediate, and at a fairly advanced stage. The foreign language classroom chosen was the French one, as French is one of Canada's official languages and where offered, its instruction is obligatory until the end of grade 8 in the Ontario school system. All 12 classes were given the appropriate levels of the Listening Comprehension Tests, which are part of the International French Achievement test battery (IEA), developed by the International Association for the Evaluation of Educational Achievement.

Population I of the IEA was administered to the grade 8 students, Population II to grade 10, and Population IV to grade 12. It was emphasized that the test results had absolutely no influence upon the students' school marks. The researchers explained that this test had been developed internationally, and that they were interested in examining its appropriateness for measuring French achievement in Ontario. The students were therefore asked to do their best, in order not to invalidate the results. The test took approximately 30 minutes.

The teachers were asked to make a seating plan of the classroom so that researchers could identify the students they wanted to select for subsequent observation without the teachers' knowledge.

During or immediately after the test period the teachers were casually asked to name the five students whom they would predict to do the best, and the five students whom they would expect to do worst. They were told that their predictions would help the researchers in judging whether the IEA test was valid for measuring achievement in Ontario French classes. It was the impression of the researchers that none of the teachers were aware at this stage that their predictions would at all influence the selection of students for observation.

On the basis of the IEA results and the teachers' predictions, six students per class were chosen for observation. In order to facilitate the selection of subjects, it would have been ideal if the top and bottom students identified by the teachers had been identical with those who scored highest and lowest on the IEA tests. On the whole the teachers' predictions were fairly accurate, but in several cases the IEA results did not match. It was thought to be of interest to include such mismatch cases whenever possible. It was hoped that classroom observation and the subsequent interviews with both the teachers and students concerned would reveal some of the underlying reasons for the discrepancies. Including mismatches meant that an equal distribution of top and bottom students, matched on IEA and teacher prediction in each class, was not always possible. However, with regard to the grand total, the number of low and high achievers, matched on the above-mentioned criteria, was equal (see page 102).

In reference to the teachers' impressions, 29 of the 72 students chosen had been predicted to score in the higher range and 31 students had been expected to score in the lower range. Those 12 students who had been additionally selected had not been mentioned by the teachers. With regard to the IEA test results, 32 of the students chosen were at the top, 31 at the bottom, and 9 scored around the class mean. On the basis of the two criterion measures mentioned above it was decided to differential among eight combinations of teacher predictions and IEA results (see Table 6).

It was originally intended to choose an equal number of male and female students at the high and low achievement levels. This proved to be impossible, due to the decreasing number of male students in grades 10 and 12. Table 7 shows the distribution of the sample according to the combination categories by grade, class, and sex.

In sum, a total of 72 students were selected, out of which 29 were male and 43 female. Twenty-two students were at the top end and 22 at the bottom end of the achievement scale, matched on both the teachers' prediction and the IEA Test results. Twenty-eight students were chosen specifically because they represented a mismatch between the teachers' predictions and the IEA results.

Since in Canada a great number of people are newly arrived immigrants, the linguistic background of the students chosen was also considered to be of interest. Seventeen students out of the total sample of 72 were bilingual (to a greater or lesser degree), with Italian being predominant as a second or original first language (44%).

Table 6 Description of combination categories

Index no. for combinations	Teachers' predictions of students' achievement level	IEA results	Combinations
1	T (Top)	T (Top)	T–T
2	T	B (Bottom)	T–B
3	T	M (Mean)	T–M
4	B (Bottom)	B	B–B
5	B	T	B–T
6	B	M	B–M
7	– (not predicted)	T	–T
8	–	B	–B

Table 7 Distribution of experimental sample according to combination categories by grade, class, and sex

		1		2		3		4		5		6		7		8	
		T-T		T-B		T-M		B-B		B-T		B-M		-T		-B	
Grades	Class No.	M	F	M	F	M	F	M	F	M	F	M	F	M	F	M	F
8	1	1	2					2				2					
	2		1	1				1	1			1					
	3	2	2					2				1					
	4		1					2	1						1		
Grade 8 TOTAL		3	6	1				7	2			4			1		
10	5	2	1								1						
	6												1	1	1		
	7				1						1			1	1		
	8	1	1	1			1	3	3						1	1	1
Grade 10 TOTAL		3	2	1	1		1	3	3		2		1	2	3	1	1
12	9	1	1						1			1					1
	10		1			1	1		1								1
	11		2		1				3		1						1
	12	1	2						2						1		
Grade 12 TOTAL		2	6		1	1	1		7		1	1			1		3
GRAND TOTAL		8	14	2	2	1	2	10	12	0	3	5	1	2	5	1	4
		22		4		3		22		3		6		7		5	

3. Procedure

3.1 Observation

After the six students in each class had been selected on the basis of the criteria discussed above, two members of the research team went into the classrooms, explaining their visit as part of a survey on the different ways in which French was taught and learned in different high schools in Ontario. The students were asked to ignore the researchers' presence as much as possible and to continue in their usual manner.

Each researcher randomly chose three of the six students for observation. The observers were seated at the back or the side of the classroom, attempting to locate themselves where they could observe the students' faces without making themselves too conspicuous. Each researcher further tried to note down different facial expressions, indicating shyness, anxiety, boredom, confusion, etc., as well as any other behavior that might be relevant to a comparison between good and poor learners.

As the length of instruction periods varied from 40 to 80 minutes the minimum total observation time was set for 250 minutes, which appeared to be a reasonable time to allow for class adjustment to the researchers' presence and variation in teaching and learning activities.

In addition to coding the classroom behavior of the six chosen students according to the categories of the observation schedule, and closely observing their behavior, each investigator also made general observations. For example, each noted the amount of time allotted to different activities, the classroom atmosphere, and the participation habits of the whole class.

At the end of the observation period the researchers thanked the teacher and students for the visit and asked if a few students, whom the researchers would name, would be willing to fill in a few questionnaires and answer some questions on their impressions of learning French. The names of the six students of the experimental sample were then called out. The additional procedures were explained to them outside the classroom.

3.2 Administration of tests

The students concerned were allowed to leave regular French classes for three separate testing sessions, each of which lasted approxmiately 30 minutes. It was emphasized that the interviews and questionnaires were confidential and had absolutely no bearing on their school marks. The tests were administered in the following order:

First session:
(1) The Stroop Color-Word Interference Test
(2) Embedded Figures Test
(3) Intolerance of Ambiguity Scale
(4) Introversion–Extroversion Scale

Second session:
(1) Category-Width Test
(2) Fear of Rejection Scale
(3) Empathy Scale

Third session:
(1) National Test Battery for Attitudes

3.3 Imitation task and student interviews

The reseachers arranged individual appointments with each of the three students whom thay had previously observed. Before the interview two cassette recorders were set up, one for the model sentences and one for the recording of the student's repetition of the sentences and the subsequent interview. It was explained to the students that the tape recorders were necessary because it would save time if the researcher did not have to take notes of what the student said.

In the imitation task, the student was asked to repeat each sentence as best he could, after he had heard it twice on the tape. He was given two practice examples. It was explained to the students that in this test the researchers were comparing the errors of French-speaking children with those of students of French as a second language. The student was repeated reassured that this test had nothing to do with his school marks.

The interview followed the basic sequence of questions outlined above. Sometimes a few questions had to be rephrased or modified, if the students did not understand them. Occasionally a question was omitted, if the researcher regarded it as inappropriate. Additional comments or questions were a result of the direct observation period.

In general, an attempt was made to make the interview as informal and also as meaningful to the student as possible. The student was assured that the interview would remain confidential, and he was encouraged to be as honest and frank as he could. Each interview lasted between 15 and 30 minutes, depending upon the student's willingness to communicate his thoughts.

3.4 Teacher interviews

In order to gain additional information about the selected students, a brief informal interview was conducted with each teacher. At the beginning, the IEA results of the entire class were presented and the teacher's comments were invited. In order to compare the school marks and the IEA results, the teachers were asked for the oral and written or the combined marks of the six students. As the IEA-subtests measured only listening comprehension, it was thought to be of interest to investigate to what degree teachers' marks and IEA results matched. The researchers asked the teachers to offer any comments or information regarding the learning behavior and general characteristics of the selected students.

3.5 Return visit to the school

Several weeks after the completion of the experimentation researchers returned to each of the six schools. They requested and reserved the permission of the teachers involved to explain to the whole class in greater detail the overall purpose and procedures of the study. In addition, some of the preliminary results were presented to the class. It was the researchers' impression that both the teachers and the students were extremely interested in the study and that they appreciated the reserchers' returning to explain it to them at greater length.

Note

1. A detailed description of the classroom environment will be presented in Part III, chapter 5, section 6.

CHAPTER 3
Results

1. Scoring and Results of Criterion Measures

Two measures of French language competence were collected. The IEA test of French achievement was used to measure primarily the comprehension component of linguistic competence while the imitation task was used to measure the production component.

1.1 IEA listening test

The IEA tests were scored for each grade, using standardized scoring sheets. The means and standard deviations for each class and grade can be found in Table 8.

As previously described, the six subjects in each class were chosen on the basis of their results on the IEA test in conjunction with their teacher's prediction of success. The means and standard deviations for the six experimental subjects chosen in each class can be found in Table 9. (It is worth noting that the means for the experimental subjects in each grade closely approximate the overall means for all students tested in each grade.)

Because of the relatively small sample, it was considered beneficial to standardize scores across grades so that in later analyses the other measures collected could be related to the same criterion for all 72 subjects. Therefore, on the basis of the mean scores for each grade, scores for the 24 experimental subjects in each of the grades were standardized.

1.2 Imitation task

The imitated sentences were transcribed by the experimenters as soon as possible after the initial testing period. If either experimenter experienced the least doubt during the process of transcription, the other was consulted so as to obtain mutual agreement about the linguistic element(s) in question.

The sentences given to the students of each grade were divided into a number of basic syntactic units for the purposes of scoring. For example, the grade 8 sentence, '*Alain lance un ballon à Henri*' was considered to be made up of the following four syntactic units: *Alain/lance/un ballon/à Henri.*

In grade 12, the sentence, '*Alain lance son ballon à Henri mais il ne l'attrape pas*' was broken up in the following manner: *Alain/lance/son ballon/ à Henri/mais/il ne/l'attrape/pas.* The division of all the sentences used can be found in Table 10.

Table 8 Means and standard deviations on IEA test of French achievement by class and by grade

	Grade 8			Grade 10			Grade 12		
	n	mean	S.D.	n	mean	S.D.	n	mean	S.D.
Class 1	24	17.42	3.91	25	19.24	4.79	27	23.22	6.54
2	23	15.96	3.70	20	20.18	6.71	31	24.84	5.65
3	28	16.54	4.58	28	14.79	4.37	24	18.43	4.35
4	28	17.07	4.60	18	19.42	8.28	16	18.31	8.28
All Classes:		16.78	4.01		18.41	5.50		21.40	6.70
	Maximum possible on IEA Pop 1 = 35			Maximum possible on IEA Pop 2 = 40			Maximum possible on IEA Pop 4 = 40		

Table 9 Means and standard deviations on IEA test of French achievement for the experimental subjects by class and by grade

	Grade 8			Grade 10			Grade 12		
	n	mean	S.D.	n	mean	S.D.	n	mean	S.D.
Class 1	6	17.30	5.24	6	20.33	7.99	6	22.50	8.89
2	6	15.70	5.20	6	22.33	10.05	6	25.83	9.11
3	6	19.00	7.40	6	16.33	7.55	6	18.17	5.56
4	6	18.30	8.12	6	18.30	8.12	6	21.67	12.04
All Classes:	24	17.58	6.30		19.33	7.95		22.04	9.01
	Maximum possible on IEA Pop 1 = 35			Maximum possible on IEA Pop 2 = 40			Maximum possible on IEA Pop 4 = 40		

Table 10 Imitation sentences divided into units

(a) Grade 8 (36 units)

(1) Alain/lance/un ballon/à Henri./

(2) Le grand chien/a mangé/la petite poule./

(3) Nous/avons acheté/des grosses oranges./

(4) Maman/m'/a donné/un beau manteau./

(5) Ton papa/a demandé/une pomme verte./

(6) Je/lui/montre des images/dans le livre./

(7) Quelqu'un/a raconté/une histoire./

(8) J'/ai acheté/des botte noires/ce matin./

(9) Les enfants/regardent/le cheval noir./

(10) Hier/j'/ai vu/mon ami François./

(b) Grade 10 (47 units)

(1) Alain/lance/un ballon/à Henri/près de l'école./

(2) Le grand chien/a mangé/la petite poule/de mon frère./

(3) Nous/avons acheté/des grosses oranges/pour le souper./

(4) Maman/m'/a donné/un beau manteau rouge/ce matin./

(5) Ton papa/a demandé/à Jean-Paul/une grande pomme verte./

(6) Je/montre/des images/qui/sont/dans le livre bleu/de Paul./

(7) Hier/quelqu'un/nous/a raconté/une belle histoire./

(8) J'/ai acheté/des bottes noires/dans le nouveau magasin./

(9) Les enfants/les/regardent/par la fenêtre/de l'école./

(10) J'/ai vu/mon ami François/avec son grand chien brun./

(c) Grade 12 (66 units)

(1) Alain/lance/son ballon/à Henri/mais/il/ne/l'/attrape/pas./

(2) Le grand méchant chien/a mangé/la petite poule blanche/de mon frère./

(3) Nous/avons acheté/des grosses oranges/que/nous/avons mangées./

(4) La maman/de mon ami/m'/a donné/son beau manteau rouge./

(5) Ton papa/lui/a demandé/une pomme verte/et/il/l'/a mangée./

(6) Maintenant,/je/leur/montre/des images/qui/sont/dans le grand livre bleu./

(7) Hier/quelqu'un/nous/a raconté/l'histoire/du petit Indien./

(8) Les enfants/les/regardent/par la fenêtre/après le déjeuner./

(9) J'/ai acheté/les bottes/que/tu/m'/as montrées/dans le magasin./

(10) Je/t'/ai vu/avec ton ami François/qui/a/un chien brun./

Table 11 Percentage of units correctly repeated of total units to be repeated on imitation task for experimental subjects

	Grade 8			Grade 10			Grade 12		
	n	mean	S.D.	n	mean	S.D.	n	mean	S.D.
Class 1	6	50.0	24.15	6	50.0	20.53	6	51.01	21.53
2	6	44.44	12.04	6	51.63	28.86	6	70.70	19.32
3	6	47.22	16.94	6	35.46	25.09	6	38.89	13.16
4	6	52.78	21.67	6	44.68	18.84	6	49.75	27.93
All Classes	24	48.61	18.24	24	45.44	22.58	24	52.59	22.94

The 10 sentences for each grade contained a different number of units, grade 8 sentences containing 36 units, grade 10 sentences 47 units, and grade 12 sentences 66 units. As a broad measure of linguistic competence based on oral production, a ratio of the number of units repeated correctly to the total number of units present was calculated for each subject. For example, if a subject in grade 8 had accurately repeated 18 units, his score on the task would be 18/36 = 50.0%. A subject had to repeat the entire linguistic unit accurately in order for it to be scored as correct. For example, if a subject repeated '*une*' *ballon* instead of '*un*' *ballon*, the whole unit would be considered incorrect. The mean scores and standard deviations for the subjects in each grade can be found in Table 11. Further descriptions of the results of the imitation task will be presented in detail later.

For the same reasons previously given for standardizing the results of the IEA tests across grades, the scores on the imitation task were also standardized across grades.

2. Scoring and Results of Other Measures

2.1 Personality and cognitive style

All the tests of personality and cognitive style were standardized tests with prescribed scoring procedures. The tests were scored by the researchers following the standard scoring procedures. The means and standard deviations for each grade can be found in Table 12.

Table 12 Descriptive statistics of cognitive style and personality variables

Variable		Grade 8	Grade 10	Grade 12
Field independence	Mean	3.76	5.48	7.25
	S.D.	3.40	4.26	4.84
Interference	Mean	0.16	0.21	0.26
	S.D.	0.07	0.10	0.10
Category width	Mean	67.92	52.21	60.25
	S.D.	16.98	20.48	15.69
Intolerance of ambiguity	Mean	59.96	58.43	54.12
	S.D.	10.32	8.52	9.08
Sensitivity to rejection	Mean	60.71	56.38	48.96
	S.D.	16.21	21.76	21.38
Extraversion	Mean	13.38	14.83	13.17
	S.D.	3.40	3.42	2.99
Empathy	Mean	31.92	35.33	36.38
	S.D.	4.24	3.63	5.67

According to the literature, the results of several of these tests (i.e. field independence, intolerance of ambiguity, and category width) were related to the sex of the subject. Analyses of Variance for these variables dividing the groups into male and female were conducted. None of the results were significant (see Table 13).

Table 13 Analyses of variance for sex differences, in field independence, intolerance of ambiguity, and category width

Variable		Mean	F ratio
Field independence	Male	6.27	1.472
	Female	5.00	
Intolerance of ambiguity	Male	58.07	0.117
	Female	57.28	
Category width	Male	63.65	1.743
	Female	57.74	

2.2 Attitude

The experimenters scored the attitude batteries and subsequently sent the raw scores to the Language Research Group in London to be tabulated. There were, in all, 25 subscales of the attitude battery. The Language Group suggested to the researchers that it was possible to combine some of the 25 subscales into several broader categories. The following are the five major composite scales the group suggested, with their respective subscales.

(1) Integrative orientation:
   (a) integrative
   (b) attitudes towards French Canadians
   (c) attitudes towards European French

(2) Instrumental orientation:
   (a) need for achievement
   (b) instrumentality

(3) Evaluation of means of learning French:
   (a) teacher evaluation
   (b) course evaluation

(4) Motivation:
   (a) motivational intensity
   (b) desire to learn French
   (c) attitudes towards learning French

(5) Lack of ethnocentrism:
    (a) interest in foreign languages
    (b) lack of ethnocentrism

2.3 Observation schedule

The coding of the observation schedule was previously described in detail (Part III, chapter 1, section 3.3). From the individual coding sheets made for each observation period, composite sheets were made for each subject, based on the total observation made on that subject.

Summation categories were then constructed from the total of the observational codings made on the subjects in the classroom. The raw scores were converted into percentages so that the results could be comparable from student to student. For example, it was important to know, not just how often a student corrected himself, but how often he did so out of the total opportunities he had for self-correction. Similarly, it was necessary to know not only how often a teacher had interrupted a student, but how often he had interrupted him out of the total number of possible occasions for doing so.

In some cases, where percentages were not applicable, the raw scores had to be standardized to make them comparable from subject to subject. For example, with reference to hand-raising, some students had 250 minutes of class time whereas others might have only had 200 because they were absent for one period. It was decided to adjust the categories concerned to a standard unit of 225 minutes. For example, if a student raised his hand 50 times in 200 minutes, his score on the variable of hand-raising was adjusted to $50 \times \dfrac{225}{200} = 56$.

The newly constructed categories were broken up into two major subdivisions: 'student-centred', and 'teacher-centred'. A list of the composite categories and the method by which the researchers attained these categories follows:

(a) Student-centred

(1) Student self-correction	Percentage of student responses in which the student corrected himself.
(2) Student self-initiated repetition	Percentage of occasions in which the student repeated a teacher's correction or providing of the answser, without being asked to do so.

(3) Student self-initiated further responding

Percentage of further student responding that was self-initiated and not the result of the teacher's clues or further explicit questioning.

(4) Student responding beyond teacher questioning

Indication of whether the student's responses were more than or equal to the number of initial questions.

(5) Student hand-raising

The number of times in 225 minutes that the student raised his hand.

(6) Student callout

The number of times in 225 minutes that the student called out a response.

(7) Student–teacher questioning

The number of times in 225 minutes in which the student asked the teacher a question.

(8) Student answers to questions asked of others before

Percentage of the total teacher questions asked of the student that had been presented to another student previously.

(9) Student complete responses

Percentage of total student responses that were complete responses.

(10) Student partial responses

Percentage of total student responses that were partial responses.

(11) Student null responses

Percentage of total student responses that were null responses, or cases in which the student said, 'I don't know'.

(12) Student continuing responses

Percentage of total student responses in which the student went on with his response.

(13) Student hesitation

Percentage of total student responses (excluding null responses) that involved hesitation or rising intonation.

(14) Student complete responses (voluntary–involuntary responses)

Indication of whether the student responses gave more, less (by 1 standard deviation [S.D.] or the same amount of complete responses on voluntary in contrast to involuntary responses.

(15) Student partial responses (voluntary–involuntary responses) — Indication of whether the student gave more, less (by 1.S.D.) or the same amount of partial responses on voluntary in contrast to involuntary responses.

(16) Student null responses (voluntary–involuntary responses) — Indication of whether the student gave more, less (by 1.S.D.) or the same amount of null responses on voluntary in contrast to involuntary responses.

(17) Student hesitation (voluntary–involuntary responses) — Indication of whether the student hesitated more, less (by 1.S.D.) or the same on voluntary in contrast to involuntary responses.

(18) Student correct responses — Percentage of total student responses that were correct.

(19) Student partially correct responses — Percentage of total student responses that were only partially correct.

(20) Student incorrect responses — Percentage of total student responses that were incorrect.

(21) Student responding above 10 times — Indication of whether the student responded more than or less than 10 times in total.

(22) Other types of voluntary clarification, correction, or elaboration — Percentage of all student voluntary responses that were elaborations, clarifications, or mutual corrections.

(b) Teacher-centred

(1) Positive feedback — Percentage of teacher evaluations that included positive feedback.

(2) Negative feedback — Percentage of teacher evaluations that included negative feedback.

(3) Teacher repetition — Percentage of student's responses (excluding null responses) that the teacher repeated.

(4) Teacher elaboration — Percentage of teacher evaluations that involved elaboration of the student's responses.

(5) Teacher clarification — Percentage of teacher evaluations that involved a clarification of the student's responses.

(6) Providing the answer

Percentage of teacher evaluations (excluding acceptance) that involved providing the answer to the student.

(7) Teacher interruption

Percentage of teacher evaluations (excluding acceptance) that involved interrupting the student.

(8) Teacher explicit correction

Percentage of teacher evaluations (excluding acceptance) that involved an explicit correction.

(9) Teacher implicit correction

Percentage of teacher evaluations (excluding acceptance) that involved an implicit correction.

(10) Teacher localization of incorrectness

Percentage of teacher evaluations (excluding acceptance) that involved localizations of incorrectness.

(11) Teacher indication of incorrectness

Percentage of teacher evaluations that involved indications of incorrectness.

(12) Teacher providing clues

Percentage of teacher evaluations (excluding acceptance) and further questioning that involved the giving of clues.

(13) Further questioning

Percentage of total teacher questions that were not initial questions.

(14) Involuntary questioning

Percentage of total questions asked of the student when he had not raised his hand.

(15) Voluntary questioning

Percentage of questions asked by the teacher of the students when they had raised their hands out of the students' total hand-raising behavior.

(16) Mutual correction

Percentage of questions asked of the student that required him to correct previous responses.

(17) Student answers to questions asked of others before

Percentage of the total teacher questions asked of the students that had been presented to somebody else previously.

2.4 Student interview

The interviews were transcribed by the researchers and transferred to cards. From this information, specific factors were isolated and data on these factors were tabulated for use in later analysis. In most cases the data for each student were tabulated on binary and ternary scales. An enumeration and brief description of these factors follows:

(1) Student perception of classroom formality — An indication by the student of whether the formality of the classroom was a match or mismatch to his preferred classroom environment.

(2) Student perception of rapport with teacher — An indication of the student's general feelings towards his teacher.

(3) Student perception of rapport with other students — An indication of the student's feelings towards the other members of the class.

(4) Student and teacher match of goals — An indication of whether the student's personal goal matched or did not match his perception of the teacher's aim.

(5) Student perception of teacher's expressed goal — An indication of whether the teacher's expressed goal (based on the teacher interview) matched or did not match the student's expressed perception of this goal.

(6) Student's general attitude — Experimenter rating (on a five-point scale) of the student's general attitude towards his learning of French in that situation.

(7) Student learning modality preference — An indication of whether the student preferred to learn orally or through the written medium.

(8) Student certainty in hand-raising — An indication of the student's feeling towards his willingness to take the risk of being wrong when he raises his hand.

(9) Student reaction to being called upon without hand-raising — An indication of the student's attitude to being called upon when he hadn't raised his hand.

(10) Student perception of whether he is asked sufficiently — An indication of the student's opinion as to whether the teacher asks him sufficiently.

(11) Student reaction to lack of comprehension

An indication of the student's response to whether he would ask a friend, the teacher, or check for himself, if he hadn't understood something.

(12) Student attitude towards teacher correction

An indication of the student's attitude to being corrected in general.

(13) Student attitude towards being interrupted

An indication of the student's preference to being interrupted as soon as he has made a mistake or to being allowed to finish responding first.

(14) Student attitude towards correcting others

An indication of whether or not the student corrects other students.

(15) Student repetition of teacher correction

An indication of whether or not the student says he repeats or does not repeat the teacher's corrections.

(16) Student reaction to teacher's use of L1 and L2

An indication of whether the student feels the teacher is using too much of L2 or too much of L1 in the classroom.

(17) Student embarrassment in speaking

An indication of whether or not the student is embarrassed to speak the language in front of the other students.

(18) Student affective remarks

An indication that the student has made further statements revealing his classroom anxiety, or fear of being rejected or laughed at.

3. Statistical Analyses

3.1 Student sex, teacher, and school

One-way Analysis of Variance were conducted for the variation of student sex, teacher, and school on the two criterion measures of linguistic competence. For none of the three variables was there a significant difference in performance. The F ratios for these analysis can be found in Table 14. It appears, at least in terms of the limited number of students studied, that there were no significant differences in linguistic competence attributable to the various levels of the three variables.

Table 14 Analysis of variance: school, teacher, sex on IEA and Imitation

Variable	F-ratio IEA	Imitation
School	0.994	1.543
Teacher	0.617	0.964
Sex	0.436	0.150

3.2 Correlational analysis with criterion measures

Subsequently, correlations were calculated between the many variables gathered from the various data collection techniques and the stardardized scores on the IEA and Imitation tests. The results of these correlations can be found in Table 15.

Table 15 Correlation of variables with standardized IEA and Imitation for all grades

(a) Personality and cognitive style	IEA Test	Imitation Test
Field independence	0.311**	0.247*
Category width	−0.099	−0.036
Interference	0.062	0.063
Intolerance of ambiguity	−0.255*	−0.230
Extraversion	−0.110	−0.136
Empathy	0.008	0.025
Sensitivity to rejection	−0.023	−0.018

(b) Attitudinal measures (Gardner et al. battery)		
Parental encouragement	0.107	0.149
Taking French next year	−0.116	−0.025
Opportunity to speak French	−0.041	0.108
Integrative orientation	0.270*	0.285*
Motivation	0.351**	0.385**
Evaluation of means of learning French	0.341**	0.406**
Instrumental orientation	0.254*	0.225
Lack of ethnocentrism	0.255*	0.204

Table 15 Correlation of variables with standardized IEA and Imitation for all grades *continued*

(c) Observation schedule	IEA Test	Imitation Test
Student self-correction	0.071	0.076
Student self-initiated repetition	0.069	0.088
Student self-initiated further responding	−0.041	0.053
Student responses beyond teacher questioning	0.115	0.164
Student hand-raising	0.495**	0.435**
Student callout	0.263*	0.220
Student–teacher questioning	−0.017	0.081
Student answers to questions asked of others before	0.264*	0.189
Student complete responses	0.422**	0.374**
Student incomplete (partial) responses	−0.206	−0.186
Student null responses	−0.256*	−0.208
Student continuing responses	−0.284*	−0.267*
Student hesitation	−0.023	−0.008
Student complete responses (voluntary–involuntary responses)	0.137	0.145
Student partial responses (voluntary–involuntary responses)	0.061	−0.026
Student null responses (voluntary–involuntary responses)	0.089	0.082
Student hesitation (voluntary–involuntary responses)	−0.015	−0.017
Student correct responses	0.387**	0.416**
Student partially correct responses	−0.250*	−0.263*
Student incorrect responses	−0.310**	−0.303**
Student responding above 10 times	0.391**	0.309**
Student voluntary clarification, correction, or elaboration	0.248*	0.227

(d) Student interview	IEA Test	Imitation Test
Student perception of classroom formality	0.097	0.127
Student perception of rapport with teacher	0.206	0.257*
Student perception of rapport with other students	0.151	0.202
Student and teacher match of goals	0.035	0.095
Student perception of teacher's expressed goal	0.008	0.054
Student's general attitude	0.418**	0.482**
Student learning modality preference	0.236*	0.225
Student certainty in hand-raising	−0.007	0.012
Student reaction to being called upon without hand-raising	0.291*	0.171
Student perception of whether he's asked sufficiently	−0.195	−0.086
Student reaction to lack of comprehension	0.293*	0.292*
Student attitude towards teacher correction	0.069	0.104
Student attitude towards being interrupted	0.123	0.226
Student attitude towards correcting others	0.391**	0.384**
Student repetition of teacher correction	0.061	−0.026
Student reaction to teacher's use of L1 and L2	0.362**	0.332**
Student embarrassment in speaking French	0.098	0.202
Student affective remarks	0.337**	0.377**

* $p < 0.05$
** $p < 0.01$

It should first be noted that the majority of variables that are correlated with success on the IEA test are similarly correlated with success on the imitation task. Even though different aspects of linguistic competence are being measured, it appears that the two tests are still measuring aspects of one overall linguistic competence. In fact, the correlation between the two criterion measures was found to be highly significant, $r = 0.792$ ($p < 0.001$).

The variables were divided into four categories based on the source of their collection:

(a) Personality and cognitive style tests
(b) Attitudinal measures (Gardner *et al.* battery)
(c) Observation schedule
(d) Student interview

The results of the correlations are described according to these four categories.

(1) *Personality and cognitive style.* Field independence and tolerance of ambiguity[1] are the only two measures of personality or cognitive style which are correlated with both criteria.

(2) *Attitudinal measures.* All of the composite scales on the Gardner *et al.* battery are correlated with success on the IEA test, while all of these measures excepting instrumental orientation and lack of ethnocentrism are correlated with success on the imitation task.

(3) *Observation schedule.* Many of the measures gathered on the basis of the observation schedule were significantly correlated with results on the two criterion measures.[2] However, several of the factors originally considered to be related to success did not result in any significant correlations; for example, student self-correction, student self-initiated further responding, and student–teacher questioning. It appears that good students, defined by the results on the criterion measures, did not demonstrate the above characteristics any more frequently than did poor students. The factors that appeared to be more related to success were ones such as student hand-raising, student callouts (on IEA only), student complete responses, and correct responses, while incorrect and partially correct responses were negatively correlated with success.

(4) *Student interview.* The student interview attempted to discover the student's attitude towards his learning environment and the subject matter, as well as to discover the student's preference for certain ways of learning in the classroom. Several measures were significantly correlated with success, such as the student's general attitude towards learning French, his attitude towards correcting others, his reaction to the teacher's use

of L1 and L2, and his indication that there was no affective component that was hindering his active use of the language in the classroom.

Even though only partially evidenced in the first correlation analysis, two of the most important variables that might be related to successful language learning in a formal situation were felt to be a student's perception of his classroom environment and his overall personality characteristics, concerning such factors as embarrassment at speaking in class or reluctance to take chances and make a fool of himself. In order to get a more accurate picture of these two variables, several of the other measures from the student interview were combined.

A new variable measuring the student's overall perception of the classroom environment was created by combining additively the following variables:

(a) student perception of classroom formality
(b) student perception of rapport with teacher
(c) student perception of rapport with other students

For the variable of student overall classroom personality, the following measures were combined additively:

(a) student certainly in hand-raising
(b) student reaction to being called upon without hand-raising
(c) student embarrassment in speaking French
(d) student affective remarks

The composite variables were then correlated with the two criterion measures. The results of the correlations appear in Table 16.

Table 16 Correlation of composite variables with criterion measures

Variable	IEA Test	Imitation Test
Student perception of classroom environment	0.268*	0.285*
Student overall classroom personality	0.361**	0.380**

It might be noted at this point that a two-way Analysis of Variance was performed to determine the effect of personality and classroom environment, and the interaction of the two, on the criterion measures. For the personality factor *Ss* were divided into two groups: those students' scores which fell above the mean on the variable Overall Classroom Personality (see above for description of variable) were considered 'high', and those which fell below the mean were considered 'low'.

The classroom environment factor included three groups: traditional, open-plan, and individualized. As can be seen from Table 17, personality was a significant factor, which suggests that those students who are more outgoing and not embarrassed to talk are more successful language learners. However, classroom environment did not prove to be a significant factor. One reason that these factors were not significant might be the small size of the sample used; only one school was open-plan and one other had individualized programs, the other ones were considered traditional. However, even though the schools were described as 'open' or 'traditional', there may have been no actual difference in the environments of the language classrooms. For example, one school was considered 'traditional' and another 'open', but actually the classrooms did not differ greatly – the same program was followed, the desks were arranged in semicircles, and the general activities in each of the classes were similar.[3]

Table 17 ANOVA for personality and classroom environment on criterion measures (F-ratio)

	IEA	Imitation
Personality	5.804*	6.230*
Classroom environment	1.514	2.637
Interaction	0.678	2.205

$p < 0.05$

3.3 Regression anaylses on criterion measures

In order to identify which personality, attitudinal, cognitive style, and behavioral factors were predictive of success on the criterion measures, stepwise regression analyses were calculated.[4] Two separate analyses were run for each criterion – one with personality, attitudinal, and cognitive style factors as predictor variables, the other with behavioral measures (from the observations schedule) as predictors. The majority of the factors that were extracted from the student interview were considered to fit into the category of personality, attitude, and cognitive style factors. Only a few, namely, student reaction to lack of comprehension, student attitude towards correcting others, and student repetition of teacher correction, were included in the behavioral category.

The results of the regression anaylses for the personality, attitudinal, and cognitive style factors appear in Tables 18 and 19.

Table 18 Stepwise regression: personality, attitude, and cognitive style on IEA

Step number	Variable entered	Multiple R	RSQ	Increase in RSQ
1	Student's general attitude	0.418	0.175	0.175
2	Student reaction to teacher's use of L1, L2	0.507	0.257	0.082
3	Field independence	0.535	0.286	0.029
4	Student learning modality preference	0.556	0.309	0.022
5	Student overall classroom personality	0.571	0.326	0.018
6	Integrative orientation	0.592	0.350	0.024

Table 19 Stepwise regression: personality, attitude, and cognitive style on imitation

Step number	Variable entered	Multiple R	RSQ	Increase in RSQ
1	Student's general attitude	0.482	0.232	0.232
2	Student reaction to teacher's use of L1, L2	0.539	0.291	0.059
3	Student attitude towards being interrupted	0.577	0.333	0.043

For both criterion measures, it appears that the rating of the student's general attitude towards his language learning situation and the student's expressed desire that the teacher use more French in the classroom are the best predictors of success. Field independence, student learning modality preference, and integrative orientation are also predictors for the IEA test. For results on the imitation task, the only other predictor was the student's attitude towards being interrupted. Although integrative orientation (of the Gardner *et al.* battery) was predictive of success on the IEA test, the general rating of the student's attitude was a much more powerful predictor of success for both criteria.

For neither of the two criteria do the personality, attitudinal, and cognitive style factors account for a great deal of the variance, i.e. 35.0% on the IEA test, and 33.3% on the imitation task.

It was considered possible that these factors may be more important predictors of success in one grade that in another. Since French is no longer compulsory in Ontario beyond the eighth grade, students who lack certain positive attitudes, personality characteristics, or cognitive styles that facilitate learning a second language in a formal situation, especially at the initial stages, may drop out as soon as they have the opportunity. In order to examine this possibility, separate regression analysis were run for subjects of each grade. The results of these analyses can be found in Tables 20 and 21.

Table 20 Stepwise regression: personality, attitude, and cognitive style on IEA by grade

Step number	Variable entered	Multiple R	RSQ	Increase in RSQ
(a) Grade 8				
1	Motivation	0.534	0.285	0.285
2	Student reaction to teacher's use of L1, L2	0.663	0.440	0.154
3	Student perception of classroom environment	0.703	0.494	0.054
4	Student overall classroom personality	0.731	0.535	0.041
5	Intolerance of ambiguity	0.758	0.575	0.040
(b) Grade 10				
1	Student's general attitude	0.477	0.227	0.227
2	Student reaction to teacher's use of L1, L2	0.536	0.288	0.060
(c) Grade 12				
1	Field independence	0.430	0.184	0.184
2	Evaluation of means of learning French	0.589	0.347	0.163

Table 21 Stepwise regression: personality, attitude, and cognitive style on imitation by grade

Step number	Variable entered	Multiple R	RSQ	Increase in RSQ
(a) Grade 8				
1	Evaluation of means of learning French	0.716	0.512	0.512
2	Student's general attitude	0.809	0.655	0.143
3	Student attitude towards being interrupted	0.863	0.745	0.090
4	Student reaction to teacher's use of L1, L2	0.902	0.813	0.068
5	Instrumental orientation	0.929	0.863	0.050
6	Field independence	0.939	0.882	0.018
7	Student overall classroom personality	0.951	0.905	0.023
8	Intolerance of ambiguity	0.957	0.916	0.011
9	Student learning modality preference	0.963	0.927	0.011
10	Student perception of classroom environment	0.970	0.940	0.014
(b) Grade 10				
1	Student reaction to teacher's use of L1, L2	0.535	0.286	0.286
(c) Grade 12				
1	Student's general attitude	0.344	0.119	0.119
2	Field independence	0.475	0.226	0.107
3	Student learning modality preference	0.561	0.315	0.089

It is clear that there are many differences in the results of each grade. The most obvious difference lies in the proportion of the variance that is accounted for by the predictors in grade 8, compared to grade 10 and 12. Cognitive style, personality, and in particular attitudinal factors appear to be more important in predicting success for both criterion measures in the lower grades than in the higher grades.

It is worth noting that intolerance of ambiguity is a predictor of success in grade 8 alone, and student reaction to teacher's use of L1 and L2 in grade 8 and 10 alone. On the other hand, field independence is a major predictor in grade 12, while elsewhere only a minor predictor of success (on the imitation task for grade 8 alone). In addition, the attitude measures appear to be most important at the intial stages (i.e. grade 8).

In order to see if there are significant differences in the scores of the grade 8, 10, and 12 students on the above-mentioned variables (subtests of attitude battery, field independence, intolerance of ambiguity, and student reaction to teacher's use of L1 and L2), Analysis of Variance were calculated. The means and standard deviations of the variables for the students in each grade can be found in Table 22, with the results of the ANOVAs in Table 23.

Table 22 Descriptive statistics of selected variables

Variable		Grade 8	Grade 10	Grade 12
Field independence	$\bar{X}$	3.75	5.48	7.25
	S.D.	3.40	4.26	4.84
Intolerance of ambiguity	$\bar{X}$	59.96	58.43	54.12
	S.D.	10.32	8.52	9.08
Integrative orientation	$\bar{X}$	67.67	62.00	69.21
	S.D.	16.00	10.87	10.75
Motivation	$\bar{X}$	44.50	44.13	51.46
	S.D.	14.19	12.05	8.57
Evaluation of means of learning French	$\bar{X}$	84.00	80.78	94.71
	S.D.	32.82	26.21	23.03
Instrumental orientation	$\bar{X}$	42.92	39.96	43.75
	S.D.	8.75	7.38	7.18
Lack of ethnocentrism	$\bar{X}$	7.88	7.91	13.37
	S.D.	8.93	7.33	5.85
Student reaction to teacher's use of L1, L2	$\bar{X}$	0.70	0.88	1.29
	S.D.	0.56	0.74	0.62

Table 23 Analysis of Variance: differences between grades on selected variables

Variable	F-ratio
Field independence	4.10*
Intolerance of ambiguity	3.51*
Integrative orientation	1.99
Motivation	2.90
Evaluation of means of learning French	1.64
Instrumental orientation	1.52
Lack of ethnocentrism	4.26*
Student reaction to teacher's use of L1, L2	5.28*

* $p < 0.05$

Significant differences for students of the three grades occurred for the following variables: field independence, intolerance of ambiguity, student reaction to teacher's use of L1 and L2, and lack of ethnocentrism and motivation.[5]

Of these variables, field independence is the only one that may be correlated with age (see Part III, chapter 1, section 2.1). The differences in the other variables can therefore be attributed to the differences in the populations of students taking French in grade 8, 10, and 12. For all the variables the means for the grade 12 students were the greatest (low intolerance of ambiguity signifying a high tolerance of ambiguity). Even though for a few of the variables grade 8 students had higher means than students of grade 10, the standard deviations were greatest in all cases for grade 8 students (excepting two in which the means for grade 8 students were indeed the lowest). This indicates that there was a greater variability in the scores of the grade 8 students – some scoring very high, others very low. This, taken in conjunction with the fact that these variables were, for the most part, better predictors of success in grade 8, substantiates the hypothesis that students who do not possess the necessary positive attitudes, personality attributes, or cognitive styles may drop French as soon as it is no longer compulsory. Therefore, it appears that at early stages of language learning in a formal situation, certain attitudinal or personality factors may in fact be necessary, though not sufficient, conditions for success; however, at later stages some cognitive style factors such as field independence may be more important.

In order to get a more comprehensive picture of the relationship between observable learning behaviors and successful second language learning in a formal situation, stepwise regression analyses were calculated, with the observed learning behaviors as predictor variables on the two criterion measures. In addition, several previously enumerated 'behavioral' measures extracted from the student interview were included in the analysis. The results of these analyses can be found in Tables 24 and 25.

The results indicate that student hand-raising was the most important predictor of success for the two criterion measures, with other factors such as student callouts and student correct or complete responses being significant but less important. But few of the other variables initially considered to be related to successful language learning, such as student repetition, self-correction, and self-initiated responding, were found to be significant predictors.

Table 24 Stepwise regression: behavioral measures on IEA

Step number	Variable entered	Multiple R	RSQ	Increase in RSQ
1	Student hand-raising	0.495	0.245	0.245
2	Student complete responses	0.575	0.330	0.085
3	Student attitude towards correcting others	0.623	0.388	0.057
4	Student callout	0.650	0.423	0.035
5	Student responding above 10 times	0.667	0.445	0.022
6	Student reaction to lack of comprehension	0.694	0.481	0.036
7	Student continuing responses	0.706	0.498	0.017
8	Student incorrect responses	0.718	0.515	0.017
9	Student attitude towards correcting others	** deleted		
10	Student voluntary clarification, correction, or elaboration	0.724	0.524	0.014

Table 25 Stepwise regression: behavioral measures on Imitation

Step number	Variable entered	Multiple R	RSQ	Increase in RSQ
1	Student hand-raising	0.435	0.189	0.189
2	Student correct responses	0.537	0.288	0.099
3	Student attitude towards correcting others	0.598	0.358	0.070
4	Student callout	0.622	0.387	0.029
5	Student reaction to lack of comprehension	0.640	0.409	0.022
6	Student continuing responses	0.659	0.434	0.025

In order to see if there were differences across grades, separate regression analyses were run for students of each grade. These can be found in Tables 26 and 27.

Table 26 Stepwise regression: behavioral measures on IEA by grade

Step number	Variable entered	Multiple R	RSQ	Increase in RSQ
(a) Grade 8				
1	Student hand-raising	0.753	0.566	0.566
2	Student attitude towards correcting others	0.802	0.643	0.076
3	Student complete responses	0.869	0.756	0.113
4	Student incorrect responses	0.923	0.852	0.096
5	Student hand-raising	** deleted		
6	Student continuing responses	0.940	0.883	0.031
7	Student questioning asked to others before	0.949	0.901	0.018
8	Student reaction to lack of comprehension	0.959	0.920	0.019
9	Student hand-raising	0.964	0.928	0.008
10	Student correct responses	0.971	0.943	0.015

Table 26 Stepwise regression: behavioral measures on IEA by grade *continued*

Step number	Variable entered	Multiple R	RSQ	Increase in RSQ
(b) Grade 10				
1	Student reaction to lack of comprehension	0.472	0.222	0.222
2	Student continuing responses	0.597	0.356	0.133
3	Student voluntary clarification, correction, or elaboration	0.716	0.513	0.157
4	Student complete responses	0.741	0.550	0.037
5	Student null responses	0.790	0.624	0.075
6	Student questioning asked to others before	0.847	0.717	0.092
(c) Grade 12				
1	Student responding above 10 times	0.496	0.246	0.246
2	Student complete responses	0.681	0.463	0.217
3	Student questioning asked to others before	0.753	0.568	0.104
4	Student partially correct responses	0.802	0.644	0.076

The results of these analyses did not differ greatly from grade to grade and from criterion to criterion. However, it is worthwhile to note that hand-raising was not a significant predictor in any of the grades excepting grade 8; moreover, in grade 8, though initially the most important predictor, hand-raising was later deleted from the stepwise regression. This might have resulted from the fact that hand-raising was highly correlated with some of the other predictors, and thus, the unique contribution of the variable lessened as the other correlated variables were entered into the equation. Alternatively, the statistical validity of the regression analysis itself may be questioned because of the small number of subjects for the analysis in each grade.

Table 27 Stepwise regression: behavioral measures on Imitation by grade

Step number	Variable entered	Multiple R	RSQ	Increase in RSQ
(a) Grade 8				
1	Student hand-raising	0.670	0.449	0.449
2	Student attitude towards correcting others	0.710	0.504	0.055
3	Student correct responses	0.739	0.546	0.042
4	Student partially correct responses	0.794	0.631	0.085
5	Student hand-raising	** deleted		
6	Student continuing responses	0.833	0.694	0.072
(b) Grade 10				
1	Student correct responses	0.540	0.291	0.291
2	Student reaction to lack of comprehension	0.598	0.358	0.066
3	Student continuing responses	0.662	0.438	0.080
4	Student null responses	0.701	0.492	0.053
5	Student complete responses	0.753	0.567	0.075
6	Student questioning asked to others before	0.823	0.678	0.111
7	Student correct responses	** deleted		
8	Student partially correct responses	0.836	0.698	0.035
(c) Grade 12				
1	Student complete responses	0.501	0.251	0.251
2	Student questioning asked to others before	0.695	0.483	0.232
3	Student responding above 10 times	0.730	0.533	0.049
4	Student reaction to lack of comprehension	0.768	0.590	0.057
5	Student voluntary clarification, correction, or elaboration	0.797	0.636	0.046

3.4 Intercorrelation of all variables

It was considered to be of interest to examine the intercorrelations of all the measures collected on the experimental students, in order to be able to examine the relationship of different variables both within the same category (based on the source of data collection), and across different categories. A correlation matrix was therefore constructed for all these variables. Due to the large number of variables collected, only the significant or near significant correlations will be presented here in tabular form (see Table 28).

The variables in the tables are once more divided into four areas coinciding with the source of the variable, i.e. personality and cognitive style, attitude battery, observation schedule, and student interview. Because of the great number of variables, only some of the more interesting intercorrelations will be discussed here.

(1) Personality and cognitive style
Field independence was negatively correlated with intolerance of ambiguity and positively correlated with the student's reaction to the teacher's use of the foreign language (i.e. that the teacher should use more French). Intolerance of ambiguity on the other hand was negatively correlated with teacher's use of L1 and L2 and negatively correlated with lack of ethnocentrism, which means that someone who was tolerant of ambiguity also wanted the teacher to use more French and was not ethnocentric. Empathy was correlated with extraversion as well as with lack of ethnocentrism. Sensitivity to rejection was found to be negatively correlated with extraversion.

(2) Attitudes
As expected, all of the five subscales of the attitude battery were intercorrelated. In addition, all of these subscales were significantly correlated with student hand-raising. Both integrative orientation and motivation were correlated with student callouts. In addition, all of the five subscales were correlated with the experimenter's rating of the student's general attitude. In all cases, except for instrumental orientation, the attitudinal measures were correlated with student perception of classroom environment. The five subscales were also all correlated with the student's reaction to the teacher's use of L1 and L2.

(3) Observation schedule
Unfortunately, there were few significant correlations between student self-correction, self-initiated repetition, self-initiated further responding, and any of the other measures collected. There was, however, a significant correlation between student self-initiated repetition and student–teacher questioning.

The variable from the observation schedule which appeared to be correlated with the greatest number of other measures was student hand-raising. Most of the measures correlated with student hand-raising were from the attitude battery or from a student interview. Hand-raising was not correlated with any personality and cognitive style variables and with only one other variable from the observation schedule.

The variable of student callout was also correlated with several of the attitude measures as well as with student–teacher questioning and student voluntary clarification, correction, or elaboration.

Many of the remaining variables of the observation schedule were each correlated with several other measures, but it is not possible to enumerate these correlations fully at this point. Only the most relevant ones have been discussed here; the others, however, can all be identified by examination of the tables provided.

(4) Student interview
The student's general attitude (rated by the experimenters after the student interview) was correlated with all of the subscales of the attitude battery. It was also significantly correlated with hand-raising, and voluntary clarification, correction, and elaboration, and to the student perception of classroom environment.

The student's attitude towards correcting others was correlated with many of the attitudinal factors and with the student hand-raising as well as with several of the other measures from the student interview.

The student's attitude towards the teacher's use of the foreign language seemed to be one of the most important variables for predicting success. From the intercorrelations conducted, it appears that those students who wanted the teacher to use more French were also field-independent, tolerant of ambiguity, and positively motivated towards the learning of French; but no other characteristics from classroom observation or from the interview were correlated with this variable.

The student's perception of the classroom environment was correlated very highly with one of the subscales of the attitude battery, i.e. evaluation of the means of learning French, as well as with the student's general attitude and hand-raising.

Surprisingly, student overall classroom personality (compiled from several measures of the interview) was not correlated with any of the other personality or cognitive style tests given. However, it was correlated with student hand-raising, responding above 10 times and several aspects of student responding (e.g. complete, correct).

Table 28 Intercorrelation of selected variables

(a) Personality and cognitive style		
(1) Field independence	*Significant correlations*	
Personality and cognitive style	Intolerance of ambiguity	−0.344**
	Sensitivity to rejection	−0.401**
Observation schedule	Student callout	0.272*
	Student–teacher questioning	0.241*
	Student null responses	−0.233*
Student interview	Student reaction to teacher's use of L1, L2	0.314**
(2) Category width		
Student interview	Student perception of whether he's asked sufficiently	0.261*
(3) Interference		
Personality and cognitive style	Empathy	0.303**
Attitudinal measures (Gardner *et al.* battery)	Lack of ethnocentrism	0.284*
Observation schedule	Student null responses	0.270*
Student interview	Student attitude towards teacher correction	−0.256*
(4) Intolerance of ambiguity		
Personality and cognitive style	Field independence	−0.344**
	Empathy	−0.268*
	Sensitivity to rejection	−0.266*
Attitudinal measures (Gardner *et al.* battery)	Motivation	−0.258*
	Instrumental orientation	−0.300*
	Lack of ethnocentrism	−0.363**
	Integrative orientation	0.231
Student interview	Student's general attitude	−0.229
	Student attitude towards being interrupted	−0.229
	Student repetition of teacher correction	−0.259*
	Student reaction to teacher's use of L1, L2	−0.331**

(5) Extraversion	*Significant correlations*	
Personality and cognitive style	Empathy	0.377**
	Sensitivity to rejection	−0.294*
Attitudinal measures (Gardner *et al.* battery)	Instrumental orientation	0.265*

(6) Empathy		
Personality and cognitive style	Interference	0.303**
	Intolerance of ambiguity	−0.268*
	Extraversion	0.377**
	Sensitivity to rejection	−0.232*
Attitudinal measures (Gardner *et al.* battery)	Lack of ethnocentrism	0.305**
	Motivation	0.273*

(7) Fear of rejection		
Personality and cognitive style	Field independence	−0.401**
	Intolerance of ambiguity	0.266*
	Extraversion	−0.294*
	Empathy	−0.232*

(b) Attitudinal measures (Gardner et al. battery)

---

(1) Integrative orientation	*Significant correlations*	
Personality and cognitive style	Intolerance of ambiguity	−0.232*
Attitudinal measures (Gardner *et al.* battery)	Motivation	0.796**
	Evaluation of means of learning French	0.608**
	Instrumental orientation	0.655**
	Lack of ethnocentrism	0.509**
Observation schedule	Student hand-raising	0.372**
	Student callout	0.301*
Student interview	Student's general attitude	0.346**
	Student perception of whether he's asked sufficiently	0.389**
	Student attitude towards teacher correction	0.272*
	Student attitude towards correcting others	0.241*

$^*p < 0.05$ $^{**}p < 0.01$

(b) Attitudinal measures (Gardner et al. battery) continued

---

(1) Integrative orientation cont. Significant correlations

| Student interview cont. | Student reaction to teacher's use of L1, L2 | 0.228 |
| | Student perception of classroom environment | 0.221 |

(2) Motivation

Personality and cognitive style	Intolerance of ambiguity	−0.258*
	Empathy	0.273*
Attitudinal measures (Gardner et al. battery)	Integrative orientation	0.796**
	Evaluation of means of learning French	0.753**
	Instrumental orientation	0.624**
	Lack of ethnocentrism	0.716**
Observation schedule	Student hand-raising	0.465**
	Student callout	0.298*
	Student null responses	−0.317**
	Student incorrect responses	−0.290*
	Student responding above 10 times	0.274*
Student interview	Student's general attitude	0.611**
	Student perception of whether he's asked sufficiently	0.269*
	Student attitude towards correcting others	0.342**
	Student reaction to teacher's use of L1, L2	0.358**
	Student perception of classroom environment	0.366**

(3) Evaluation of means of learning French

Attitudinal measures (Gardner et al. battery)	Integrative orientation	0.608**
	Motivation	0.753**
	Instrumental orientation	0.520**
	Lack of ethnocentrism	0.513**

Observation schedule	Student hand-raising	0.389**
	Student complete responses	
	(vol.–invol. responses)	0.239*
	Student correct responses	0.281*
	Student incorrect responses	−0.329**
	Student responding above	
	10 times	0.343**
Student interview	Student general attitude	0.613**
	Student attitude towards teacher	
	correction	0.282*
	Student attitude towards	
	correcting others	0.291*
	Student reaction to teacher's use	
	of L1, L2	0.321**
	Student perception of classroom	
	environment	0.577**

(4) Instrumental orientation

Personality and cognitive style	Intolerance of ambiguity	−0.300*
	Extraversion	0.265*
Attitudinal measures	Integrative orientation	0.655**
(Gardner *et al.* battery)	Motivation	0.624**
	Evaluation of means of learning	
	French	0.520**
	Lack of ethnocentrism	0.406**
Observation schedule	Student self-initiated further	
	responding	0.293*
	Student hand-raising	0.333**
	Student incorrect responses	−0.234*
Student interview	Student general attitude	0.358**
	Student reaction to teacher's use	
	of L1, L2	0.262*

(5) Lack of ethnocentrism

Personality and cognitive style	Interference	0.284*
	Intolerance of ambiguity	−0.363**
	Empathy	0.305**
Attitudinal measures	Integrative orientation	0.509**
(Gardner *et al.* battery)	Motivation	0.716**
	Evaluation of means of learning	
	French	0.513**
	Instrumental orientation	0.406**

(b) Attitudinal measures (Gardner et al. battery) continued

(5) Lack of ethnocentrism cont. *Significant correlations*

Observation schedule	Student hand-raising	0.272*
	Student complete responses	−0.404**
	Student incorrect responses	−0.234*
	Students responding above 10 times	0.378**
Student interview	Student and teacher match of goals	−0.250*
	Student's general attitude	0.492**
	Student repetition of teacher correction	0.300*
	Student reaction to teacher's use of L1, L2	0.382**
	Student perception of classroom environment	0.250*

(c) Observation schedule

(1) Student self-correction   *Significant correlations*

Observation schedule	Student self-initiated further further responding	0.232*
	Student hesitation	−0.228
Student interview	Student reaction to lack of comprehension	0.225

(2) Student self-initiated repetition

Observation schedule	Student–teacher questioning	0.367**
Student interview	Student attitude towards teacher correction	0.242*

(3) Student self-initiated further responding

Attitudinal measures (Gardner *et al.* battery)	Instrumental orientation	0.293*
Observation schedule	Student self-correction	0.232*
Student interview	Student learning modality preference	−0.274*
	Student reaction to teacher's use of L1, L2	0.247*

(4) Student responses beyond teacher questioning

Observation schedule	Student hand-raising	0.225
Student interview	Student repetition of teacher correction	−0.224

(5) Student hand-raising

Attitudinal measures (Gardner *et al.* battery)	Integrative orientation	0.372**
	Motivation	0.465**
	Evaluation of means of learning French	0.389**
	Instrumental orientation	0.333**
	Lack of ethnocentrism	0.272*
Observation schedule	Student responses beyond teacher questioning	0.225
Student interview	Student's general attitude	0.507**
	Student learning modality preference	0.321**
	Student reaction to lack of comprehension	0.317**
	Student attitude towards correcting others	0.318*
	Student perception of classroom environment	0.241*
	Student overall classroom personality	0.317**

(6) Student callout

Personality and cognitive style	Field independence	0.272*
Attitudinal measures (Gardner *et al.* battery)	Integrative orientation	0.301*
	Motivation	0.298*
Observation schedule	Student–teacher questioning	0.283*
	Student null responses (vol.–invol. responses)	0.222
	Student voluntary clarification, correction, or elaboration	0.313**

(7) Student–teacher questioning

Personality and cognitive style	Field independence	0.241*
Observation schedule	Student self-initiated repetition	0.367**
	Student callout	0.283*
	Student voluntary clarification, correction, or elaboration	0.231

(c) Observation schedule *continued*

(8) Student null responses	Significant correlations	
Personality and cognitive style	Field independence	−0.233*
	Interference	−0.270*
Attitudinal measures	Motivation	−0.317**
(Gardner *et al.* battery)	Lack of ethnocentrism	−0.280*
Observation schedule	Student null responses (vol.–invol. responses)	−0.582**
	Student hesitation (vol.–invol. responses)	0.274*
Student interview	Student reaction to teacher's use of L1, L2	−0.428**

(9) Student hesitation		
Attitudinal measures (Gardner *et al.* battery)	Lack of ethnocentrism	0.416**
Observation schedule	Student self-correction	−0.228
Student interview	Student learning modality preference	−0.268*
	Student perception of whether he's asked sufficiently	0.267*
	Student reaction to lack of comprehension	−0.406**
	Student attitude towards being interrupted	−0.234*
	Student attitude towards correcting others	0.226
	Student repetition of teacher correction	0.223

(10) Student complete responses (vol.–invol. responses)		
Attitudinal measures (Gardner *et al.* battery)	Evaluation of means of learning French	0.239*
Observation schedule	Student null responses (vol.–invol. responses)	−0.312**
	Student hesitation (vol.–invol. responses)	0.239*
Student interview	Student perception of classroom environment	0.255*

(11) Student null responses (vol.–invol. responses)

Observation schedule	Student callout	0.222
	Student null responses	−0.582**
	Student complete responses (vol.–invol. responses)	−0.312**
	Student hesitation (vol.–invol. responses)	−0.307**
Student interview	Student reaction to teacher's use of L1, L2	0.292*

(12) Student hestitation (vol.–invol. responses)

Observation schedule	Student null responses	0.274*
	Student complete responses (vol.–invol. responses)	0.293*
	Student null responses (vol.–invol. responses)	−0.307*
Student interview	Student reaction to teacher's use of L1, L2	−0.271*

(13) Student voluntary clarification, correction, or elaboration

Observation schedule	Student callout	0.313**
	Student–teacher questioning	0.231
Student interview	Student's general attitude	0.306**

(d) Student interview

---

(1) Student and teacher match of goals

Student interview	Student learning modality preference	0.232*

(2) Student's general attitude

Personality and cognitive style	Intolerance of ambiguity	−0.229
Attitudinal measures (Gardner *et al.* battery)	Integrative orientation	0.346**
	Motivation	0.611**
	Evaluation of means of learning French	0.613**
	Lack of ethnocentrism	0.343**
	Instrumental orientation	0.358**

(d) Student interview continued

---

(2) Student's general attitude cont.

Observation schedule	Student hand-raising	0.507**
	Student voluntary clarification, correction, or elaboration	0.306**
Student interview	Student attitude towards correcting others	0.384**
	Student perception of classroom environment	0.547**
	Student overall classroom personality	0.335**

(3) Student learning modality preference

Observation schedule	Student self-initiated further responding	−0.274**
	Student hand-raising	0.321**
	Student hesitation	−0.268*
Student interview	Student and teacher match of goals	0.232*

(4) Student perception of whether he's asked sufficiently

Personality and cognitive style	Category width	−0.261*
Attitudinal measures (Gardner *et al.* battery)	Integrative orientation	0.390**
	Motivation	0.269*
Observation schedule	Student hesitation	0.267*

(5) Student reaction to lack of comprehension

Attitudinal measures (Gardner *et al.* battery)	Lack of ethnocentrism	−0.337**
Observation schedule	Student self-correction	0.225
	Student hand-raising	0.317**
	Student hesitation	−0.406**
Student interview	Student attitude towards correcting others	0.248*
	Student repetition of teacher correction	−0.293*

(6) Student attitude towards teacher correction

Personality and cognitive style	Interference	−0.256*
Attitudinal measures (Gardner *et al.* battery)	Integrative orientation	0.272*
	Evaluation of means of learning French	0.282*
Observation schedule	Student self-initiated repetition	0.242*
Student interview	Student perception of classroom environment	0.222

(7) Student attitude towards being interrupted

Personality and cognitive style	Intolerance of ambiguity	−0.229*
Observation schedule	Student hesitation	−0.234*

(8) Student attitude towards correcting others

Attitudinal measures (Gardner *et al.* battery)	Integrative orientation	0.241*
	Motivation	0.342**
	Evaluation of means of learning French	0.291*
	Lack of ethnocentrism	0.230
Observation schedule	Student hand-raising	0.318**
	Student hesitation	0.226
Student interview	Student's general attitude	0.384**
	Student reaction to lack of comprehension	0.248*
	Student reaction to teacher's use of L1, L2	0.233*
	Student perception of classroom environment	0.251*

(9) Student repetition of teacher correction

Personality and cognitive style	Intolerance of ambiguity	-0.259*
Attitudinal measures (Gardner *et al.* battery)	Lack of ethnocentrism	0.300*
Observation schedule	Student responses beyond teacher questioning	−0.224
	Student hesitation	0.223
Student interview	Student reaction to lack of comprehension	−0.293*

(d) Student interview *continued*

---

(10) Student reaction to teacher's use of L1, L2

Personality and cognitive style	Field independence	0.314**
	Intolerance of ambiguity	−0.334**
Attitudinal measures	Integrative orientation	0.228
(Gardner *et al.* battery)	Motivation	0.358**
	Evaluation of means of learning French	0.321**
	Instrumental orientation	0.262*
	Lack of ethnocentrism	0.382**
Observation schedule	Student self-initiated further responding	0.247*
	Student null responses	−0.428**
	Student null responses (vol.–invol. responses)	0.292*
	Student hesitation responses (vol.–invol. responses)	−0.271*
Student interview	Student attitude towards correcting others	0.233*
	Student overall classroom personality	0.225

(11) Student perception of classroom environment

Attitudinal measures	Motivation	0.366**
(Gardner *et al.* battery)	Evaluation of means of learning French	0.577**
Observation schedule	Student hand-raising	0.241*
	Student continuing responses	−0.232*
	Student complete responses (vol.–invol. responses)	0.255*
	Student incorrect responses	−0.290*
Student interview	Student's general attitude	0.547**
	Student attitude towards teacher correction	0.223
	Student attitude towards correcting others	0.251*

(12) Student overall classroom personality

Observation schedule	Student hand-raising	0.317**
	Student complete responses	0.375**
	Student incomplete (partial) responses	−0.221
	Student continuing responses	−0.267*
	Student correct responses	0.357**
	Student responding above 10 times	0.257*
Student interview	Student's general attitude	0.335*
	Student reaction to teacher's use of L1, L2	0.225

Notes

1. In fact a high score on this test indicates intolerance of ambiguity, and this score was negatively correlated with success. In other words, tolerance of ambiguity is positively related to success on the two criteria.
2. Due to the fact that many of the students did not respond very often, some of the variables derived from observation were based on a small number of occurrences. Separate analyses were run for only those Ss who responded more than 10 times during the observation period. These results did not differ by any appreciable extent from the original analyses.
3. A more detailed description of these programs will be presented in a later section, see Part III, chapter 5, section 6.1.
4. The stepwise regression analysis was adapted from Buhler (1971) for use with P Stat.
5. All variables $p < 0.05$, excepting motivation $0.05 \, p < 0.10$.

CHAPTER 4
Discussion of Statistical Results

The results of the experimentation demonstrated the feasibility of and the need for this type of research. It was evident that certain personality characteristics, cognitive styles, and attitudes were more significant for success than others, and that their significance varied at different stages of language learning. Unfortunately, few learning strategies and techniques were identified.

1. Learning Strategies

Initially, the investigators expected that by observing language learners in their language learning situation over a prolonged period it would be possible to isolate specific techniques or strategies; they now feel that this approach has not been successful. The indices of overt language learning behaviors they had selected for observation, such as student self-correction, student-initiated repetition, student–teacher questioning, and student self-initiated further responding were infrequent and in addition, did not appear to differentiate between successful and unsuccessful learners. Other techniques such as circumlocution, silent repetition, or role-playing occurred rarely, if ever.

One or both of the following explanations may account for the failure to identify strategies using such an observation schedule.

(1) The investigators may not have spent enough time in the classroom, so that it was impossible for systematic patterns of learning behavior to be evidenced. If the observers had spent an additional two weeks in the classroom, these techniques and the differences between the patterns of learning behavior between good and poor learners might have become more apparent. The researchers were nevertheless of the opinion that further observation of the same type for even an additional month would probably not have resulted in the identification of any additional learning strategies and techniques. The observation schedule was nevertheless extremely useful in identifying other relevant aspects of teacher–student interactions, which will be described in detail at a later point.

(2) Very few overt and systematic techniques or strategies are ever displayed in the language classroom. Simple behavioral phenomena such as hand-raising and repetition occur, and can be observed, but it is impossible to observe more complex or important but covert forms of learning behavior in the daily classroom routine. Perhaps they can be observed only when the student's language learning is tied to more specific tasks.

Alternatively, there are more indirect means of assessing cognitive processes underlying language learning behavior. In fact, many researchers have recently begun to systematically develop such methods in an attempt to identify these processes. The majority of them (for example, Dulay and Burt, 1974; Bailey, Madden and Krashen, 1974; Hakuta, 1974; Selinker, Swain and Dumas, 1975) have been analyzing language production data in the hope of describing the systematic processes which may account for the language that second language learners are producing.

But research of this type, though extremely valuable to the field of second language learning research, poses several other problems. Many of the researchers have formulated general hypotheses about the processes of second language learning solely on the basis of the order of acquisition of a small set of morephemes. However, morpheme acquisition may be wholly unrepresentative of other aspects of second language learning. Furthermore, the practice of inferring language learning *processes* solely on the basis of language *product* is tenuous.

In fact, what would be needed in future research would be a combination of this latter kind of research with research of the type initiated in the present project, albeit with necessary modifications. As previously stated, if language learning is to be studied it cannot be observed solely in a classroom; the performance of language learners on individual learning tasks would have to be carefully followed. Researchers could develop learning tasks in which selected linguistic material is presented to learners. Students' performance on a variety of exercises and tasks measuring the learning of various aspects of these materials could be closely monitored. In addition, the language learner himself could be consulted and asked to describe what he is doing and why. The learning tasks would be both tools for the rigorous monitoring of second language learning behavior and foci for the learner's reporting about the strategies he may be employing. This would be done in conjunction with the collection of language production data on a longitudinal basis, so that the identified processes could be related to the linguistic product and to the processes independently inferred from the linguistic product. With such research it is hoped that we will be able to discover more about the strategies and processes of second language learning.

In the present study, even though it was not possible to identify learning strategies by simple classroom observation to any great extent, other important relationships between cognitive style, personality characteristics, attitudes, and successful language learning were nevertheless evidenced. The results of the stepwise regression analalyses predicting the outcomes in the measures of linguistic competence (IEA and Imitation) using the cognitive style, personality, and attitudinal factors were indicative of several relationships (see Tables 18–21).

2. Productive vs. Receptive Competence

There did not seem to be any major differences in the cluster of variables that were predictive of success for the two criterion measures. In other words, the personality, attitudinal, and cognitive style traits that were predictive of success were, in most instances, the same for productive (imitation) and receptive (IEA) competence. This finding was not totally expected. One might have predicted that certain cognitive styles or personality characteristics might have been more related to one of the linguistic skills than to another. For example, it might have been expected that extroversion would be more related to success on productive skills than on receptive skills; similarly, student overall classroom personality. On the other hand, one might have thought that eye-minded students would have been less adept in the productive than in the receptive skills.

The lack of differences may be attributable to the fact that the tests were not adequately measuring the aspects of linguistic competence they were designed to. The IEA Test of French Acheivement was developed as an international test and some of the vocabulary items that were included in the test may not have been familiar to the students in the Ontario school system. As a matter of fact, some of the teachers indicated to the investigators that they were certain that the students were unfamiliar with several of the vocabulary items contained in the test.

As for the imitation test, it was not developed as a strict measure of oral production for use with the present sample, but was designed for use with young children in an 'immersion' program. It was desirable, nonetheless, to use the same test, so that the results of the two groups could subsequently be compared. However, the sentences still had to be modified from the original set used with the 'immersion' children, for they were found to be too difficult for the adolescents in the regular program.

It may be because of these weaknesses in the construct validity of the criterion measures that there were so few differences in the nature of the variables that were related to the two aspects of linguistic competence. It should nevertheless not be overlooked that ideally one would like to be able to differentiate between the various skills contributing to success in second language learning; perhaps certain factors are related to specific skills whereas others are related to totally different skills. In future research, other French language tests would have to be developed to measure more rigorously the various skills contributing to an overall linguistic competence. With valid criterion measures, clusters of variables related to these specific skills could be isolated.

3. I.Q. and Language Aptitude

At this point it should be reiterated that it was unfortunately impossible to administer any I.Q. or language aptitude tests to the sample. Since the investigators were already at the limit of the time they were allowed to remove the students from their regular programs, it was decided that it was only possible to concentrate on a subset of the possible measurable factors. It was considered beneficial to select those factors which other researchers had for the most part neglected, and consequently, no measures of I.Q. and language aptitude were given. We are unable to speculate on how the results of factors such as I.Q. and aptitude would have compared with the measures of personality characteristics, cognitive style, and attitude in predicting success on the criterion measures.

4. Attitude

In conjunction with many other studies in the field (e.g. Gardner and Smythe, 1975a) it was confirmed in this research that attitude and motivation were in many instances the best overall predictors of success in second language learning. However, our results may add several qualifications to this general trend of results. It appears that attitude may be more important at certain stages of language learning than at others. In addition, positive attitude may be a necessary but is certainly not a sufficient condition for success in learning a second language.

Furthermore, most of the studies that have related attitudes to success in second language learning haves found that students possessing an integrative motivation are more likely to succeed than students with an instrumental motivation. However, the results of this study are not so clearcut. As a matter of fact, many of the results of the regression analyses (see Tables 20 and 21) indicates that some of the other attitudinal measures of the battery appeared to be much more predictive of success than were either integrative or instrumental motivation.

These discrepencies, however, may have been due to the form of the test and the combination of subscales used in the present study. The attitude battery that was administered to the students was an experimental shortened version of the Language Research Group's National Test Battery (Form A). The test consisted of approximately one half of the items contained in the original battery. In addition, the researchers at the Language Research Group were experimenting with different combinations of the 25 subscales of the test, and the make-up of the several possible combinations. Therefore, the lack of agreement between this study and the preceding ones may be attributable to this factor.

It is also interesting to note that the attitude measure constructed by the investigators on the basis of the interviews with the students, i.e. student's general attitude, appeared to be the best overall predictor of success for both criterion measures and for students at different stages of second language learning (see Tables 18 and 21). This measure can be described as an indication of how a student perceives his individual language situation and his general attitude towards learning the language in this particular situation.

If indeed such a measure is as good a predictor of success in various aspects of second language learning as it appears to be, then perhaps more attention should be paid to encouraging means of collecting such information, from both a theoretical and a practical point of view. In other words, a brief, but carefully designed, interview with a student may indicate a great deal more about his overall attitude towards language learning, and therefore the probability of his success, than the results of an involved attitude battery. Of course, the total time involved in such an assessment would be greater than that of a group testing situation, but this does not mean that it would be impossible for a teacher, a head of a language department, or another responsible person whom the student trusted to spend fifteen or twenty minutes speaking individually with students about their feelings towards language learning. In addition to gathering information about their general attitude, teachers would be able to entertain students' specific opinions about their language learning preferences and ideas for change.[1] Furthermore, students would probably not forget the feeling that teachers were interested and willing to consider their ideas and suggestions.

The hypothesis that attitude may be more crucial at the beginning stages of language learning was substantiated by the differences in the results of the various regression analyses for each grade, the Analysis of Variance between grades, and also by the greater amount of variance accounted for by these factors in grade 8 than in the later grades (see Tables 20, 21, and 23). Since attitude appears to be most important early in language learning, it is suggested that methods of fostering students' positive attitudes towards their second language learning situation at the earliest possible time be encouraged, otherwise there is a very real possibility that many students will drop out.

5. Cognitive Style and Personality

As this study has been able to demonstrate, attitude is not the only factor in success, and in fact can in no way be construed as a sufficient condition. Several cognitive style and personality characteristics are important predictors of successful language learning, and again, some of these factors may be more crucial at one stage of language learning than at others.

For example, it appears that those students who have a high intolerance of ambiguity may have great difficulty in coping with the amount of ambiguity present in the second language classroom, and therefore may drop the subject as soon as possible. This possibility was strengthened by the fact that tolerance of ambiguity was a significant predictor of success for both criteria only in grade 8, while the results of the Analysis of Variance indicated that grade 10 and grade 12 students were both significantly more tolerant of ambiguity than grade 8 students (see Tables 20, 21 and 23). Similarly, reaction to the teacher's use of French in the classroom,[2] which is highly related to tolerance of ambiguity, was a significant predictor for both criterion measures in grade 8 and grade 10, but for neither in grade 12.

At later stages of second language learning in a formal situation, it appears that other cognitive style factors, for example, field independence, are more important. In fact, field independence was the single most significant predictor of success on both criteria for grade 12, while it was not significant in any of the other grades (except as a minor predictor of success on imitation in grade 8) (see Tables 20, 21, and 23).

Certain cognitive styles or personality factors may be more important predictors of success at certain stages of language learning than at others, as has already been discussed. Future research should attempt to isolate more of these factors and investigate their theoretical relationship to the processes and stages of second language acquisition. In a later section (see Part III, chapter 5, section 2.2), findings from this study which relate the cognitive style of the student to the language he was producing will be reported upon. This is but one of the many paths that should be followed in opening up this important area of research.

Even though there were a few test measures of cognitive style and personality factors, i.e. field independence and intolerance of ambiguity, that were related to successful second language learning, the results of the majority of the cognitive style and personality tests administered did not yield any systematic relationships to the criterion measures. The explanation as to why this was the case may be provided by either of the following factors. (1) There were indeed no relationships between the variables and the criteria; in other words, the original hypotheses about the relationships of these cognitive style and personality measures to language learning were not confirmed. Or (2), the constructs these tests were supposed to be measuring were in fact not being adequately measured by these tests.

The investigators tend to believe the latter. Especially with regard to the personality measures, they were not convinced of the construct validity of some of the tests administered. In other words, they do not believe, for example, that a higher score on the extroversion scale indicated that a student was in fact an 'extrovert' in the language classroom. After interviewing the students and observing them in their classrooms for an extensive period of time, they felt that by the end of the testing period they knew each of the students assigned to them quite well. Yet, they were later surprised to see gross discrepancies between their opinions about the students and the results of the tests of Extroversion and Sensitivity to Rejection. Students who had reported that they were extremely shy and embarrassed, afraid to speak out in class and afraid that people were laughing at them, and whom the investigators regarded as being introverted on the basis of classroom observation, often scored no differently on the extroversion scale than did students who reported being 'extroverted' and acted accordingly.

As a result of some of these misgivings, an alternative personality measure was constructed, based upon students' responses in the interview. This variable[3] could best be described as an indication by the student of his general classroom personality, including fear of being laughed at, or being embarrassed when speaking, or not putting up his hand until he was certain he knew the response, etc.

The results of the analyses indicate that this measure was a better predictor of success on both criteria than were any of the other personality measures given, apart from intolerance of ambiguity (which may be more of a combination of cognitive style and personality than strictly a personality measure).

There is thus a need for other and better measures of the personality factors thought to be related to language learning. This is especially so with variables like empathy. The investigators were from the outset wary of using the Hogan set for measuring aspects of empathy directly related to language learning, despite the overall validity of the test. The results tend to confirm their doubts.

6. Interviews

In addition to providing a great deal of information about the students' cognitive styles, personality factors, ideas for change and preferences in learning, the student interviews also confirmed the fact that many learning behaviors cannot be observed objectively in the language class as it is widely conducted. During their interviews several students indicated that they used techniques for learning in the classroom which were invisible to any observers, such as attempting to answer to themselves every question asked by the teacher. Others stated that they frequently used certain strategies for learning which were outside of the classroom altogether. Some of these behaviors will be enumerated in Part III, chapter 5, section 3.

Information about the relationships of different personality characteristics, cognitive styles, and attitudes to different learning environments is based primarily on the interviews conducted with the students. The results of the statistical analyses comparing the various learning environments (i.e. traditional, open-plan, and individualized) were considered tentative because of the small sample from each environment and because of the many similarities evidenced across different programs. The investigators therefore felt that the Analysis of Variance examining the interaction between overall classroom personality and environment resulted in non-significance (see Table 17). However, there were descriptive results from the student interviews that demonstrated the importance of the relationships between the learning environment and student learning behavior, personality, cognitive style, and attitude. These will be described in detail in a later section (see Part III, chapter 5, section 3).

The interviews also identified several general important predictors of success, such as learning modality preference – i.e. those students who reported themselves as ear-minded tended to be more successful than eye-minded students. In addition, the information gathered from the interviews substantiated many of the findings of the more formal testing sessions, and in general indicated that useful information could be found on the reasons for success and failure in language learning by talking to the learners themselves.

The evidence of interrelationships among variables gathered from the multiple sources is substantiated by the many positive correlations to be found in the pages of the intercorrelation matrix (see Table 28). There were also many relationships among variables that were not easily explainable. For example, student hesitation in responding was correlated with lack of ethnocentrism, and negatively correlated with student learning modality preference and student reaction to lack of comprehension. The reason for this apparent lack of systematicity is probably that there were too few subjects and too many variables. It was for just this reason that a factor analysis on the data was considered inadvisable.

Even though these relationships should be regarded cautiously, several interesting examples can be extracted (see Table 28). A student who said that he wanted the teacher to use more French in the classroom was likely to be tolerant of ambiguity, field independent, have generally positive attitudes, likely to initiate further responding, and generally to correct other students when they had made errors. Some one who was tolerant of ambiguity was likely to be field independent, insensitive to rejection, not ethnocentric, have high instrumental orientation, and want the teacher to use more French in the classroom. If more subjects had been tested, it would have been possible to identify such clusters of interrelated variables more reliably.

In sum, the multiplicity of sources of data on the various factors related to successful language learning proved quite useful. Discussions of the weaknesses and strengths of these research instruments should prove helpful for future research in the area. Such cross-sectional correlational studies as the present one can indicate general trends in the relationships between personality, cognitive styles, attitudes, overt learning behavior and success or failure in the classroom second language learning. The study has indicated, for example, that several personality factors, cognitive style, and attitudinal factors are related to successful language learning and at which stages they are most operative. The major weakness of such a study, however, lies in the fact that one cannot relate these factors directly to processes of second language acquisition. This can only be accomplished through a longitudinal case study.

Notes

1. Detailed accounts about the students' preferences and ideas for change will be presented in Part III, chapter 5, section 3.
2. The students were asked whether they felt the teachers were using too much English or French or just about the right mixture of the two.
3. For a more detailed description of this variable, see Part III, chapter 3, section 3.3.

CHAPTER 5
Detailed Discussion of Special Aspects

1. Introduction

Sections D and E of the main study dealt primarily with the results and discussions of the statistical interrelationships among the variety of variables collected and their relationships to the criterion measures of success on receptive (IEA) and productive (Imitation) competence. However, in presenting and discussing these results, it was not possible to elaborate on any parts of the study that were not directly connected to the statistical relationships between personality, cognitive style, attitude or learning behavior, and success or failure in second language learning.

The following section therefore presents several of these aspects of the main study which demand a more detailed description. This section should provide useful information, both theoretical and practical, about some of the more interesting facets of the main study. These are:

Imitation Task Results
Student Interview
Differential Teacher Treatment
Case Studies of Selected Students
General Information about Classroom Activities and Atmosphere

2. Imitation Task Results

As previously described in Part III, chapter 3, gross measures of linguistic productive competence were attained for each subject on the imitation task. A score was obtained by calculating the total number of linguistic units a subject had repeated correctly out of the total number of units in each set of sentences. This provided the researchers with a measure of linguistic productive competence which could be used in addition to the measure of receptive competence attained from the IEA test. (As noted previously, these two measures of linguistic competence were significantly correlated, $r = 0.792, p < 0.001$.)

Some of the further findings from the imitation task will now be presented, under two main topics:

(1) the acquisition of linguistic structures
(2) the relationship of cognitive style to language product

2.1 Acquisition of linguistic structures

As explained in Part III, chapter 1, section 1.2, the sentences of the imitation task were adapted from a set of sentences used as one of several measures of the French language competence of grade 1, 2 and 3 Anglophone children in an 'immersion' program. Initially, it was hoped that comparisons could still be made between the performance of the older students in the regular program with the younger children in the 'immersion' program. However, at the time of writing the results of the study of the immersion program children were not available.[1]

The results of the imitation task were transcribed onto cards, with indications of the substitutions, omissions, and correct responses given by every subject. These results were then summed for students within each grade so that indications of the general level of acquisition, as well as the substitutions made, were available for each grade.

Because not all structures and vocabulary items were identical in the different sets of sentences given to the students of each grade, most of the discussion will be limited to those structures that were present in all sets and hence comparable across grades.

The structures that will be discussed are:

(a) articles
(b) possessive pronouns
(c) prepositions
(d) indirect and direct object pronouns
(e) verbs (past tense)

The results for the students in each grades can be found in Table 29 (a–e). In each part of the table the majority of exemplary structures for each of the five superordinate categories listed above are presented. For each individual structure, the following information is provided in each table. After the name of the structure, the total number of occurrences of the structure in all the sentences given to students of that grade appears in brackets. For example, if '*la*' appeared once in the set of 10 sentences for 24 students of grade 8, the total number of occurrences of '*la*' was $24 \times 1 = 24$.

Table 29 Imitation of various structures

(a) Articles

Grade 8

LE (72) Correct – 50.0, Subst. – 22.2

Substituted by	a	b
les	37.5	8.3
la	31.2	6.9
des	6.2	1.4
une	6.2	1.4
de	6.2	1.4
un	6.2	1.4
mon	6.2	1.4

LA (24) Correct – 29.2, Subst. – 41.7

Substituted by	a	b
le	50.0	20.8
une	30.0	12.5
mon	10.0	4.2
un	10.0	4.2

UN (48) Correct – 50.0, Subst. – 8.3

Substituted by	a	b
la	50.0	4.2
une	25.0	2.1
le	25.0	2.1

Grade 10

LE (96) Correct – 52.1, Subst. – 9.4

Substituted by	a	b
un	44.4	4.2
la	22.2	2.1
les	11.1	1.1
ton	11.1	1.1
des	11.1	1.1

LA (48) Correct – 31.2, Subst. 47.9

Substituted by	a	b
le	95.7	45.8
les	4.3	2.1

UN (48) Correct – 35.4, Subst. – 27.1

Substituted by	a	b
une	38.5	10.4
son	23.1	6.2
la	7.7	2.1
des	7.7	2.1
mon	7.7	2.1
le	7.7	2.1
les	7.7	2.1

Grade 12

LE (96) Correct – 62.5, Subst. – 11.4

Substituted by	a	b
la	45.4	5.2
un	12.3	3.1
les	18.2	2.1
mon	9.1	1.0

LA (72) Correct – 62.5, Subst. – 23.6

Substituted by	a	b
le	58.8	13.9
un	17.6	4.2
les	11.8	2.8
ma	11.8	2.8

UN (24) Correct – 45.8, Subst. – 45.8

Substituted by	a	b
le	45.4	20.8
une	36.4	16.7
des	9.1	4.2
son	9.1	4.2

Table 29 Imitation of various structures *continued*
(a) Articles *continued*

Grade 8

UNE (48) Correct – 29.2, Subst. – 27.1

Substituted by	a	b
un	61.5	16.7
des	15.4	4.2
l'	7.7	2.1
la	7.7	2.1
de	7.7	2.1

DES (72) Correct – 29.2, Subst. – 34.7

Substituted by	a	b
de	48.0	16.7
une	16.0	5.6
un	8.0	2.8
les	4.0	1.4
l'	4.0	1.4
mon	4.0	1.4
du	4.0	1.4
d'	4.0	1.4
le	4.0	1.4
la	4.0	1.4

Grade 10

UNE (48) Correct – 20.8, Subst. – 27.1

Substituted by	a	b
un	76.9	20.8
l'	15.4	4.2
les	7.7	2.1

DES (72) Correct – 36.1, Subst. – 34.7

Substituted by	a	b
de	36.0	12.5
les	24.0	8.3
le	20.0	6.9
d'	12.0	4.2
une	4.0	1.4
un	4.0	1.4

Grade 12

UNE (24) Correct – 37.5, Subst. – 33.3

Substituted by	a	b
un	50.0	16.7
le	50.0	16.7

DES (48) Correct – 35.4, Subst. 43.7

Substituted by	a	b
les	57.1	25.0
le	14.3	6.2
de	14.3	6.2
un	4.8	2.1
d'	4.8	2.1
une	4.8	2.1

Table 29 Imitation of various structures *continued*

(b) Possessive pronouns

Grade 8

MON (24) Correct – 50.0, Subst. – 12.5

		a	b
Substituted by	un	66.7	8.3
	une	33.3	4.2

TON (24) Correct – 70.8, Subst. – 16.7

		a	b
Substituted by	un	50.0	8.3
	ta	25.0	4.2
	le	25.0	4.2

Grade 10

MON (48) Correct – 43.7, Subst. – 12.5

		a	b
Substituted by	un	66.7	8.3
	son	33.3	4.2

TON (24) Correct – 75.0, Subst. – 12.5

		a	b
Substituted by	le	66.7	8.3
	mon	33.3	4.2

SON (24) Correct – 20.8, Subst. – 45.8

		a	b
Substituted by	le	27.3	12.5
	une	27.3	12.5
	un	27.3	12.5
	des	9.1	4.2
	mes	9.1	4.2

Grade 12

MON (48) Correct – 66.7, Subst. – 4.2

		a	b
Substituted by	l'	50.0	2.1
	son	50.0	2.1

TON (48) Correct 47.9, Subst. – 35.4

		a	b
Substituted by	mon	58.8	20.8
	ta	11.8	4.2
	le	11.8	4.2
	la	11.8	4.2
	une	5.9	2.1

SON (48) Correct 45.8, Subst. – 14.6

		a	b
Substituted by	un	57.1	8.3
	ma	14.3	2.1
	le	14.3	2.1
	sa	14.3	2.1

Table 29 Imitation of various structures *continued*

(c) Prepositions

	Grade 8	Grade 10	Grade 12

Grade 8

À (24) Correct – 20.8, Subst. 8.3

		a	b
Substituted by	en	100.0	8.3

DANS (24) Correct – 50.0, Subst. – 12.5

		a	b
Substituted by	à	100.0	12.5

Grade 10

À (48) Correct – 33.3, Subst. – 10.4

		a	b
Substituted by	*après de*	40.0	4.2
	de	20.0	2.1
	en	20.0	2.1
	avec	20.0	2.1

DANS (48) Correct – 37.5, Subst. – 20.8

		a	b
Substituted by	*à*	70.0	14.6
	de	30.0	6.2

PRÈS DE (48) Correct – 6.2, Subst. –33.3

		a	b
Substituted by	*à*	56.2	18.7
	après de	18.7	6.2
	en	12.5	4.2
	pour	6.2	2.1
	avec	6.2	2.1

Grade 12

À (24) Correct – 45.8, Subst. – 4.2

		a	b
Substituted by	*en*	100.0	4.2

DANS (48) Correct – 45.8, Subst. – 14.6

		a	b
Substituted by	*à*	57.2	8.3
	de	28.6	4.2
	in	14.3	2.1

PRÈS DE (0)

(c) **Prepositions** *continued*

Grade 8	Grade 10	Grade 12

Grade 10

PAR (24) Correct – 45.8, Subst. – 25.0

Substituted by		a	b
	à	66.7	16.7
	de	16.7	4.2
	dans	16.7	4.2

DE (72) Correct – 52.8, Subst. – 12.5

Substituted by		a	b
	à	88.9	11.1
	de le	11.1	1.4

AVEC (24) Correct – 54.2, Subst. – 4.2

Substituted by		a	b
	dans	10.0	4.2

POUR (24) Correct – 58.3, Subst. – 0

Grade 12

PAR (24) Correct – 25.0, Subst. –33.3

Substituted by		a	b
	à	75.0	25.0
	de	12.5	4.2
	dans	12.5	4.2

DE (48) Correct – 62.5, Subst. – 4.2

Substituted by		a	b
	à	62.5	4.2

AVEC (24) Correct – 70.8, Subst. – 0

APRÈS (24) Correct 45.8, Subst. – 29.2

Substituted by		a	b
	près	28.6	8.3
	à	14.3	4.2
	à prendre	14.3	4.2
	devant	14.3	4.2
	par	14.3	4.2
	after	14.3	4.2

Table 29 Imitation of various structures *continued*
(d) Indirect and direct objects
(i) Direct objects

	Grade 8	Grade 10	Grade 12
	M' (24) Correct – 25.0, Subst. – 0	M' (24) Correct – 34.5, Subst. – 0	M' (48) Correct – 52.1, Subst. – 4.2

Grade 8

LUI (24) Correct – 50.0, Subst. – 8.33

Substituted by		a	b
	leur	50.0	4.2
	les leur	50.0	4.2

Grade 10

NOUS (24) Correct – 25.0, Subst. – 0

Grade 12

M' (48) Correct – 52.1, Subst. – 4.2

		a	b
Substituted by	*l'*	50.0	2.1
inversion:	*à me donné*	50.0	2.1

LUI (24) Correct – 45.8, Subst. – 20.8

		a	b
Substituted by inversion:	*à lui demandé*	80.0	16.7
	la	20.0	4.2

NOUS (24) Correct – 41.7, Subst. 12.5

		a	b
Substituted by	*la*	33.3	4.2
	quelqu'un	33.3	4.2
inversion:	*a raconté nous*	33.3	4.2

LEUR (24) Correct – 54.2, Subst. – 20.8

		a	b
Substituted by	*la*	20.0	4.2
	lui	20.0	4.2
	te	20.0	4.2
	le	20.0	4.2
inversion:	*à leur*	20.0	4.2

Table 29 Imitation of various structures *continued*

(d) Indirect and direct objects

(ii) *Indirect objects*

Grade 8	Grade 10	Grade 12
	LES (24) Correct – 33.3, Subst. – 20.8	*LES* (24) Correct – 12.5, Subst. – 16.7
	a *b*	*a* *b*
	Substituted by *le* 80.0 16.7	Substituted by *le* 75.0 12.5
	la 20.0 4.2	*la* 25.0 4.2
		T' (24) Correct – 70.8, Subst. – 0
		L' (m) (24) Correct – 25.0, Subst. – 0
		L' (f) (24) Correct – 33.3, Subst. – 33.3
		a *b*
		Substituted by *lui* 100 33.3

Table 29 Imitation of various structures *continued*

(e) Verbs (past tense)

Grade 8

3rd REG. (96) Correct – 28.1, Subst. – 46.9 (e.g., *a mange*)

Substituted by	a	b
p.p.	40.0	18.7
Ph	17.8	8.3
E	13.3	6.2
av	11.1	5.2
word sub	6.6	3.1
apres	4.4	2.1
word sub + p.p.	4.4	2.1
Pres	2.2	2.1

1st REG. (24) Correct – 79.2, Subst. – 20.8 (e.g., *avons mangé*)

Substituted by	a	b
Ph	40.0	8.3
av	20.0	4.2
Pers (a)	20.0	4.2
Pers + av (avez)	20.0	4.2

Grade 10

3rd REG. (96) Correct – 37.5, Subst. – 37.5

Substituted by	a	b
p.p.	51.3	20.8
Ph	15.4	6.2
word	7.7	3.1
av	7.7	2.1
Pers (avons)	5.1	1.0
Pres	2.5	1.0
Apres	2.5	1.0
E	2.5	1.0
aller	2.5	1.0
Ph + Pers	2.5	1.0

1st REG. (24) Correct – 58.3, Subst. – 16.7

Substituted by	a	b
aller	50.0	16.7
p.p.	12.5	4.2
av	12.5	4.2
word	12.5	4.2
word order	12.5	4.2

Grade 12

3rd REG. (120) Correct – 45.0, Subst. – 36.7

Substituted by	a	b
p.p.	36.4	13.3
Pres	18.2	6.7
Apres	11.4	4.2
Pers (avons)	9.1	3.3
av	6.8	2.5
Phon	6.8	2.5
E	4.5	1.6
Epres	2.3	.8
word sub	2.3	.8
Aller	2.3	.8

1st REG. (48) Correct – 56.2, Subst. – 16.7

Substituted by	a	b
p.p.	25.0	4.2
av	25.0	4.2
word sub	25.0	4.2
Ph	12.5	2.1
Pers (a)	12.5	2.1

(e) Verbs (past tense) *continued*

Grade 8

1st REG. (24) Correct – 91.7, Subst. – 8.3

(e.g., *ai mangé*)

Substituted by		a	b
Ph		100	8.3

1st IRREG. (24) Correct – 50.0, Subst. – 20.8

(e.g., *ai vu*)

Substituted by	a	b
av	20.0	4.2
Pres	20.0	4.2
Inver	20.0	4.2
word sub	20.0	4.2
Pers + av (avez)	20.0	4.2

Legend

model	*a mangé*
av	*a*
p.p.	*mangé*
Pres	*mange*
Apres	*a mange*
E	*est mangé*
Epres	*est mange*
Pers (avons)	*avons mangé*
aller	*va mangé*
Ph	*a mandé*
word sub	*a dîné*

Grade 10

1st REG. (24) Correct – 75.0, Subst. – 16.7

Substituted by		a	b
	Ph	50.0	8.3
	av	25.0	4.2
	Ph	50.0	8.3

1st IRREG. (24) Correct – 83.3, Subst. – 4.2

Substituted by		a	b
Ph		100	4.2

Grade 12

1st REG. (24) Correct – 91.7

1st IRREG. (24) Correct – 62.5, Subst. – 20.8

Substituted by		a	b
	av	60.0	12.5
	p.p.	20.0	4.2
	ai avais vu	20.0	4.2

2nd REG. (24) Correct – 58.3, Subst. – 20.8

Substituted by		a	b
p.p.		80.0	16.7
		20.0	4.2

Next, there is an indication of the percentage of correct repetitions of the structure out of the total number of occurrences. For example, if the total number of occurrences of '*la*' was 24, and the subjects repeated it correctly 12 times, the percentage correct would have been 50.0%. Following the percentage of correct imitations, there is a number indicating the percentage of substitutions made for these structures out of the total numbers of occurrences of the structures. For example, if '*la*' occurred 24 times and substitutions were made for it 6 times, the percentage of substitutions would be 25.0%.

In addition, there is a tabulation of the substitutions for each of the individual enumerated structures with two percentages following each: (a) the percentage of the total number of substitutions that were made using this form; (b) the percentage of the total occurrences of the model structure that were substituted by this individual form. For example, if '*la*' occurred 24 times and there was a total of 6 substitutions, the percentage of substitutions would be 25.0%. If '*le*' was substituted for '*la*' 4 out of these 6 times, (a) would be 4/6 or 66.7%, while (b) would be 4/24 or 16.7%.

Articles

From Table 29a, it is clear that the competence of the subjects, on the articles enumerated, increases for the most part from grades 8 to 12 (evaluated by the percentages of correct imitations out of the total number of occurrences of the structure). However, the major point to note is the increasing overgeneralization of the form '*le*' up to and including grade 10 and the subsequent differentation of the two forms '*le*' and '*la*' by grade 12. For grade 8 students, '*la*' is correct only 29.2% of the time, and '*le*', while correct 50% of the time, is substituted for '*la*' 20.8% of the time. In grade 10, the correct repetition of '*la*' has only increased to 31.2%, while the substitution of '*le*' for '*la*' has increased to 45.8%. In other words, by grade 10, '*le*' is being used for '*la*' more often than '*la*' is being used correctly. However, by grade 12 '*la*' is correct 62.5% of the time (exactly the same as the correctness of '*le*'), and is substituted by '*le*' only 13.9% of the time.

The results lead to the conclusion that the choice of gender for the definite article is fairly random at grade 8, with '*le*', however, being the form which is somewhat more prevalent. By grade 10, '*le*' has become the overgeneralized form, while by grade 12, the accurate differentiation of the two forms appears to be underway.

The only other forms that appear to be commonly substituted for '*le*' and '*la*' are the plural form '*les*' and the indefinite masculine article '*un*'.

With regard to correct formation of gender of the indefinite articles, a similar trend to that of '*le*' and '*la*' is evident in the substitution of '*un*' for the feminine form '*une*' – grade 8 performance being random, grade 10 students substituting '*un*' for '*une*', and grade 12 students in the process of acquiring the form.

As for the indefinite plural '*des*', the most prevalent error in grade 8 is the substitution of '*des*' by '*de*'. However, this error decreases from grade to grade, while the substitution of '*des*' by '*les*' increases.

Possessive pronouns

It appears from the data that the correct formation of the possessive pronoun does not increase from grade to grade. As a matter of fact, the correct repetition of '*ton*' decreases from grade 10 to grade 12. The most common type of substitution appears to be the substitution of an indefinite or definite article for the possessive pronoun. Interestingly, the substitution of the possessive pronoun of one person for another, e.g. '*mon*' for '*ton*' was much more frequent than a gender substitution, e.g. '*ma*' for '*mon*'. Unfortunately, there were no feminine possessive pronouns in the model sentences, but the infrequency of substitution of the feminine form for the masculine form of the pronoun is but another indication of the general trend of the prior acquisition of the masculines (or unmarked) form.

Prepositions

Subjects seemed to have had greater difficulty with some prepositions than with others. An examination of the peformance of the subjects at each grade level on individual prepositions would be extremely valuable for teachers, for it would provide them with possible indications of difficulty levels of prepositions. They could then provide remedial work for those structures that appeared to be most difficult. The utility of results of such an imitation task to teachers applies to all structures, not only to prepositions.

It is interesting to note that the preposition '*à*' is evidently the preposition most often substituted for other prepositions. It is also apparent that for the most part the proficiency of the subjects on the individual prepositions given increases from grade to grade.

Indirect and direct object pronouns

Indirect object: Unfortunately, there are not many points of comparison from grade to grade, because different indirect object pronouns were present in each grade, with the grade 12 task containing the greatest number of indirect objects. For the only indirect object pronoun that was contained in sentences for all grades, i.e. '*m'*', it is evident that subjects perform better with increasing grade level.

It is also interesting to note that there were many inversions of the indirect object pronouns, in other words, instances in which the object pronoun was placed after the verb or between the auxiliary and past participle instead of in front of both. This inversion corresponds to the word order of English, and not French. Surprisingly, none of these inversions occur in any grade other than grade 12. In addition, all of the inversions of the pronoun '*lui*' are of the form '*a lui demandé*' and not '*a demandé lui*'. Purely from the point of view of interference, one might expect that the latter type of inversion would precede the former one. However, the present data do not support this hypothesis.

Direct object: There were no direct object pronouns in the grade 8 task, only one in grade 10, and four in grade 12. At first glance, it appears that '*t*'' is acquired to a much greater extent than are any of the other direct object pronouns. However, this is probably an artifact of the task, in that '*t*'' appears right at the beginning of the model sentences, while the other pronouns do not. Memory plays a part in an imitation task (Naiman, 1974) and the primacy of '*t*'' in the sentence may be crucial to its high accuracy of repetition. It is for this reason that an imitation task should be designed so that the structure one is interested in appears in different parts of the sentence, to neutralize the effect of memory.

Past tense of verbs

Before discussing the results of the past tense verbs, two things must first be noted. First, the verbs were tabulated not by occurrences of individual verbs but by categories based on the person of the verb and on whether the verb was regular (i.e. 1st conjugation) or irregular. For example, '*a mangé*' and '*a donné*' were considered to be two occurrences of the category third person regular, whereas '*ai vu*' was considered to be occurrence of the first person irregular.

Secondly, the errors made on these verbs were categorized into cases that could be applied to all categories of the verbs. A description of these various error types with reference to a model appears in the Legend of Table 29e.

Turning to the data, it is clear that there are a great number of different types of substitutions made by the students. However, the most frequent substitution in nearly all categories of verbs was 'pp' – i.e. the formation of the past tense with the use of the past participle only, omitting the auxiliary. This substitution does not really decrease from grade 8 to grade 12, appearing, therefore, to be a common and persistent error. With more data of this type, hypotheses could be generated about the processes or strategies that resulted in its production, as well as some of the other types of errors.

In addition, it may be noted from the table that many of the verb categories, e.g. first person regular, appeared to be acquired better than others, e.g. third person regular. For the imitation task used in the present study, this may be the case because this form occurred at the beginning of the sentence while the others did not. However, if the position of the various structures in the sentences had been adequately controlled, comparisons among these different categories would have been more valid. For example, differences between the acquisition rate of '*avons mangé*' as opposed to '*a mangé*' could be explained by such factors as perceptual or phonetic saliency, or by uniqueness of function in that '*a*' has more than one semantic function in French, while the function of '*avons*' is unique. The generation of hypotheses such as these from similar imitation data could lead to the development of language acquisition universals.

2.2 The relationship of cognitive style to language product

For the purposes of the present study, gross criterion measures of second language competence alone were sufficient. There were time constraints in addition; the subjects were already being tested on many other measures. Copious language production data were therefore not collected from each student. Nevertheless, by analyzing the language produced on the imitation task it was possible to test several hypotheses about the relationship of cognitive style to language product.

In order to analyze the language produced by the students on the imitation task in a more systematic fashion, several new distinctions had to be made with regard to the data. Students may approach the problem of dealing with structures they do not know on the imitation task in different ways. Some students may choose to substitute the structures of which they are uncertain with alternative ones. Other students, when repeating the sentence, may omit just those structures they do not know, while still others may omit not only the structures they do not know, but give up and omit the rest of the structures that follow as well. It was necessary to distinguish these three alternatives. For example, in the sentence, '*La maman de mon ami m'a donné son beau manteau rouge,*' a student unfamiliar with the form '*m'*' might have said:

(1) La maman de mon aim lui a donné son beau manteau rouge.

Another student might have said:

(2) La maman de mon ami a donné son beau manteau rouge.

While a third type of student might have only said:

(3) La maman de mon ami.

When scoring the indirect object '*m*'' the first student's response would have been counted as a substitution, the second student's response as an omission type 1, and the third as an omission type 2. The definition of an omission type 2 was that the item omitted had to be contained in a unit that was omitted in conjunction with at least one other consecutive unit. For example, in sentence 2, '*m*'' formed the whole unit omitted, while the preceding and following units were not omitted. Therefore, in sentence 2, the omission of '*m*'' was considered an omission type 1. On the other hand, in sentence 3, '*m*'' and at least one more unit following '*m*'' were omitted, and therefore, this was counted as an omission type 2.

For each subject, a tabulation was made for each part of speech in the sentences provided. Depending upon how the subject imitated the sentence, each part of speech was put under one of four categories, i.e. correct, substitution, omission type 1, or omission type 2. Therefore, for each subject, a cumulative record exists of his performance in every part of speech according to these four categories. In addition, a cumulative record exists for the sum total of all the parts of speech for each subject.

With the information gathered in the cumulative records, the experimenters felt they had enough data to look at the relationship of learning styles to the language produced by the subjects.

For example, field dependent learners are characteristically distracted by irrelevant stimuli. When presented with a large stimulus array, they find it more difficult to select the relevant stimuli from the entire field. In terms of second language learning, field dependent learners may find it more difficult to attend to known features of the language when they are included in a long stream of the second language. They may be more likely to disregard the whole array because they find it too difficult to select the features they know.

On the imitation task, it was considered that field dependent learners might be more inclined, therefore, to omit whole segments of sentences instead of repeating at least the specific units they knew which were embedded in larger unknown segments. To test this hypothesis, subjects were divided into field dependent and field independent learners. In each grade, field dependent learners were defined as those who scored at least one standard deviation below the mean for the grade on the Embedded Figures Test; field independent learners were those who scored at least one standard deviation above the mean.

It was hypothesized that in imitating, field dependent learners would be more likely to omit items in large segments (omission type 2) than in small segments (omission type 1) in relation to the total number of units they were able to repeat correctly. The results of a t test between the two groups confirmed the hypothesis (t $= 1.71, p < 0.05$).

It was also evident that certain types of errors were committed more frequently by field dependent learners. For example, in the sentence, '*Hier quelqu'un nous a raconté une belle histoire*', field dependent learners were more likely to be distracted by the *nous* in juxtaposition to the '*a*' and say '*quelqu'un* nous avons *raconté*' than field independent learners. This type of error indicates that field dependent learners were more distracted by the immediate stimulus field.

Another hypothesis tested about the relation of cognitive style to language production concerned broad and narrow categorizers. A broad categorizer may construct very broad generalizations about the language he is learning, under which he subsumes a number of examples that do not really fit or are only partially related. In a sense, he is overgeneralizing in his inclusion of many inappropriate examples in order to fulfill his tendency towards broad generalizations. The narrow categorizer may make very fine precise distinctions, so that every example has its own rules. Therefore, it was felt that when a broad categorizer was confronted with a structure of which he was uncertain, he would be more likely to substitute another form for this structure (overgeneralize a rule to include this specific case) than would a narrow categorizer.

In terms of the imitation task, it was hypothesized, therefore, that broad categorizers would have a greater ratio of substitutions to type 1 omissions than would narrow categorizers. To test this hypothesis, those scoring more than one standard deviation above the mean on the Category Width test for each grade were considered broad categorizers; those scoring more than one standard deviation below the mean were considered narrow categorizers. A t test measuring the differences between the two groups was non-significant, $t = 0.52$.

Other hypotheses could have been tested if more language data had been collected from each subject. Similarly, if more data had been collected more information about specific learner's strategies or processes could have been inferred. For example, one student consistently overgeneralized the masculine form of the definite article, '*le*', in all instances where the definite article was required. Other subjects consistently used the past participle form alone, omitting the auxiliaries, in the formation of the past tense. If the data had been collected on a more longitudinal basis, the acquisition of many structures could have been traced for each student. With this information, it would have been possible to infer many language learning strategies and compare the different strategies used by subjects with differing cognitive styles. In addition, data of this type could be of practical use to teachers. The discovery of the order of acquisition and difficulty of level of many structures would be helpful in syllabus planning and remediation.

3. Student Interview

The researchers felt that an investigation of the student interviews more detailed than the basic statistical analyses of all the variables reported in Part III, chapter 3, should be undertaken. Therefore, tabulations were calculated to indicate the break-up of student responses to the interview items, according to the eight groups of students defined by combinations of teacher predictions and IEA results, as previously described (see Part III, chapter 2, section 2). The interview items produced the following variables.

(1) Studentperception of classroom formality

(2) Student perception of rapport with teacher

(3) Student perception of rapport with other students

(4) Student and teacher match of goals

(5) Student's general attitude

(6) Student learning modality preference

(7) Student certainty in hand-raising

(8) Student reaction to being called upon without hand-raising.

(9) Student perception of whether he is asked sufficiently

(10) Student reaction to lack of comprehension

(11) Student attitude towards teacher correction

(12) Student attitude towards being interrupted

(13) Student attitude towards correcting others

(14) Student repetition of teacher correction

(15) Student reaction to teacher's use of L1, L2

(16) Student affective remarks

Out of the total number of 16 variables only five differentiated significantly between the eight different combinations of student selection criteria, namely variable 2 – student perception of rapport with teacher; variable 5 – student's general attitude; variable 13 – student attitude towards correcting others; variable 15 – student reaction to teacher's use of L1, L2; and variable 16 – student affective remarks. The frequency distribution of the above mentioned variables is presented in Table 30.

Table 30 Frequency distribution of student response to interview items according to combination of teacher predictions and IEA-results

(a)

Variable	Scale	Interpretation of Scale	Combinations of Teacher Predictions and IEA-Results								Row Totals
			B-B	-B	T-B	B-M	T-M	B-T	-T	T-T	
Student perception of rapport with teacher	0	dislikes teacher	3	0	1	2	0	2*	1	0	9
	1	neutral	9	4*	1	2	0	0	3	3	22
	2	likes teacher	10	1	2	2	3	1	3	19	41
Column Totals			22	5	4	6	3	3	7	22	72

* high individual cell x^2 Table $x^2 = 29.67$ $(p < 0.01)$

(b)

Variable	Scale	Interpretation of Scale	Combinations of Teacher Predictions and IEA-Results								Row Totals
			B-B	-B	T-B	B-M	T-M	B-T	-T	T-T	
Student's general attitude	1	experimenter rating of student's attitude 1 – 5	0	0	0	1*	0	0	0	0	1
	2		5	1	1	1	0	0	0	0	8
	3		4	1	0	3	0	2	3	1	14
	4		12	3	3	1	2	1	3	11	36
	5		1	0	0	0	1	0	1	10*	13
Column Totals			22	5	4	6	3	3	7	22	72

* high individual cell x^2 Table $x^2 = 48.46$ $(p < 0.05)$

Table 30 Frequency distribution of student response to interview items according to combination of teacher predictions and IEA-results *continued*

(c) Variable	Scale	Interpretation of Scale	Combinations of Teacher Predictions and IEA-Results								Row Totals
			B-B	-B	T-B	B-M	T-M	B-T	-T	T-T	
Student attitude towards correcting others	0	Student does not correct others	3	2*	0	0	1	0	1	0	7
	1	Student sometimes corrects others	5	0	3*	2	2	2	1	1*	16
	2	Student always corrects others	9	3	1	1	0	1	4	20*	39
Column Totals			17	5	4	3	3	3	6	21	62

* high individual cell χ^2 Table $\chi^2 = 31.36$ ($p < 0.01$)   (This question was not responded to by 10 students)

Table 30 Frequency distribution of student response to interview items according to combination of teacher predictions and IEA-results *continued*

(d) Variable	Scale	Interpretation of Scale	Combinations of Teacher Predictions and IEA-Results								Row Totals
			B-B	-B	T-B	B-M	T-M	B-T	-T	T-T	
Student reaction to teacher's use of L1, L2	0	Student would like the teacher to use more L1	13	2	0	0	0	1	2	0*	18
	1	proportion of L1 and L2 is OK	8	1	3	4	2	2	3	15	38
	2	Student would like the teacher to use more L2	1	2	1	1	1	0	2	7	15
		Column Totals	22	5	4	5	3	3	7	22	71

* high individual cell x^2 — Table $x^2 = 29.47$ ($p < 0.01$) — (This question was not responded to by 1 student)

Table 30 Frequency distribution of student response to interview items according to combination of teacher predictions and IEA-results *continued*

(e)

Variable	Scale	Interpretation of Scale	Combinations of Teacher Predictions and IEA-Results								Row Totals
			B-B	-B	T-B	B-M	T-M	B-T	-T	T-T	
Student affective marks	0	Student expressed class anxiety, etc.	15*	1	4	2	0	1	2	5	30
	1	Student did not experience class anxiety, etc.	7	4	0	4	3	2	5	17	42
		Column Totals	22	5	4	6	3	3	7	22	72

* high individual cell x^2 Table $x^2 = 19.07 \ (p < 0.01)$

As can be seen in Table 30a, the majority of the students interviewed explicitly stated that they liked their teacher (56.9%). Only very few students (12.5%) expressed a dislike of their teacher, whereas the rest (30.6%) were neutral. It is interesting to see that not only top students had a favorable attitude towards their teacher, as one might have hypothesized, but also bottom students. However, when redistributing the students according to teachers' predictions, it became apparent that a considerably higher proportion of top-predicted than bottom-predicted students liked their teacher (82.8% vs. 41.9%). Of those few students who expressed a dislike of their teacher 77.8% were bottom-predicted, including two students who scored very highly on the IEA test. This might indicate that the teacher conveys his positive as well as negative expectations to the students and thus affects their attitude towards him.

Generally speaking, however, it is worth noting that the student's feelings toward the teacher were not a highly significant variable influencing success or failure.

With respect to variable 5 – student's general attitude – the general frequency distribution, as presented in Table 30b, illustrates that students with a negative attitude towards learning French in that particular learning situation are not successful. No statements can be made about the cause-and-effect relationship of lack of success and negative attitude. The number of top students increases with a higher degree of positive attitude. It is very interesting that more bottom than top students show a fairly high degree of positive attitudes (4 on evaluation scale). This indicates that a positive attitude, even though extremely important, does not guarantee success. These results support the outcome of the separate regression analyses run for subjects of each grades (see Tables 20 and 21 and discussion following in Part III, chapter 3, section 3.3).

The third significant variable was student attitude towards correcting others. As shown in Table 30c, it is mainly the good students who correct others. This finding coincides with the correlation analysis of the above variable and both criterion measures (IEA test and imitation task).

As to the next variable – student reaction to teacher's use of the students' mother tongue or the second language – it is significant that mainly poor students would like the teacher to use more English (L1). The majority of students (53.5%) felt that the proportion of L1 and L2 in the classroom was adequate. Of the remaining 15 students who expressed the wish to hear more of L2, the majority (60%) were students with high scores on the IEA test. In general, this finding coincides with the positive correlations of this variable with the criterion measures.

Table 30e, representing the distribution of variable 16 – student affective remarks – indicates that classroom anxiety, a high fear of rejection, and similar feelings may be related to failure. Again, no statement can be made about the cause-and-effect relationship of failure and anxiety.

As the responses to the other interview items did not yield significant distributions, the results will be presented by simply describing several trends.

Out of the remaining 11 variables, three differentiated very little between good and poor students. These were variable 1 – student perception of classroom formality; variable 11 – student attitude towards teacher correction; and variable 14 – student repetition of teacher correction. The results were as follows: for 83.3% of the students, the classroom environment matched their individual preferences in terms of either formality or informality. Out of the total number of students, 95.8% did not mind being corrected by the teacher. As to student repetition of teacher correction, the majority of the students indicated that they usually repeat the teacher's correction (88.7%; the question was not answered by 10 students).

The remaining interview items will be presented in the order of the list of variables given above (see Part III, chapter 5, section 3). The answers to the question about the student's perception of rapport with other students (variable 3) indicated that the majority of the students (63.9%) interviewed felt that they got along well with their fellow students. The next variable – student and teacher match of goals – yielded an almost equal distribution. Out of the total number of 62 students who responded to the question, 51.5% considered that their personal goals were generally met by the learning content and classroom activities.

Variable 6 referred to the student's learning modality preference. The frequency distribution across the eight groups of students, defined by combinations of teacher predictions and IEA results, showed that 48.5% of the students considered themselves to be eye-minded. In other words, they felt that they learned better through the written medium. Of the remaining number of students 50% expressed a preference for learning aurally and 50% indicated that they were neither eye- or ear-minded. Differences between those students who were predicted to score low on the IEA test and actually did so and their counterparts at the top appear to be negligible. However, when redistributing the students on the basis of their scores on the IEA listening comprehension test, it becomes apparent that more bottom students are eye-minded. Of those students who considered themselves to be ear-minded 64.7% scored high on the IEA test. This finding supports the result of the initial regression analysis (see Table 19).

Replies to these question of whether the student, when raising his hand, is willing to take the risk of being wrong or not (variable 7) indicated that the majority of the students interviewed (62.9%) would prefer to be certain before volunteering an answer. Though differences between top and bottom students are slight, the latter group tends to prefer certainty before volunteering a response.

With respect to variable 8 – student reaction to being called upon – the distribution shows that 68.2% of the students do not mind being called upon by the teacher when they have not raised their hands. It is worth noting that of those students (16.7%) who minded being called upon 81.8% were bottom-predicted students.

The following interview item (variable 9) referred to the question of whether the student felt that the teacher asked him sufficiently. Out of the total number of students who responded to this question (58) only 5.2% wanted to be asked less frequently; 67.2% felt that they were asked often enough; and 27.6% wanted to be asked more often. It is interesting to note that more bottom than top students wanted to be asked more frequently. This may indicate that they feel neglected or that they recognize the need for greater participation.

Responses to the following item – student reaction to lack of comprehension – (variable 10) indicated that almost an equal number of students either ask a friend when they have not understood something (43.9%) or the teacher (39.4%). Only 16.7% of the students preferred to seek clarification on their own. It is interesting that 55.2% of those students who would ask a friend were teacher-predicted bottom students. Of those students who would ask the teacher 57.7% were teacher-predicted top students. These findings may indicate that bottom students are afraid of asking the teacher, thus revealing their ignorance and possibly exposing themselves to criticism.

The last item to be considered is variable 12 – student attitude towards being interrupted. When interviewed, most students had definite opinions about whether they would like to be interrupted when making an error or whether they would prefer to finish their response. Out of the total number of 63 students who responded to this question 38.1% opted for being interrupted, 54% preferred to finish their response first, 7.9% were neutral to the question.

Other aspects covered by the interviews with the students will be described in more general terms, as the answers do not lend themselves to statistical tabulations. Several questions were answered by an insufficient number of students. Others, when answered to, were not clear. Therefore, they were excluded from the general description.

In order to investigate the students' insights into the ways they learn a languages, they were asked about techniques or study habits they might have developed. Unfortunately, only 26 students responded to the question. Most of the techniques mentioned referred to the acquisition of vocabulary. Eleven students mentioned that they read the *new* words, mostly in conjunction with their English equivalents. Seven students reported that they wrote either the French word or also the English equivalent. One student indicated that he preferred learning new words in the context of a sentence rather than as isolated items. Another student stated that she attempted to stimulate her memory by relating the words to the situation in which she learned them. She also compared them to English whenever the English and French version appeared to be similar. Two students reported that they consciously visualized the spelling when reading the French words or saying them aloud.

Twelve students indicated that they normally learned grammar by doing specific exercises and by memorizing the rules.

In order to increase their aural and oral competence six students stated that they occasionally listened to the radio or watched television; one student repeated sentences while listening. Four students mentioned that from time to time they had the chance to speak with native speakers. Others indicated that once in a while they spoke French with their friends – 'just for fun'. One student who felt a great need for more oral practice was taking conversation classes with a tutor after school hours.

One of the more general questions asked of the students dealt with their impressions of the difficulty or facility they experienced in learning French. Out of the total number of students responding 52.9% felt that learning French was an easy task; 30% regarded it as difficult; 17.1% differentiated between various aspects of language learning, some of which they felt were easy and others difficult. It is interesting that 23.8% of those students who were predicted to score low on the IEA-test and actually did so considered learning French to be easy. The explanation may be found in the teacher's marks for these students. Some of these bottom-predicted students actually received grades not greatly different from the mean of the sample chosen in each class, so did not perceive themselves as being bottom students. Thus, their opinions about their ease in learning French coincided with the general trend that students perceive ease or difficulty in learning French according to the marks they receive.[2]

When asked to indicate why learning French presented difficulties, students who scored in the low or medium range on the IEA-test frequently complained about lack of comprehension. A few also indicated that they were not interested in learning French. However, as previously mentioned, some of the bottom students displayed great interest in learning French, in spite of their limited success. Several students mentioned that they had bad memories which caused difficulty in learning a language. Others attributed the difficulties they experienced in learning French to the fact that they were nervous, tense and afraid of speaking in class.

Among other reasons mentioned were lack of background in English grammar and the way French was taught. One student made the interesting comment that he considered language learning to be more difficult than studying another subject due to the oral nature of language – 'a language is something you have to learn by speaking it every day'.

Of those students who were predicted to score highly on the IEA-test and actually did so, several indicated that they really enjoyed learning French. A few students felt that their good memory helped them learn French. Among other students' comments on their experience in learning French were: (a) it was felt to be essential to listen carefully – 'you just have to open your ears'; (b) it was considered to be necessary to work with consistency and diligence; (c) language learning was regarded as a continuum – 'languages always come easy – everything flows, you have to know one thing to know the next thing, so in that way it builds up and you're using it constantly.

Some good as well as many poor students were bored; however, some students were successful despite their boredom with the course and the way it was being taught.

Those students who had an Italian background generally felt that knowing Italian made learning French easier.

It became apparent in the interviews that very few students had had the chance of meeting native speakers of French. Those who had spent some time with native speakers enjoyed these contacts very much. Using the languages in a real communication situation also made them aware of the shortcomings of the classroom learning situation. One student realized that when actually using the language, she talked without thinking too much about grammar. She commented, 'to spend so much time on grammar seems to be a kind of waste.'

When asked to indicate their goals in learning French, 52.9% of the students answered that they would like to be able to speak the language. The emphasis on speaking and communication increased slightly in the upper grades. Individual grade 8 students differentiated between specific goals, such as 'understanding the language', 'writing and speaking French', 'being able to respond to teachers' questions in French', and 'reading French'. One student mentioned that through learning French he hoped to learn something about French-speaking people.

Students of grade 10 and 12 were more in agreement about their goals. As indicated before, the wish to be able to communicate ranked first, followed by the combined goal of speaking and understanding, as well as comprehension alone. Two grade 10 students and four grade 12 students indicated that they wanted to acquire all the linguistic skills. One student explicitly stated that she would like to become bilingual.

A great number of students felt a need to use the language more actively than they were doing. The desire for more oral practice (conversations, discussions) was particularly strong in grade 12 (75%). In this context a few students mentioned that they would rather emphasize fluency than always be corrected for grammatical errors. It was further indicated that grammar should be taught based upon actual usage by native speakers. Among other suggestions for change were:

(a) more cultural material, exchanges with Quebec, greater emphasis on Quebec French
(b) no language laboratory
(c) more plays, more reading
(d) group work, smaller classes, and ability grouping.

The students of grade 10 were less in agreement about what they wanted to change. Five students wanted more audio-visual and audio-lingual material in French (TV, movies, records); some expressed the desire for more conversational practice. One student, who indicated that she would prefer less emphasis on grammar, compared second language acquisition with first language acquisition, pointing out that one learns to *speak* one's mother tongue long before one focusses on grammar. A few students felt that the stories they read should be more relevant to their age group and should resemble real life more. Of those students who had worked with 'individual packages' (which will be described more fully in a later section), 50% wanted to increase the time spent on such material. Group work was also among the suggestions made. Two of the grade 10 students who were in an open plan school were dissatisfied with the lack of formality in their learning environment and expressed the wish for greater structure.

The students of grade 8 made fewer suggestions for change. Of the students, 25% wanted more French games. A few students wanted to see more films, TV, etc., and do more reading. Three very good students felt that they would benefit from a more homogeneous class.

Answers to the questions about students' likes and dislikes were closely related to the classroom activities in which they were presently engaged. As to the grade 8 students, five students enjoyed everything they were doing and three did not really like anything. In both groups there were top and bottom students. Of those activities which were liked the ones mentioned most often were, in descending order of frequency, grammar exercises (i.e. filling-in-the-blanks on special grammar work sheets, conjugation, etc.), conversation (i.e. asking each other questions, skits), reading aloud, and games. However, the same activities were also disliked by some students.

There appeared to be no consistent pattern in good and poor learners' preferences. There is, however, an indication that those students who appeared to be very shy did not particularly like oral work. Poor students tended to prefer written work, such as grammar exercises. If exercises were constructed in such a way that almost everyone could do them, the poorer learner would probably experience a certain sense of achievement. However, as indicated above, other variables such as personality characteristics may play a role in the development of students' preferences.

A third of grade 10 students greatly enjoyed reading. The next activity, given preferential ranking, was conversations (including oral descriptions of pictures), followed by language laboratory exercises (such as repeating sentences after the voice on the tape). As in the grade 8 classes, both positive and negative attitudes towards the same activity could be found, especially towards language lab exercises. There also were four students (predominantly good students) who liked everything and one student (predicted top, but low IEA score) who disliked everything.

Coinciding with the explicit desire for a great opportunity to speak French, 50% of the grade 12 students stated that they liked oral activities, i.e. conversations, discussions, etc. In this context, the French 'assistant' program and the involvement of French native speakers of the community were regarded very favorably by 25% of the students. Acting out plays or situations, even though an oral activity, was mentioned only by five students, probably because acting requires theatrical abilities which are not demanded for ordinary conversations. Of the grade 12 students, 41.7% considered reading very enjoyable. Among the remaining activities liked by students were, in descending order of frequency, working on individual projects, grammar exercises, and exercises with tapes, such as repeating sentences or answering questions.

When explicitly asked to indicate what they did not enjoy, seven students expressed their dislike of grammar exercises. One student mentioned that grammar should be learned by speaking the language; it should be given a meaningful context. Another student indicated that she would prefer to learn grammar through reading. Five students (good as well as poor learners) also mentioned that they did not enjoy acting out plays and giving oral presentations in front of the class. Reading was also disliked by some students. It appears, however, that their criticism was mainly directed towards the stories in the textbook used (*Ici on Parle Francais* and *French II*). A few good students considered the stories boring, a few poor students felt frustrated because of their lack of comprehension.

Generally speaking, the students' answers to the question about their likes and dislikes, though not very explicit show that most students form opinions about classroom activities they have to do and, in most cases, develop positive as well as negative attitudes towards them. Students' criticisms and suggestions could be more constructively used if students were induced to reflect about their learning situation so as to identify reasons for their negative or positive reactions towards specific learning tasks and activities. Indeed, they might be able to change their attitudes and contribute to changes in their learning environment. It is *not* suggested that teachers follow students' every whim. However, language learning in general might be more effective if the students' ideas were used more frequently. Thus the learner would take an active part in deciding how he would like to learn. Such a situation might be of particular importance in the case of older students.

The great variety of opinions stated, even within one class, supports the conviction of many teachers and educationists that different ways of individualizing learning will have to be found. Students' insights into their difficulties and individual preferences could be used to their greater benefit. Thus, for example, some students could be allowed to listen to the foreign language passively for limited periods of time; they could be given a choice of different material (films, filmstrips, records) and content (cultural, documentary, entertaining). Others who prefer to use the language might want to select from different oral activities, i.e. describing pictures, inventing stories, discussing specific topics, or acting out situations and plays. These suggestions are by no means original. The important point, however, is to give individual learners or groups of students the chance of choosing from a variety of activities, at least from time to time, so that they can participate in the development of a personal language learning strategy.

4. Differential Teacher Treatment

As previously mentioned in Part III, chapter 1, section 4 on foci in classroom observation, the results of several research studies indicated that teachers treat students they consider good learners differently from those students they consider poor learners.

It is hoped that classroom observation would answer some of the questions initially raised about differential teacher treatment. The questions were as follows:

(1) Does the teacher ask good and poor students different types of questions?
(2) Does he ask good students more questions than he asks poor students?
(3) Does he ask good students more often when they have not indicated that they would like to respond?
(4) Does he react differently to their native langauge insertions?
(5) Does he react to their responses with more, or les, feeling?
(6) Does he use responses given by good students more often as correct models for classroom repetition?
(7) Does the teacher interrupt good students less frequently than poor students?
(8) Does he correct good students in a different way from poor students?
(9) Does he ask good students more often to correct other students?
(10) Does he provide them more or less frequently with clues before or during their responses; what kind of clues (intra, inter, or extralingual) does he give to good and poor students?
(11) Does he make good students repeat his corrections more or less frequently?

We originally intended to do an Analysis of Variance on *all* variables indicated by the questions. However, after the observation and coding of classroom behavior over an extended time, it became apparent that many behavioral aspects considered to be indicative of differential teacher treatment rarely occurred. Several items found inappropriate because of their infrequency had to be excluded from the subsequent Analysis of Variance.

The original question 1, referring to whether the teacher asks good and poor students different types of questions, was not fully answerable by the data collected from the observation schedule. As previously described (see Part III, chapter 1, section 3.3) the observation schedule allowed for the coding of ten different types of questions. Questions asking for specific information (Category A1) were the type of questions predominantly presented (83.9%). Therefore, questions of this type were not included among the variables for the Analysis of Variance. (For an exact breakdown of the types of questions asked of each experimental sample, see Part III, chapter 5, section 6.3.) The only types of teacher questions which appeared to be meaningful in terms of differential treatment were category A2, teacher 'elicits general information' and category A9, teacher 'elicits correction'. The latter had been explicitly considered in the original question 9.

Several other variables were excluded from the analysis for a variety of reasons. For example, in addition to the infrequent occurrences of native language insertions (see question 4), the classroom observers felt at the end of the observation period that their reliability in coding English insertions was insufficient.

The form of teacher behavior referred to in question 6 was also rare and therefore not considered as a separate item in the subsequent analysis. Instead, any teacher initiated classroom repetition of a student answer was subsumed under the general category of 'repetition of student answer' (see Part III, chapter 1, section 3.3).

The question of whether the teacher makes good students repeat his correction more or less frequently (number 11) proved difficult to answer. It became evident in some of the student interviews that repetition of the teacher's correction was an expected reaction, since the teacher had repeatedly told the students to do so. As this background information was obtained accidentally and only for a few classes, it was decided to disregard this item in an analysis of differential teacher treatment.

The remaining aspects of teacher behavior indicated in the initial list of questions were supplemented by additional categories from the observation schedule, coded during classroom observation. The complete list of the variables considered is as follows:

(1) Voluntary questioning
(2) Involuntary questioning
(3) General questions
(4) Mutual correction
(5) Student answers to questions asked to others before
(6) Providing the answer
(7) Positive feedback
(8) Negative feedback
(9) No feedback
(10) Teacher repetition
(11) Teacher elaboration
(12) Teacher clarification
(13) Further questioning
(14) Teacher interruption
(15) Teacher explicit correction
(16) Teacher implicit correction

(17) Teacher localization of incorrectness
(18) Teacher indication of incorrectness
(19) Teacher providing clues

(For a more detailed explanation of the variables see Part III, chapter 3, section 2.3.)

The majority of the enumerated variables occurred relatively infrequently. Consequently, the statistical validity of the Analysis of Variance was reduced. The following table presents the percentages of students out of the total sample of 72 to whom the teacher reacted in any of the ways indicated by the variables.

As can be seen in Table 31, only 7 out of 19 variables occurred more than 50% of the time, which means that only 7 types of teacher behavior applied to at least 50% of the students, involuntary questioning occurring most frequently (96%) of the students) followed by teacher questioning of a student when he had raised his hand and volunteered to answer (89% of the students).

Table 31 Percentage of students out of total sample receiving aspects of teacher treatment

Variables of teacher treatment	Percentage of students reacted to
(1) Voluntary questioning	89
(2) Involuntary questioning	96
(3) General questions	17
(4) Mutual correction	16
(5) Student answers to questions asked to others before	26
(6) Providing the answer	31
(7) Positive feedback	28
(8) Negative feedback	4
(9) No feedback	54
(10) Teacher repetition	69
(11) Teacher elaboration	19
(12) Teacher clarification	22
(13) Further questioning	69
(14) Teacher interruption	40
(15) Teacher explicit correction	60
(16) Teacher implicit correction	7
(17) Teacher localization of incorrectness	35
(18) Teacher indication of incorrectness	14
(19) Teacher providing clues	53

For the Analysis of Variance, the experimental sample was divided into three groups, based upon the teachers' predictions about the achievement level of the students concerned. The first group consisted of 31 students, predicted to be low achievers; 12 non-predicted students constituted the second group; and 29 top students formed group 3.

Table 32 presents the results of the Analysis of Variance with the 19 enumerated variables including the means for the three different groups.

Table 32 Analysis of Variance on variables of teacher treatment for teacher predicted bottom, top, and non-predicted students, including means of variables

Variables from classroom teacher observation	Bottom students	Non-predicted students	Top students	F-ratio
	Means	Means	Means	
(1) Voluntary questioning	29.49	32.62	27.10	0.23
(2) Involuntary questioning	60.74	56.86	38.33	4.20*
(3) General questions	0.91	1.67	3.29	1.52
(4) Mutual correction	1.02	0.0	1.42	1.03
(5) Student answers to questions asked of others	1.68	2.17	4.77	2.0
(6) Providing the answer	9.86	0.93	7.48	1.20
(7) Positive feedback	1.04	5.4	2.13	4.07*
(8) Negative feedback	0.54	0.0	0.18	0.69
(9) No feedback	8.2	6.13	6.61	0.23
(10) Teacher repetition	12.6	12.9	16.41	0.59
(11) Teacher elaboration	0.86	1.35	2.01	0.91
(12) Teacher clarification	1.22	1.57	1.71	0.18
(13) Further questioning	13.86	10.20	11.78	0.83
(14) Teacher interruption	12.20	14.94	12.30	0.06
(15) Teacher explicit correction	20.78	12.99	23.02	0.54
(16) Teacher implicit correction	0.81	3.97	1.03	1.47
(17) Teacher localization of incorrectness	5.06	13.97	7.56	1.39
(18) Teacher indication of incorrectness	1.05	0.93	4.47	2.23
(19) Teacher providing clues	12.56	9.78	10.56	0.22

The Analysis of Variance was significant for only two variables of teacher behavior, namely 'involuntary questioning' (F = 4.20) and 'positive feedback' (F = 4.07). Despite their limited statistical validity, the results, when based upon the differences in means, reveal certain trends which allow tentative interpretations. Generally speaking, the results confirm the original hypothesis about the existence of differential treatment of students by the teacher. This in itself is not surprising, as different types of students have different needs, which the teacher should attempt to meet. However, some forms of teacher behavior may favour one particular group disproportionately. For example, it appears that those students whom the teacher considers to be high achievers receive significantly more praise than low achievers, despite the fact that the latter probably need more encouragement than the former. Considering the results for the two extreme groups, the bottom and the top students, it becomes evident that good students receive more positive and less negative feedback than poor students (see variable 7, 8). It has to be kept in mind that teacher feedback was only coded when the teacher's emotional reaction to a student differed from the general classroom atmosphere as created by the teacher.

In addition, its appears that teachers tend to repeat answers given by good students more often than those of poor students (see variable 10). It seems that poor students more frequently receive no feedback from the teacher after they have responded to a question (see variable 9).

Furthermore, low achievers are asked significantly more often when they have *not* raised their hands. This may be considered a threatening situation for the student. However, it is also possible that the student interprets being called upon as a gesture of encouragement by the teacher. A clear interpretation of this aspect of teacher behavior will have to take into consideration the general context of its occurrence, the student's personality, and the classroom atmosphere.

It is a positive indication of compensatory teacher treatment that teachers tend to give poor students more clues to a correct answer (see variable 19). Furthermore, whenever they volunteer to give a response, the teachers appear to give the poorer students a greater chance of responding than the better ones.

In order to demonstrate the pattern of teacher treatment in terms of teacher-afforded response opportunities, four different groups were established, based upon the means of voluntary and involuntary questions and response behavior for the experimental sample in each class. The first mean was calculated on the basis of the total percentage of times the teacher gave the student the opportunity to respond in relation to the number of times he had raised his hand (a). The second referred to the percentage of times in which the student was called upon by the teacher when he had *not* raised his hand in relation to the total number of responses (b).

The four groups mentioned above are as follows: group 1 consists of those students who are *above* the mean of both variables (a) and (b); group II includes those students who are *below* the mean of both variables (a) and (b); group III indicates those students above the mean of (a) and below the mean of (b); group IV includes those students who fall below the mean for variable (a) and above the mean for variable (b). The total number of students included is 54, out of which 29 are top students and 25 bottom students. Those students who never raised their hands at all and those who were not predicted by the teachers were excluded. As shown in Table 33, less than half of the students concerned (42.59%) were given the opportunity to respond more often when they had volunteered to do so than when they had not raised their hands. This form of teacher treatment appears to be positive in that it displays a supportive attitude by the teacher and should ideally apply to *all* students.

Table 33 Distribution of bottom and top students according to the degree of teacher afforded voluntary and involuntary response opportunities

	Teacher predictions	
Categories	*Bottom student*	*Top student*
I above (a) above (b)	2	2
II below (a) below (b)	5	13
III above (a) below (b)	9	10
IV below (a) above (b)	9	4

Legend $x^2 = 5.257^*$

(a) = *voluntary student responses*
student hand-raising

(b) = *involuntary student responses*
total number of student responses

An interpretation of the above data in terms of possible *negative* effects on students would therefore be in reference to the students in Groups II and IV (57.41% of the total). Group II indicates a great disregard of the students on the teacher's part. More top students than bottom students fall into this category (13% vs. 5%). However, since good students usually have a higher degree of motivation, this lack of teacher attention would probably not have such a negative effect upon them as on low achievers.

As to group IV, a greater number of bottom students are asked more often when they have not raised their hands. It would appear to be more gratifying and encouraging for a student to be asked proportionately more often when he has volunteered to respond than to be called upon by the teacher when he may or may not know the answer. Again, this form of teacher behavior, as indicated in group IV, may have a more negative bearing upon bottom students.

In general, the significant X^2 indicates that the top and bottom students were not evenly distributed among the four groups. Teachers appear, therefore, to treat top and bottom students differently with regard to the two variables (a) and (b), sometimes, unfortunately, to the benefit of one group and to the detriment of the other.

In summary, on the basis of the sample of teachers and students selected in the present study it appears that teacher-differentiated treatment does exist, but not to any great extent. This treatment may benefit the good student to the detriment of the poor student, or vice versa. What is important, however, is that teachers be made aware of the possibility that they may be treating students they consider to be successful or unsuccessful differently. They should be sensitive to the fact that their differential treatment could have adverse effects on students, especially on the unsuccessful ones.

5. Case Studies of Selected Students

In order top give an indication of the quantity of information that was gathered about each student, six case studies will be presented. They illustrate some of the so-called 'match' and 'mismatch' cases, i.e. cases in which the teachers' predictions of the students' results on the IEA Listening Comprehension Test did or did not coincide with the actual scores.

The first two case studies represent matches; namely the case of an unsuccessful language learner (Student A) and of a successful one (Student B). The following four descriptions demonstrate various types of mismatches.

(1) Student C was predicted top and did poorly.
(2) Student D was expected to score very low and scored high.
(3) Student E was predicted bottom and attained an average result on the IEA test.
(4) Student F was not named by the teacher, but belonged to the group of students who scored high.

It has to be noted that none of the six case studies is representative of all the other members of any of these categories. That is to say, for example, not all students who were predicted to score in the bottom range and actually did so had the same characteristics and views. The students selected for the presentation had offered interesting insights and opinions during the interviews. It was therefore considered to be of general interest to record this information in the present report.

5.1 Case Study One

NAME: Student A

GRADE: 12

SEX: F

Student A was predicted to score within the bottom range on the IEA French Listening Comprehension Test. Her score was the second lowest of the whole class. She was chosen for observation as an illustration of a case in which the teacher's prediction matched the actual IEA result. Her general low level of competence in the language was substantiated by her low score on the Imitation Task.

Student A was observed for five periods totalling 240 minutes, which included one period of silent study of the 'individual package' (see Part III, chapter 5, section 6.1). During the period of observation Student A raised her hand twice and gave a total of four responses. She appeared to be attentive, very jovial and relaxed, obviously enjoying some of the activities, for example, the preparation of situations which was subsequently acted out. She was not afraid of telling the teacher that she did not understand certain things. She frequently talked to another student in class, a semi-native speaker of French, sometimes asking for explanations, at other times just talking socially. The observer also overheard Student A expressing to a friend her enjoyment of learning French.

Student A's positive attitude towards the learning of French also revealed itself in the interview. She indicated that French was her favorite subject and expressed a general love for languages: 'It just appeals to me to know another language.' Student A indicated a preference for communication skills. She thoroughly enjoyed the conversation classes with French-speaking members of the community. She considered it more important to convey her ideas than to be grammatically correct. Outside the classroom she occasionally listened to the French radio station and talked to her friend in French – 'for fun'.

Student A was very aware of her difficulties, especially with certain grammatical aspects. She reported that the teaching of French in the school she had first attended was rather poor. Changing to her present school in grade 9, she took a summer course in French, which helped her to catch up to a certain extent. Her self-criticism was evident in her remark that she should work harder at home.

When asked to comment on her rare participation, Student A replied: 'Normally I am wrong and I feel like a dummy.' She emphasized that she did not suffer personally from this experience. However, she would usually wait until she was absolutely certain before raising her hand. She therefore wanted the teacher to call upon her more often, so that she would learn to express herself better.

In response to the final question, whether the French language sounded strange to her and whether she was embarrassed to speak it, Student A commented: 'English is weird, not French.'

The teacher's remarks about Student A coincided with the general picture presented above. According to the teacher, Student A was a 'beautifully adapted person,' not afraid of making mistakes, very motivated, and a hard worker. She was an average student in all subjects. The teacher was puzzled that the student so far had not achieved the results she deserved, considering her favorable personal attributes.

Student A illustrates a case in which it would be worth investigating in more detail the type of learning problem encountered. Her score on the Embedded Figures Test was very low, and at the grade 12 level field independence was found to be a significant predictor of success.

If measures of intelligence and language aptitudes had been available to the researchers, a clearer picture of the student's difficulties might have been attained.

5.2 Case Study Two

NAME: Student B

GRADE: 12

SEX: M

This case study was selected in order to describe study habits and classroom behavior of an excellent student in more detail. Of all grade 12 students, Student B scored highest on the IEA Listening Comprehension Test (95% correct) and also did best on the Imitation Task; he repeated all units, with 95% of them correct. However, he scored a little below the mean on the Embedded Figures Test, and in general field independence was predictive of success at the grade 12 level.

Student B was observed for a period of 315 minutes. During that time he raised his hand 59 times and gave a total of 52 answers, 71% of which were voluntary. He appeared to be very attentive and replied to many difficult questions. His answers were always correct. His pronunciation of French was very good and his general oral performance was excellent. He gave the impression of being serious and calm. Occasionally the teacher joked with him. She showed her respect for him by asking him a few times if he would have given the same answer as someone else. His fellow students seemed to regard him as a respected authority in many areas. Student B was asked by several students to explain questions in subjects other than French.

Asked about his personal goal in learning French, Student B stated: 'I'd like to know how to speak French – fluently; I'd like to be bilingual, as this is a bilingual country.' In addition to his own personal motivation to learn French, Student B indicated that he had also been positively influenced by his mother, who knew French very well. On occasion he spoke to her in French.

The impression that Student B was very diligent and conscientious proved to be correct. When asked about his study habits, Student B mentioned that he prepared himself carefully for tests: 'I usually make up my own questions – the questions I expect to get.' With respect to learning techniques, he reported that he preferred to learn vocabulary in the context of a sentence: 'I can't look just at a whole list – I have to take one sentence at a time.' As to grammar, he mentioned that the teacher sometimes related a grammar rule in French to a grammar rule in English, 'but that's not how I learn; I just learn it by French grammar; I know my French grammar, but not my English grammar. I learn by the exercises.' As mentioned above, Student B occasionally spoke French with his mother. He also reported that he sometimes watched the French TV station. Other than that he had no contact with French outside the classroom.

Although Student B's participation was not extraordinarily frequent, the interview revealed that he always paid attention. He explained: 'Even if she [teacher] doesn't ask me, I ask the question to myself and compare it to the answer another student gives . . . It doesn't really matter if she asks me or not.' He further reported that if the student's answer varied from his own and if he was not sure about the correctness of his own, he immediately checked with the teacher.

When questioned what he would do when he did not know a word while responding, Student B indicated that he sometimes inserted English and sometimes attempted to circumlocute: 'Even though I use the incorrect structure, I still get the meaning across.' However, he emphasized for him to be correct than to convey the meaning.

The interviewer got the impression that many of the classroom activities presented no challenge to Student B. He indicated that he disliked learning 'basic stuff' and having to repeat sentences etc., and that he was bored by having to answer questions on stories. He expressed a desire for more creative work, free conversations and debates. Coinciding with his serious disposition, Student B disliked acting out plays. Despite the fact that he enjoyed certain activities less than others, Student B's participation was always consistent.

In the teacher interview, the teacher mentioned that she had great respect for Student B and was particularly grateful for his co-operation and willingness to go along with everything 'despite his high calibre'. She felt that she had a good rapport with him and indicated that she showed him her appreciation. The teacher described Student B was mark-conscious, intelligent, and displaying a wide range of interests. She reported that he had organized study habits, always did his homework, and was always noticing mistakes in the classroom. She further stated that he was enriching the class and was respected by his fellow students.

Student B's case study illustrates that many learning strategies and techniques are not overt and therefore cannot be observed in the classroom. The student's self-reported strategies and techniques coincide with several of the strategies developed by the successful adult langauge learners (see Part III, section 2.3). He is an example of someone who involves himself actively in the language learning process and accepts responsibility for his progress. The interview with Student B was very informative. It might be beneficial to all students in a class, the successful as well as the unsuccessful, if they communicated their individual language learning experiences to one another.

5.3 Case Study Three

NAME: Student C

GRADE: 10

SEX: F

Student C is one of the few cases in which the teacher predicted that the student would score high on the IEA test but the student scored in the bottom range. Student C got the lowest score in a class of 18 students. The teacher's marks for Student C's oral and written performance were slightly above the mean of marks for the students observed. On the second criterion measure, the imitation task, the number of units repeated correctly ws slightly above the mean for the grade 10 students.

Student C was observed for a total of 240 minutes. During this time she raised her hand once and called out eleven times, which was not as frequent as many of the other students in her class. Since students in this school, an 'open plan' school, were not required to raise their hands before answering, callouts were equated with hand-raising. Callouts were counted as responses when they were taken up by the teacher. Student C gave a total of seven answers, out of which only one was a voluntary response, i.e. the student had volunteered to answer either by raising her hand or by calling out. Student C asked the teacher five times for an explanation. She generally appeared to be quite attentive, but gave the impression of being very reserved and cool.

The observer expected Student C to transfer her apparent reserve towards him. The investigator was surprised at the student's frankness and outspokenness during the subsequent interview. Student C had very strong opinions about the learning environment she found herself in, the open plan system. She explicitly stated that she would prefer a stricter teacher who would force the students to do their homework, and give more tests and rules. She would also prefer to be in a class where the student had to raise his hand: 'You can be smart, but if you're shy you never talk out and the teacher thinks you can be stupid.' She further reported that she preferred a closed classroom, since she was frequently distracted by the noise from other classes. Her general comment was: 'You learn more in an old-fashioned school.' Student C indicated that she got along well with her fellow students, but not so well with the teacher. Student C was the only one to indicate that the teacher was nicer than usual during the period of observation.

Though the student's expressed goal in learning French, namely to be able to speak the language, generally matched her perception of the teacher's emphasis, she indicated that she did not really like any of the activities in the classroom. Student C reacted very negatively towards the exercise with earphones, where each student had to repeat sentences and answer questions. She felt that those sessions were 'lousy, everyone fools around mumbling the words'. Student C regarded nearly all activities as a waste of time, with the exception of tests and conversations about everyday incidents.

When asked to comment on her achievement in French in comparison with other subjects, Student C reported that French was her weakest subject. She felt that the difficulties she ws experiencing this year were due to the way French was taught but also admitted that she could push herself to do better.

With respect to her infrequent participation, Student C remarked that she was embarrassed to speak French in class. 'I know I'm not that good, so I'm kind of afraid . . . I say it to myself and make sure it's right before I put up my hand. I can say it in my mind o.k., but when I have to say it out loud, I get all tense.'

When questioned whether she minded being called upon by the teacher, Student C replied that she did a little bit, but she realized that it was good for her and she should be asked more often. 'You're put on the spot and you have to think about it.'

Student C further mentioned that she usually asked the teacher for an explanation if she had not understood a point: 'I want to know why, I don't want to just do it.' In the case of teacher correction, she would repeat the corrected aspect. Student C indicated that she wanted to be interrupted when making a mistake and that she neither minded nor particularly liked being corrected. She admitted that she did not like being wrong.

When asked if she would like the teacher to use more or less French in class, Student C replied that the teacher should speak more French and should also insist that the students use less English.

At the end of the interview, Student C remarked that although she did not like the way French was taught in this school, she felt that it was important to continue learning it, especially since she wanted to go to university.

In the interview with the teacher, Student C was described as a very sensitive and serious student, who had difficulties with certain concepts. She also mentioned that the student frequently asked for explanations after class. The teacher was shocked at the student's low IEA result but could not offer any explanation.

Based upon the information available there was no reason for the student to do so badly. She even scored above average on the Embedded Figures Test. The only possible explanation we can offer is that the student's general dissatisfaction with the learning environment resulted in a negative reaction to most aspects of her French language learning situation, including the tests given to her by the investigators.

5.4 Case Study Four

NAME: Student D

GRADE: 10

SEX: F

Student D represents one of the three more extreme mismatch cases, in which the student was predicted to score in the bottom range on the IEA test but actually scored fairly high. Out of a class of 25, Student D's score was the sixth highest. The teacher's overall mark for her was the lowest of the students observed in this class. As to the measure of productive competence, the Imitation Task, Student D scored just below the mean.

Student D was observed for 350 minutes. During that time she raised her hand 73 times, which was just below the mean of the experimental sample in this class. She gave a total of 21 answers, out of which 18 were given when she had volunteered to respond.

She appeared to be very vivacious, outgoing, and at times showed a great deal of enthusiasm in the classroom. She also chatted a great deal with other students and was not always attentive.

In the interview Student D stated that her goal in learning French was to be able to understand what people were saying. This matched her perception of the teacher's emphasis in teaching.

When asked to relate her feelings about the classroom environment, Student D reported that she liked the teacher and her fellow students and that she especially enjoyed the informal classroom atmosphere: 'I can say whatever I want; you don't have to be embarrassed, if you say the wrong answer.' She generally liked all activities in the classroom, with the exception of some of the grammar exercises, and had no suggestions for future changes.

With regard to her perception of the difficulty or ease of learning French, Student D reported that French was her best subject, but that she did not consider herself to have special abilities: 'French is my best subject, because I really enjoy it.' She indicated that she could learn by hearing and did not need to see words written down. She further remarked that she attempted to speak French with as good an accent as she possibly could.

With respect to other aspects of classroom behavior, Student D mentioned that she usually raised her hand only when certain her response was correct. She did not mind, however, being corrected and wanted to be interrupted when making an error.

In the interview with the teacher, Student D was described as being lazy, nonchalant, not conscientious, and inattentive. The teacher explained that Student D came from an 'enriched'[3] class, the level of which was above her ability.

The case of Student D might illustrate a case in which a student is labelled unsuccessful by previous teachers and treated by other teachers accordingly. The student appears to have the ability to succeed: she did well on the IEA and imitation tasks, and was also extremely tolerant of ambiguity. No explanation can be offered here as to why she performs so poorly in her classroom tests, when it appears that she can succeed.

5.5 Case Study Five

NAME: Student E

GRADE: 12

SEX: M

Student E represents another example of a mismatch case, though less extreme than the two previous ones. He was predicted to score low on the IEA test but scored just below the class mean. This case was selected for presentation because it illustrates the negative effects that learning conditions inappropriate for the needs of an individual student may have.

Student E was observed for 350 minutes. He struck the observer as being very uninterested and bored. He raised his hand only seven times and gave one response; this occurred when he had not volunteered to respond.

Based upon the impressions gained during the period of observation, the interviewer did not expect Student E to be very outspoken during the interview. However, when given the opportunity the student expressed very explicit opinions about how he wanted to learn. His major criticism was of the formality of the classroom, the teacher-centredness, and the teacher's emphasis on grammatical accuracy.

In his view, the proportion of teacher talk to student talk was too high. He stated that his goal in learning French was to be able to express himself and he considered grammar to be secondary. However, in his class 'everything has to be grammatically right, so you don't get to express yourself'. He mentioned that at the beginning of the school year he got 'nailed' by the teacher; as a result he withdrew: 'I pegged her as a bad teacher, so I don't get involved.'

Since he felt that he was not allowed to attempt to communicate and make errors, Student E stopped participating in class: 'When you're asked a question I hesitate because I know she's going to stress grammar and nail me on grammar.' He indicated that he felt embarrassed and stupid when giving a wrong answer.

Student E indicated that he considered grammatical exercises out of context as useless. He preferred to be able to relate them to actual usage. Student E expressed a great desire for more oral work: 'Oral work is where you learn your French — when you get used to talking, you put the pronouns in the right place.'

Student E reported that French was difficult for him because he considered languages harder than any other subject, and furthermore because he had no background in English grammar. He felt, however, that he had a very good memory. 'Once I've learned them [the words], I don't forget them.' He also indicated that generally he had no difficulty in understanding the teacher's French.

In addition, the Imitation Task, administered during the interview, revealed that Student E's productive competence was reasonably good. He scored around the mean of the grade 12 students.

In the interview with the teacher, Student E was described as lazy and inattentive. The teacher reported that she had had a serious talk with the student, trying to convince him that she cared about his progress. She was beginning to notice a change in him and had the impression that he was starting to work.

Despite the fact that the student's reaction to the teacher can be criticized as somewhat immature and hypersensitive, this case study nevertheless indicates that not all students should be taught in the same way. Whereas some feel the need of constant correction in order to be absolutely certain about each new form and structure, others are put off when constantly corrected, and resist any further efforts on the part of the teacher. It may be advisable to allow the latter type of student greater freedom in his attempts to communicate if this prevents stifling his interest in learning a language.

A student like Student E might have fared better under a less structured program, since he scored extremely high on the Embedded Figures test and was thus very field independent.

5.6 Case Study Six

NAME: Student F

GRADE: 8

SEX: F

Student F was initially selected for observation as one of the so-called mismatch cases. She scored second highest in her class on the IEA-Listening Comprehension Test but was not mentioned by the teacher as a potential top student. Her IEA score was between the scores of the two top-predicted students.

If one compares the teacher's marks for Student F with the marks given to the two top-predicted students, it is evident that Student F's marks for oral performance were lower than the marks of the other two students; however, her mark for written work is between them. In retrospect, we hypothesize that teachers, when asked to name a student at random, might recall an active participator more readily than a very quiet one.

Student F was observed a total of 225 minutes. She appeared to be very attentive. However, she raised her hand only 39 times in comparison to the 222 and 134 times the two top-predicted students volunteered to answer. Student F frequently displayed hesitation before finally putting up her hand. During the period of observation she gave a total of 13 answers, of which only 4 were voluntary.

The overall impression of Student F, that she is quiet, soft-spoken and very shy, was confirmed during the interview with her. She appeared to be very nervous and was unable to repeat the sentences of the Imitation Task. Out of the total number of grade 8 students (24), she had repeated the third lowest number of imitation units.

In the course of the interview, Student F began to relax and willingly answered all questions. She began to learn French in grade 4, and the program followed was exclusively oral until grade 6. Student F had had to change schools very often and was now in her eighth. She remarked that it was very confusing to change schools so frequently, since the students in every new school were at a different level, either behind or ahead of her. Initially, she had difficulties catching up with the other students in the present school. She mentioned that she now obtained good marks in all subjects; French was not her favorite subject, though she considered it to be 'O.K.'

Student F felt that French was fairly easy for her, because she had started at an early age. She further indicated that she had a good memory for vocabulary.

With regard to her feelings about the class and the teacher, Student F indicated that she now liked the teacher much better than at the beginning of the year. Initially he had wanted her to talk, but he was now leaving her alone. When questioned about the class atmosphere, she commented: 'It's all right; but some kids make fun of you, if you don't say the right things'.

This also applies to other classes. She further mentioned that she usually became shy and embarrassed when she had to talk in front of the class. The language itself, however, did not sound funny or strange to her: 'I can speak it quite easily, just under pressure I can't do it.'

Coinciding with this dislike or fear of oral tasks, she expressed a preference for written work. She also indicated that she learned better by writing down French words, etc. Her general comment on the classroom activities was: 'It's all helpful, I just don't really like it.'

When asked to comment on her infrequent participation, she reported that she was afraid of saying something wrong and of making a fool of herself. She therefore preferred to wait until she was absolutely certain before raising her hand. She also mentioned that frequently when she knew the correct answer the wrong one would come out when she opened her mouth. She therefore preferred to compare her answer to the reply given by another student. Student F further indicated that she would prefer not to be confronted by the teacher and asked to respond. However, she did not mind being corrected by the teacher.

Even though she generally understood the teacher well, Student F mentioned that she would like the teacher to use slightly more English, when introducing new vocabulary, for example, in order to increase her level of comprehension. That Student F might have wanted greater structure in the program was substantiated by her extremely low mark on the Embedded Figures test.

After the interview the teacher was asked his impressions of her. He confirmed that she was a very shy and nervous. He considered her to be very intelligent and reported that her tests were excellent. He also mentioned that he had confused her with another student and initially considered her to be a student of low ability. Her written work, however, absolutely astounded him and he had to change his opinion of her.

The case of Student F illustrates that certain personality characteristics, such as extreme timidity, have to be taken into consideration in making learning settings more suitable to individual needs. Student F might gradually be able to overcome her shyness and fear of oral participation by working in small groups, perhaps even without the teacher being present. To allow students like her to remain orally passive would probably reduce their anxiety and increase their confidence.

6. Classroom Activities and Atmosphere

In addition to the statistical data, we gathered a great deal of descriptive information in the classrooms, because we needed a record of the learning context of the students under observation. This information conveys an impression of the overall classroom atmosphere and the factors that contribute to it – the teacher, the students, and the classroom activities – which are not otherwise discernible from the hard data collected.

6.1 General description of classes observed

As was stated earlier, observation and testing were carried out in twelve classes from six schools. Two classes of grade 8 students were selected from each of schools A and B, and one grade 10 and one grade 12 class were selected from each of schools C, D, E, and F.

In school A the students in grade 8 (1) numbered 25, and in grade 8 (2), 24. A female teacher taught (1) and a male teacher taught (2). The school was architecturally open, but this did not affect the French classes, which took place in portables located outside the main building. In both classes the students' desks were arranged in semi-circles.

The situation in school B was quite different from the situation in school A. The classes were larger – grade 8 (3) had 32 students and grade 8 (4) had 31 students. Both classes were taught by the same male teacher. School B was more traditional in style, which was also reflected in the French classes, where the desks were arranged in rows.

School A and school B used different programs; school A used *Ici on Parle Français* and school B used *Le Français International*. However, both schools had the same amount of time allocated to the teaching of French. In each case, the students received 45 minutes of instruction on four days in a six-day cycle, which worked out to an average of 150 minutes a week. All four classes were observed for 225 minutes for the purposes of the report. During some of the observation time in school B, the classes were taught by a student teacher, but the change of teacher was not long enough to make a significant difference in the observations.

The grade 10 and grade 12 classes chosen from schools C, D, and F all followed the program *Ici on Parle Français*. Schools C and D were considered 'traditional' in type and school F 'open', but in all the classes the desks were arranged in semicircles. In school E, the programs followed in grades 10 and 12 were *French I* and *French II*, which offers a much more 'traditional', 'grammar-translation' approach than *Ici on Parle Français*. In these classrooms the desks were arranged in rows. Although school E was also considered 'traditional', the curriculum for the French classes contained some 'individualized' components.

Table 34 General description of classes observed

School	A			B		C	D			E	F	
Grade	8_1	8_2	8_3	8_4	10_1	12_1	10_2	12_2	10_3	12_3	10_4	12_4
Number of students	25	24	32	31	27	29	22	33	33	26	20	18
Male	12	11	19	13	12	6	6	8	17	7	6	6
Female	13	13	13	18	15	23	16	25	16	19	14	12
Teacher	F	M		M	F	F		F		F	F	
Seating plan	Semi-circle			Rows		Semi-circle	Semi-circle			Rows	Semi-circle	
Type of school	Open except French (in portables)			Traditional		Traditional	Traditional (French curriculum has individualized segments)				Open	
Semester (S) or Non-Semester (NS)	NS			NS		S	NS			NS	S	
Program Followed	ICI			ICI		ICI	ICI			French I French II	ICI	

Table 34 General description of classes observed *continued*

Length of Period in Minutes	45 min. for 4 days in 6-day cycle	70 min. 70 min. 60 min. 2 x 40 min. 4-day cycle	45 min. per day 4-day cycle	2 x 45 min. every 2nd day 4-day cycle	40 min. 40 min. 40 min. 60 min. 60 min. 6-day cycle	65 min. per day
Average minutes per week	150	350	225	225	200	325
Total minutes observed	225 (50 taught by student teacher)	350 (15 taught by student teacher)	225	315 (70 taught by student teacher)	240	260

In the four grade 10 classes and four grade 12 classes observed, the number of pupils in each class varied considerably, as can be seen in Table 34. However, only in school F might the number of students be related to a factor other than general policy or convenience – the particularly low number of students in each class could coincide with the fact that the school follows an 'open' concept, which is more workable with smaller classes. All eight classes were taught by female teachers, and in schools D and E, grades 10 and 12 were taught by the same teacher.

The French program in schools C and F worked on a semester system, which would account for the greater amount of instruction time per week – 350 minutes in school C and 325 minutes in school F as compared to 225 minutes in school D and 200 minutes in school E. Except in the case of school F, the classes were observed for at least one week. Grade 12 in school D was observed for an extra day since a student teacher had taught for 70 minutes during the week of observation.

This information, as well as a breakdown of the instruction time into class periods, is summarized in Table 34.

6.2 Description of classroom activities

In the classrooms, the observers recorded not only interactions between the teachers and the selected students but also class activities and the approximate time devoted to each. The different activities were then listed and an attempt was made to calculate the total amount of time spent on each activity during the period of observation in a particular class. Then the percentage of time spent on each activity, based on the total time a class was observed, was calculated, the percentages across grade levels, and finally, the total percentage of time for each activity. These results are shown in Table 35.

However, because of various problems the figures in Table 35 are only rough estimates and should be interpreted cautiously. In the first place, not all the activities were mutually exclusive – that is, two or more of the activities enumerated might be occurring at the same time, such as 'review of previous material' and 'use of blackboard'. In this case, the same time would have been recorded for both activities. Secondly, it was often difficult to distinguish clearly between two activities, for example, between 'review of previous material' and 'classroom exercises: oral'. However, a sincere attempt was made in the recording and calculating of figures to remain consistent, so that such problems would not create a great imbalance or bias in the results. Not all classes were observed for an equal amount of time, but this problem was alleviated through the calculation of percentages.

Table 35 Percent distribution of activities in classrooms observed

Activities	A/8 (1)	A/8 (2)	B/8 (3)	B/8 (4)	Grade 8 Average	C/10 (1)	D/10 (2)	E/10 (3)	F/10 (4)	Grade 10 Average	C/12 (1)	D/12 (2)	E/12 (3)	F/12 (4)	Grade 12 Average	Grand Total Average
Grammar presentation and drill	2.7	15.6	12.9	23.6	13.7	6.6	7.6	1.3	2.7	4.6	5.1	9.8	—	—	3.7	7.3
Vocabulary presentation and drill	2.2	0.9	4.4	2.7	2.6	7.4	12.9	7.5	11.2	9.8	2.9	2.5	3.3	—	2.2	4.9
Pronunciation explanation and drill	4.0	—	7.6	7.1	4.7	—	—	—	—	—	—	0.6	—	—	0.2	1.6
Classroom exercises: oral	24.4	13.3	48.0	40.0	31.4	12.0	18.7	9.2	20.8	15.2	16.0	21.3	6.7	11.2	13.8	20.1
Classroom exercises: written	14.7	38.2	8.0	1.8	15.7	10.0	6.7	0.8	1.2	4.7	13.4	6.7	6.3	5.0	7.9	9.4
Review of previous material	2.2	—	13.8	4.0	5.0	5.1	4.9	2.5	11.2	5.9	—	13.3	—	5.8	4.8	5.2
Reading (and drill): by teacher	8.9	4.4	—	2.7	4.0	4.3	—	—	3.1	1.9	4.9	1.6	—	6.5	3.3	3.1
Reading (and drill): by student	8.9	2.2	1.8	1.8	3.7	1.4	—	7.5	—	2.2	—	2.9	7.9	—	2.7	2.9
Translations	—	—	—	1.8	0.5	—	—	1.3	—	0.3	3.4	1.3	—	7.7	3.1	1.3
Prose/poetry not from text	—	—	—	—	—	—	—	—	—	—	—	3.5	11.3	—	3.7	1.2
Classroom tests: oral	6.2	—	—	—	1.6	1.4	—	—	—	0.4	—	—	—	7.7	1.9	1.3
Classroom tests: written	—	—	—	—	—	4.3	1.8	4.2	3.8	3.5	7.1	—	—	—	1.8	1.8
Homework ('taking up')	7.1	—	3.6	—	2.7	6.3	4.4	3.3	14.2	7.1	8.9	—	16.3	6.5	7.9	5.9
Oral discussion (conversation)	—	—	—	5.8	1.5	—	2.2	—	—	0.6	—	21.0	—	—	5.3	2.5
'Culture'	—	11.1	—	—	2.8	—	—	—	—	—	—	—	—	—	—	0.9
Miscellaneous (singing, games, etc.)	8.0	7.6	—	3.1	4.7	12.9	2.7	—	—	3.9	1.4	—	9.6	10.8	5.5	4.7
Language Lab	—	—	—	—	—	—	—	11.3	6.2	4.4	—	—	—	4.6	1.2	1.9
Use of blackboard: by teacher	3.1	7.6	20.9	14.7	11.6	4.3	16.4	1.3	—	5.5	3.1	10.2	2.1	1.9	4.3	7.1
Use of blackboard: by student	—	7.1	4.4	—	2.9	7.4	4.0	—	—	2.9	2.9	7.3	4.2	2.7	4.3	3.7
Other visual aids (overhead, video)	0.9	3.1	6.7	1.8	3.1	5.4	—	2.5	6.9	3.7	8.6	7.3	—	—	4.0	3.6
Use of props	—	—	3.1	7.1	2.6	—	—	—	9.2	2.3	—	—	—	—	—	1.6
Use of records, tapes	—	—	7.1	6.2	3.3	—	4.9	—	—	1.2	—	—	2.1	—	0.5	1.7
Administration: instruction, correction of tests, announcements	—	—	—	0.4	0.1	2.0	2.2	5.0	8.1	4.3	2.3	—	2.1	10.4	3.7	2.7

Table 36 Description of dichotomous categories

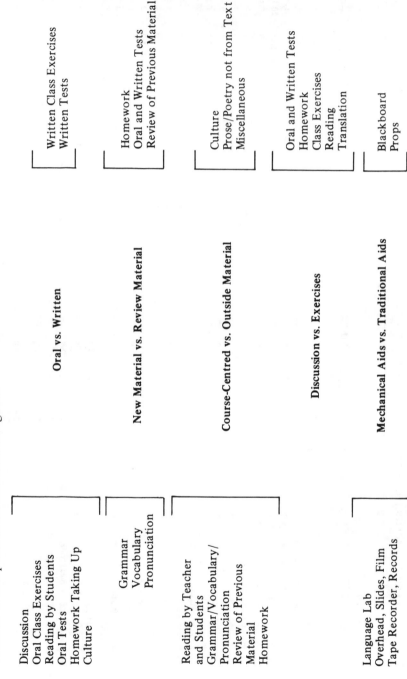

Oral vs. Written
- Discussion
- Oral Class Exercises
- Reading by Students
- Oral Tests
- Homework Taking Up
- Culture

versus
- Written Class Exercises
- Written Tests

New Material vs. Review Material
- Grammar
- Vocabulary
- Pronunciation

versus
- Homework
- Oral and Written Tests
- Review of Previous Material

Course-Centred vs. Outside Material
- Reading by Teacher and Students
- Grammar/Vocabulary/Pronunciation
- Review of Previous Material
- Homework

versus
- Culture
- Prose/Poetry not from Text
- Miscellaneous

Discussion vs. Exercises

versus
- Oral and Written Tests
- Homework
- Class Exercises
- Reading
- Translation

Mechanical Aids vs. Traditional Aids
- Language Lab
- Overhead, Slides, Film
- Tape Recorder, Records

versus
- Blackboard
- Props

The figures are nevertheless beneficial to the extent that they convey a general impression about the types of activities that take place in language classes and how much they can vary from class to class. For example, it is interesting how little time was devoted to discussion or conversation. This is especially surprising since most of the observed classes followed programs that emphasize the development or oral skills. In only one class was there a discussion of any cultural aspects associated with the target language. On the other hand, there was a fair amount of oral exercise and drill in most classes, although again the amount varied considerably from class to class.

From Table 35, the activities were subsequently grouped into broader dichotomous categories. A description of these categories can be found in Table 36. The number of minutes for the activities in a group were summed and a percentage calculated based on the total number of minutes a class was observed. This was done for each individual class, across grade levels, and also for all the classes together, to produce a total percentage (see Table 37). Though the activities associated with each category are mutually exclusive, individual activities sometimes appear in several. Although the same difficulties outlined above concerning Table 35 apply to Table 37, some important general trends can be identified from the latter.

It is clear, for instance, that in most classes oral activities played a greater role than written activities. This probably reflects the greater emphasis in recent times on the development of oral skills in language classes. However, there was still very little emphasis given to free discussion as opposed to the more structured activities like class exercises, tests, reading, etc.

In all but four cases, a greater percentages of time wsa devoted to review material than to the presentation of new material. Of the four exceptions, three of the cases were grade 8 classes. This might be a result of the fact that the students in grade 8 are in the early stages of learning French. They would therefore be more likely to receive a higher proportion of new material than students in grades 10 and 12, where the material learned in the earlier grades would be reviewed.

From Table 37 it can also be seen that all the classes used course-centred material more extensively than outside material. Finally, traditional aids were used more than mechanical aids, even though 'traditional aids' does not include pictures. Pictures were frequently used, but it was not clear from the observations when they were used or for how long.

6.3 Description of teacher elicitations and evaluations

Another interesting aspect of classroom activities is related to the teachers' interactions with the students, namely the types of question the teachers

Table 37 Percent distribution of classroom activities in dichotomous categories

Activities	School/Grade (Class No.) A/8(1)	A/8(2)	B/8(3)	B/8(4)	Grade 8 Average	C/10(1)	D/10(2)	E/10(3)	F/10(4)	Grade 10 Average	C/12(1)	D/12(2)	E/12(3)	F/12(4)	Grade 12 Average	Total Average
ORAL vs. WRITTEN	46.6	26.6	53.4	47.6	43.5	21.3	23.1	22.2	35.0	25.3	24.9	45.2	30.9	25.4	31.6	33.5
	14.7	38.2	8.0	1.8	15.7	11.4	6.7	0.8	1.2	5.0	20.5	6.7	6.3	5.0	9.6	7.6
NEW MATERIAL vs. REVIEW MATERIAL	8.9	16.5	24.9	33.4	20.9	14.0	20.3	8.8	13.9	14.2	8.0	12.9	3.3	–	6.0	13.7
	15.5	–	17.4	4.0	9.2	17.1	11.1	10.0	29.2	16.8	16.8	13.3	16.3	20.0	16.6	14.2
COURSE-CENTRED MATERIAL vs. OUTSIDE MATERIAL	36.0	23.1	20.5	41.9	30.4	31.1	29.8	22.1	39.3	30.6	21.8	30.7	27.5	18.8	24.7	28.5
	8.0	18.7	–	3.1	7.4	12.9	2.7	–	–	3.9	1.4	3.5	20.9	10.8	9.1	6.8
DISCUSSION vs. EXERCISES	–	–	–	5.8	1.4	–	2.2	–	–	.5	–	21.0	–	–	5.2	2.4
	70.2	58.1	61.4	48.1	59.4	39.7	33.4	26.3	43.1	35.6	53.7	33.8	37.2	44.6	42.1	45.7
MECHANICAL AIDS vs. TRADITIONAL AIDS	.9	3.1	13.8	8.0	6.4	5.4	4.9	13.8	13.1	10.6	8.6	7.3	2.1	4.6	5.6	7.6
	3.1	7.6	24.0	21.8	14.1	4.3	16.4	1.3	9.2	7.8	3.1	10.2	2.1	1.9	4.3	8.7

asked and the types of evaluation they gave after the students had responded. It was possible to collect these data from the entries on the coding sheets used during classroom observations. Table 38 presents the percentages occurrence of teacher questions by class and grade. (For a full description of the categories see Part III, chapter 1, section 3.3.)

As shown in Table 38, the type of question occurring most frequently is Category 1 – eliciting specific information. The mean percentages per grade indicate that the use of type 1 questions decreases in grade 12; however, the mean for grade 10; is higher than for grade 8. Since classroom activities and teaching content in the individual classes determine to a great extent the type of question asked, one cannot generalize this finding beyond the present situation.

The elicitation of general information (type 2 question) occurred most frequently in grade 12, followed by grade 10. Evidently, it is generaly limited to one or two classes. This fact may again be due to the teaching content during the period of observation. It could, however, also be a teacher characteristic or a result of the learning environment.

All the remaining types of question occurred rather infrequently. If this result can be generalized, teachers should be made aware of the fact that they are not using a broad enough variety of possible elicitations of clarification, elaboration, and mutual correction. These elicitations might draw the students' attention to important aspects of the learning process.

In sum, in the classes observed teachers appear to favor questions eliciting specific information. This finding was common to all grades. It would be worth investigating the variation of types of elicitations in clearly distinguishable learning environments, such as open plan compared to traditional schools. There were not enough samples of different classes illustrating different environments to make such a study possible.

Table 39 presents the percentage occurrences of different types of teacher evaluations by class and grade. As can be seen in this table, many evaluative aspects, as developed and defined for the observation schedule (see Part III, chapter I, section 3.3), did not occur very frequently; for example, positive and negative feedback, elaboration, clarification, implicit and explicit correction.

The type of feedback a teacher may offer to a student can vary greatly. In the present study, for example, positive teacher feedback, which was only coded when distinguishable from the general classroom atmosphere, was only occasionally evidenced. Negative feedback was coded extremely rarely. With regard to the category of 'no feedback', it is apparent that even though the total average across grades is low, the percentage occurrence in all grade 8 classes is fairly high.

Table 38 Percentage occurrences of teacher questions by class

Grade	Questions*	Type 1	Type 2	Type 3	Type 4	Type 5	Type 6	Type 7	Type 8	Type 9	Type 10
8	Vol.	67.8								4.4	3.3
	Invol.**	18.9								2.2	3.3
	Vol.	42.9	7.1			2.4		2.4			2.4
	Invol.	28.6	2.4								11.9
	Vol.	60.3				8.7				1.6	3.2
	Invol.	22.2				0.8					0.8
	Vol.	65.9				1.6					2.4
	Invol.	26.0				0.8					0.8
Average	Vol.	59.2	1.8	–	–	3.2	–	–	–	1.4	2.8
	Invol.	23.9	0.6	–	–	0.4	–	0.8	–	0.6	4.6
10	Vol.	76.6	0.8	0.9				0.8		1.6	1.6
	Invol.	15.6		0.9							3.1
	Vol.	43.0	2.8			0.9		1.9			0.9
	Invol.	41.1				1.9					5.6
	Vol.	52.8								2.8	2.8
	Invol.	38.9									2.8
	Vol.	36.1	9.8	3.3				1.6			1.6
	Invol.	44.3		1.6				3.3			
Average	Vol.	52.1	0.9	1.1	–	0.2	–	1.1	–	1.1.	1.3
	Invol.	35.0	2.5	0.6	–	0.5	–	0.8	–	–	3.3

Table 38 Percentage occurrences of teacher questions by class *continued*

		(1)	(2)	(3)	(4)	(5)	(6)	(7)	(8)	(9)	(10)
12	Vol.	73.3				1.7		1.7		1.7	5.0
	Invol.	16.7									
	Vol.	53.5	10.3	1.9				0.6		0.6	1.9
	Invol.	25.8	2.6								3.2
	Vol.	45.8		4.2	2.1	2.1		2.1		2.1	14.6
	Invol.	25.0				2.1					
	Vol.	33.3									2.4
	Invol.	50.0								2.4	11.9
Average	Vol.	51.5	2.6	1.5	0.5	1.0	–	0.6	–	1.7	1.1
	Invol.	29.4	0.7	–	–	0.5	–	0.5	–	–	8.7
Total Average	Vol.	59.3	1.7	0.9	0.2	1.5	–	0.6	–	1.4	1.7
	Invol.	29.4	1.3	0.2	–	0.5	–	0.7	–	0.2	5.5

*Questions:
- (1) Elicits specific information
- (2) Elicits general information
- (3) Elicits clarification
- (4) Elicits elaboration
- (5) Elicits repetition of preceding statement
- (6) Elicits recommencement of previous response
- (7) Elicits confirmation of comprehension
- (8) Elicits a complete response
- (9) Elicits correction
- (10) Elicits other activities

**Vol. = Voluntary, Invol. = Involuntary

Teachers elaborated student response extremely rarely (1.9%). They also hardly ever gave a clarification, i.e. an explanation of the way a correct answer was arrived at (1.7%). However, the category of 'repetition of student response', which is a way of reinforcing the student, was frequently evidenced (15.2%).

When correcting students, the teachers for the most part corrected explicitly (19.2%). Of the other types of corrections coded in the present study, 'localization of incorrectness' was the next most common corrective feedback (8.3%). The other two, i.e. 'indication of incorrectness' and 'implicit correction', were rare.

One of the most frequently occurring categories was 'interruption'. This form of teacher behavior may cause confusion for certain types of students. It is therefore suggested that teachers ask their students if they want to be interrupted or prefer to finish their response before being corrected.

Another aspect of teacher evaluation potentially beneficial to students is that of giving clues. As indicated in Table 39, the percentage of clues given was higher than the percentage of occasions in which the teacher provided the answer. This indicates that teachers usually give the students the opportunity of finding the answer themselves.

As a result of the classroom observation, it is believed that in general teachers' evaluations could be made more effective if they responded to students' responses more specifically. For example, they could offer the students more elaborations and clarifications of their responses. In correcting, they could localize the errors instead of giving mainly explicit corrections. Similarly, they could give the students more clues rather than reject their responses or offer them no feedback at all. Further research should be conducted on such recommendations.

6.4 Classroom atmosphere

While recording classroom activities the observers also jotted down their impressions of classroom atmosphere and teaching activities. From these notes another investigator made two lists of descriptive statements selected from the most frequent comments. The observers were then given the lists and asked to rate the teachers and classroom atmospheres on a five-point scale ranging from 1, agreement with the statements, to 5, disagreement (i.e. agreement with the opposite).

Table 39 Percentage occurrence of teacher evaluations by class

	Grade 8	Grade 8 Average	Grade 10	Grade 10 Average	Grade 12	Grade 12 Average	Total Average
Positive Feedback	3.5	2.9	0.6	2.0	5.2	2.9	2.6
	3.4		5.6		5.1		
	4.2		–		1.2		
	0.6		1.9		–		
Negative Feedback	0.9	0.2	–	–	–	0.3	0.1
	–		–		–		
	–		–		1.2		
	–		–		–		
Partial Rejection	17.3	13.8	19.3	19.5	10.5	19.3	17.5
	15.1		14.2		10.2		
	9.4		26.5		27.8		
	13.2		18.0		28.8		
Rejection	11.7	13.9	9.5	10.0	7.8	10.3	11.4
	21.1		5.8		9.4		
	9.6		15.1		7.4		
	13.1		9.6		16.7		
No Feedback	10.6	11.9	2.4	3.0	6.6	5.8	6.9
	13.2		4.5		5.4		
	14.4		–		7.6		
	9.2		5.0		3.4		
Repetition	21.7	13.2	7.7	15.2	20.8	17.2	15.2
	20.7		23.1		23.1		
	8.3		1.9		9.9		
	2.2		27.9		15.0		

Table 39 Percentage occurrence of teacher evaluations by class *continued*

	Grade 8	Grade 8 Average	Grade 10	Grade 10 Average	Grade 12	Grade 12 Average	Total Average
Elaboration	– 3.4 – –	0.9	4.1 2.1 –	2.0	2.6 2.8 3.7 1.7	2.7	1.9
Clarification	0.9 1.7	0.7	1.8 2.1	1.9	1.3 3.2 2.5 3.3	2.6	1.7
Providing Answer	16.7 3.7 3.7 3.2	6.8	– 3.0 – 3.8	6.8	5.3 5.8 2.9 10.3	6.1	6.6
Interruption	7.1 14.8 5.6 6.3	8.5	1.9 21.2 28.6 12.1	16.0	21.1 – 26.5 10.3	14.5	13.0
Explicit Correction	11.9 40.7 5.6 17.5	18.9	25.0 15.2 23.8 15.2	19.8	21.1 3.8 20.6 27.6	18.9	19.2
Implicit Correction	2.4 – – –	0.6	1.9 – – –	0.5	5.3 – 2.9 3.4	2.9	1.7
Localization of Incorrectness	9.5 3.7		11.5 9.1		21.1 1.9		

Category							
Indication of Incorrectness	7.4 / 4.8	6.4	14.3 / —	8.7	2.9 / 13.8	9.9	8.3
Further Questioning	— / 11.1 / —	4.8	3.8 / —	1.7	10.5 / 7.7 / 8.8	6.8	4.4
Grammar	7.9	12.5	3.0	16.2	—	10.5	13.0
Emphasis	2.6 / 8.6 / 16.7 / 22.1	2.7	11.2 / 13.3 / 15.1 / 25.0	2.2	3.9 / 16.2 / 17.3 / 8.3	4.4	3.1
Intralingual	2.2 / 3.1 / 2.4 / 2.9	3.2	2.8 / 5.8	3.6	9.1 / 3.4 / 2.1 / 2.9	5.3	4.0
Extralingual	8.9 / — / 3.7 / —	1.9	5.6 / 1.9 / 3.4 / 3.4	0.9	13.6 / 3.4 / 4.2	1.4	1.4
Extralingual	2.2 / 3.1 / 2.4 / 4.9	3.2	1.4 / 11.5 / 10.3 / 8.5	7.9	6.9 / 8.3 / 2.9	4.5	5.2
Crosslingual	3.1 / —	0.8	—	—	—	—	0.3

Table 40 Average ratings of teacher and classroom

(a)

Teacher	Grade 8				Grade 10				Grade 12			
generally friendly	2	3.5	2	2	2	1	4	2	3	1	3	4
good classroom control	1.5	4	2	2	2.5	2	4	3	1.5	1.5	2	3
method of presentation flexible	1.5	2	4	4	3	5	2	3	2	4	2	2
presentation clear, organized	2	5	2	2	2	1.5	3.5	3.5	1	1.5	4	3.5
seeks out inactive students	4.5	4	4	4	3	4	4	3.5	4	4	4	4
spreads attention evenly over class	5	3.5	4	4	3.5	4	3	3.5	3	4	3.5	2
varies activities frequently	2	4.5	1.5	2	2.5	2	3	3.5	3	1.5	3	3.5
sensitive to individual and class needs	3.5	4.5	3	3.5	2	2	5	3.5	4	2	4	4.5
uses little English	2	2	1	1	3.5	2	4	2	2	2	4	5

Table 40 Average ratings of teacher and classroom *continued*

(b)

Classroom	Grade 8				Grade 10				Grade 12			
atmosphere friendly	2	3.5	2	2	2	1.5	4	2	3	2	2	2.5
class interaction formal	1.5	2.5	4	4	3.5	3	2	5	1.5	3.5	3	5
class generally quiet	4	1	3.5	1.5	2	3	4	3.5	5	1.5	2	4.5
students attentive	1	4	2	2	2	2	4	3	2	1.5	2	4
students interested	2	4.5	2	1	2	2	4	3.5	2	1.5	4	4
student participation voluntary	1	3	3	2.5	2.5	2.5	2.5	2	2.5	2	3	3
student/teacher rapport good	2	4	2	2	2	2	4	2.5	2.5	1	3	4
class generally teacher-dominated	1.5	2	4	4	2	3	1	3	2	4	2	1

```
1 ——— 5
agreement   disagreement
```

No consultation was permitted between the observers while they carried out this task. The inter-judge reliability in these two measures was found to be 0.85. The two separate ratings were subsequently averaged and the results appear in Table 40. Again, the table must be interpreted cautiously since the observations about the teachers and classroom atmosphere are based on subjective impressions, even though the observers attempted to be as objective as possible.

Nevertheless, teachers generally did not seek out inactive students and very often gave most of their attention to certain students. This could be due to the fact that teachers often concentrated on one segment of the class, generally the centre, and virtually ignored the periphery. Thus, less outgoing students or students who did not wish to participate actively would be called upon less frequently if they did not sit in the centre.

From the table, there also appears to be a direct relationship between the frequency with which teachers varied the activities and the students' interest and attentiveness.

One final observation based on Table 40 is that most teachers used little English in the class. However, whether this was a general trend or characteristic of the classes under observation could not be determined.

6.5 Conclusion

Although it was not regarded as a major component of the present study to collect or evaluate data concerning the teachers, the classroom atmosphere, and classroom activities, it was considered necessary to extract some useful descriptive information of the learning context from the general comments the observers recorded while they were in the classrooms. Not many studies have presented a detailed account of the actual activities in languages classrooms. Perhaps the preliminary approach to this area undertaken here will serve as an impetus for future research.

Notes

1. Some of the data collected and analyzed have now been reported in Swain, M. 'Changes in errors, random or systemic?' *Proceedings of the Fourth International Congress of Applied Linguistics*, vol. 2. Stuttgart: Hochschulverlag, 1976.
2. The discrepancies between teachers' marks and their predictions for a few students were explained in the informal interviews with the teachers. Occasionally predictions were caused by impressions of the students which were not based upon marks, such as confusion of names and persons, personality clash between teacher and student, etc.
3. In an enriched class the student is exposed to second language material additional to the regular program.

PART IV
Conclusions

The principal findings of the adult interview study and the main classroom study will now be summarized in point form, followed by suggestions for future research and the presentation of several practical implications.

1. Major Findings

1. Major findings of the adult interview study

(1) The interview study generally confirmed the kinds of strategies which the Rubin-Stern inventories had suggested, but it was found necessary to reduce and order the Stern list of ten strategies to a more systematic arrangement of five (see Part II, chapter 1, section 4.3). The study was also able to identify a large number of techniques that good language learners employ.

(2) While this study indicated certain attributes common among good language learners, especially with regard to strategies and techniques they had employed or would employ, it also illustrated the complexity and individuality of each learning situation and career (See Part II, chapter 1, section 5).

(3) Looking at different case studies suggested that perceived (but not measured) aptitude was less of a crucial factor than attitude to language learning, persistence, and willingness to adapt to varied learning situations over prolonged periods of time (see Part II, chapter 1, section 5).

(4) From the point of view of research methodology, reporting in retrospect combined with predicting on the basis of a hypothetical language learning situation, such as was demanded by the interview procedure, was productive to a certain extent. But it left the investigators conscious of the fact that many aspects of the learning process were probably missed by this particular approach.

2. Major findings of the classroom study

One general conclusion arising out of the adult interview study was that in view of the exploratory nature of the entire project, it would be unwise to attempt to focus exclusively on learning strategies and techniques. This study, as well as other language learning research, has confirmed the conviction that strategies and techniques form only a part of language learning. It is therefore important to related them to personality and motivational factors in the learner, and to other less obvious aspects of the learning process.

Consequently, the main classroom study was conceived in more comprehensive terms. It was designed to explore various learner and learning factors, the learning environment (i.e. the teacher and teaching), the strategies and techniques consciously employed by the learner, and the learning outcome, through a variety of means, such as observation, personality and cognitive style tests, French achievement tests, teacher interviews, and student interviews.

The findings of the main study can be divided into those related to learning and those related to teaching.

2.1 Findings related to learning

(1) Strict observation in language learning classrooms does not reveal language learning strategies or specific techniques other than fairly obvious indicators; for example, participation or nonparticipation in classroom activities. In other words, on the basis of mere classroom observation neither teachers nor trained observers can be expected to identify whether or not these students are successfully learning, and whether or not they are employing useful learning techniques (see Part III, chapter 4).

(2) On the other hand, the interviews with the students about their language learning experiences made it possible to identify and describe some strategies and techniques and to reveal the students' learning difficulties as well as their preferences and goals in learning French (see Part III, chapter 5, section 3).

(3) Certain personality and cognitive style factors are related to success in language learning. The present study identified two such factors as important: tolerance of ambiguity and field independence. In the early stages, factors such as tolerance of ambiguity may be more related to success than at later stages, while factors such as field independence may be crucial at more advanced levels (see Part III, chapter 4).

(4) Students with different cognitive styles, as described above, appear to use different learning and communication processes. Evidence for this can be found in differences in the errors produced by field dependent and field independent learners (see Part III, chapter 5, section 2.2).

(5) Attitudes to the language learning situation play an important role in successful language learning, perhaps to a greater degree than either the integrative or instrumental orientations identified in the studies by Gardner and Lambert (1972). It should be noted that Gardner in recent work has also taken into account a wider range of motivational factors (Gardner and Smythe, 1975a) (see Part III, chapter 4).

(6) Positive attitudes to language learning appear to be a necessary but not a sufficient condition for success. In fact, attitude as a determining factor of language learning success may be most important at the initial stages (see Part III, chapter 4).

(7) A great deal more about language learning may be discovered by consulting learners directly in a carefully constructed interview than by standardized personality and attitude tests. In an interview, learners, except perhaps very young ones, are able to contribute useful information about (a) their goals in language learning (most students expressed preference for oral competence rather than written competence); (b) classroom activities and learning techniques (interviewees expressed preference for more or fewer oral activities, more or less L1 support); and (c) teacher–student interaction (students had views on interruption of communication by the teacher and on teacher correction).

2.2 Findings related to teaching

(1) The teachers emphasized question-and-answer techniques to provide language practice. Discussions on topics related to the country, people, and culture, or to some general topics of interest to the students were infrequent.

(2) In order to see whether the classroom environment is different for good and poor students, the research paid particular attention to differences in treatment given by teachers to poor and good students respectively. In general, teacher differential treatment of good and poor students does not occur to any great extent. However, there are indictors that certain tendencies towards differential treatment do exist which some-

times benefit good students to the detriment of poor students, while at other times they benefit poor students at the expense of good students. In addition, it was found that teachers occasionally ignore whole segments of the class (see Part III, chapter 5, section 4).

(3) In spite of the large numbers of students with whom they have daily classroom contacts, on the whole teachers are able to identify their good and poor students accurately. They can provide characterizations of these students which refer to (a) behavioral indices, (b) personality and motivational indices, (c) intellectual or linguistic abilities, and (d) environmental factors. But these characterizations commonly consist of broad surface features; they are generally not diagnostic or analytical. They appear to reflect the teacher's preoccupation with curriculum and the progress of the class as a group rather than with the problems of individual students.

(4) Many expected forms of teacher elicitations and evaluations coded in the observation schedule occurred only rarely: e.g. asking for or providing clarifications and elaborations, eliciting mutual correction, repeating students' responses and localizing errors in student responses (see Part III, chapter 4).

2. Suggestions for Further Research

(1) The study set out to identify strategies and techniques of good language learners. This initial purpose assumed secondary importance as it became apparent that the investigation of other factors such as personality characteristics, cognitive styles, attitudes, and learning environments was crucial. It would be useful to return to the original purpose of the present investigation and to undertake the following inquiry: (1) to study critically the different inventories of learning strategies and techniques and to develop an exhaustive list, clearly related to a language learning model; (2) to devise a study similar to the present one but with instruments such as observation schedules, interviews, and tests that are specifically designed to seek confirmation (or rejection) of the strategy inventory; (3) to devise an experimental program to test the teachability of the identified strategies and techniques.

(2) A teacher questionnaire inquiry similar to the one attempted at the initial stages of the present study would be useful, (a) because teachers have close and regular contact with students during the learning process and are, therefore, in a position to make interesting observations, and (b)

because such a study would reveal teachers' perceptions of learning processes, and of students' learning difficulties.

(3) Cross-sectional studies such as the present main study have merits for the preliminary identification of relationships among different variables related to language learning. But language learning is a complex process involving long periods of time, usually hundreds of hours of instruction and contact spread over several years. Therefore, a longitudinal case study approach is needed to investigate the learning processes. Such research could combine the periodic collection of language production data with case study procedures, such as have been employed in the present main study. An important further instrument of investigation would be the monitoring of learning behavior on specific learning tasks accompanied by the learner's explanation of his learning procedures.

(4) In this study, the absence of an empirical scheme analyzing language teaching was felt to be a disadvantage and led to *ad hoc* inquiries on relevant aspects of teaching. Research should therefore be conducted into the identification and classification of teaching techniques and into the effectiveness of alternative techniques for different kinds of students.

(5) Some specific issues arose from the present investigation.

(a) Learners with different cognitive styles may be predisposed to different language learning processes. Hence a study of cognitive style in relationship to language production would be valuable.

(b) Different classes of variables, identified in the present study – personality, cognitive style, attitude, learning strategy – may be of varying importance at different stages of language learning and in different learning environments. The investigation of this problem would require larger samples of learners, of different stages, and of different environments. In addition, it would be useful to test the effectiveness of individualizing language learning by grouping students according to various common personality and cognitive style factors as well as shared learning preferences.

(c) The combination of attitude testing and interviewing in the present research has suggested the possible advantage of research into the use of the interview as an alternative means of obtaining the same information as standardized tests of personality and attitude, but at greater depth and without the disadvantage of test procedures.

(d) One of the major omissions of the present study, necessitated by the limitation of possible instruments, was the absence of any language aptitude tests such as the Carroll-Sapon MLAT or EMLAT or the Pimsleur PLAB. In a future study it would be desirable to investigate the relationships of aptitude as manifested in language aptitude tests, and the strategies and other processes employed by language learners.

(6) Some of the findings of the present study are thought to be tentative because the test instruments were often not ideally suited to this investigation. Further inquiries should be associated with the development of appropriate new tests or measures. Different cognitive style and personality tests more closely related to language learning would be advantageous. A variety of more accurate criterion measures of specific aspects of language competence greater than at present available is needed. Methods of eliciting language production data other than the Imitation Task would be valuable. Equally necessary are more refined methods of learner interviews which would render this instrument a valid and reliable research tool.

3. Some Practical Implications

What has this study told us of value to the classroom teacher and the teacher trainer? It will be remembered that this investigation was planned as an exploratory inquiry; it did not set out to answer the immediate concerns of classroom practitioners.

Nevertheless, two years of intensive investigation of learners and their learning experiences have led to certain conclusions which should interest the practitioner. Among these, the following are particularly noteworthy: (1) the diagnostic use of the model; (2) possibilities and dangers in identifying learner factors; (3) the applicability of learning strategies and learning techniques; (4) the student's view of teaching; and (5) applications to teacher education.

The diagnostic use of the model

We began the inquiry with a model of the learner with certain characteristics in a given social context (Figure 1). This learner was described as receiving input from teaching and from the L2 environment. The individual's learning processes – his strategies, techniques, and mental processes – were said to lead to a learning outcome, a certain level of proficiency or interlanguage with its characteristic error patterns. What has interested us – as it has other investigators – has been to find relationships (a) between learner characteristics, learning processes, and learning outcomes, and (b) between teaching and learning processes and learning outcomes.

At the end of this study, this model seems to us as appropriate and relevant to the purposes of research as it was at the beginning. In our view, it is also a useful tool for teachers or student teachers who want to gain a better understanding of their own students as language learners. The model represents the complexities of the interaction between the various factors involved. It can, therefore, be used as an instrument of analysis in teaching–learning situations.

We have had some evidence in this study that teachers do not normally attempt to look closely into causal relationships that may determine success or failure. In other words, it has been our impression that in spite of daily contact with the same students, teachers frequently do not consider their progress in an analytic or diagnostic manner. There are good reasons for this. The teacher teaches a whole class and focusses more on the whole group than on individual students. But taking note of individual differences does not necessarily involve a complete shift of focus. It is more a matter of being sensitive to the possible range of differences among individual students and to their causal relationships, and knowing the concepts with which to analyse learning. These skills can be exercised in classes of any size. What the teacher may need is the knowledge of what to look for in trying to help the good learner to reach his objective and the problem student to overcome his difficulties. An analytical scheme of the kind developed by recent research on language learning may be found helpful by teachers in assisting them in this process of understanding. In many instances, it may simply confirm what good practitioners intuitively know and practise; however, as was pointed out before, it is one of the objects of research of this kind to make more explicit and systematic the knowledge implicit in the best practice.

Possibilities and dangers in identifying learner factors

What has this study told us about the language learner? Among learner characteristics we have paid particular attention to personality and cognitive style in relation to L2 learning and found some evidence – in spite of difficulties in assessing it – that such features as tolerance of ambiguity, field independence, and extroversion have some bearing on language learning. From the Adult Interview Study we also found that language background and past learning experience significantly shape an individual's career as a language learner. If we add to that information the available findings on language aptitude and motivation and attitudes we have a whole array of factors to bear in mind in attempting to understand the learner.

Such knowledge should help the teacher see that students cannot be expected to respond alike to teaching. It should also help students analyze their own characteristics and adjust their learning as far as possible to what they know about themselves. One of our interviewees was fully aware that her lack of extroversion stood in the way of making the language contacts she felt were essential for successful second language learning. She tried to force herself to overcome this deficiency.

At the same time it is important not to stereotype these differences and to recognize that we are only beginning to understand such L2 learner characteristics systematically. The study as a whole suggests that *the* successful or good language learner, with predetermined overall characteristics, does not exist. There are many individual ways of learning a language successfully. The study has shown that some of the existing stereotypes do not apply. For example, some people believe that a good language learner has to be musical, or have a high language aptitude or an exceptionally good memory. The Adult Interview Study indicated that these qualities may not be essential.

It should also be pointed out that the analyses of learner factors are certainly not intended for selection purposes.

'Student A is an introvert.'

'Student B has a low score on the language aptitude test.'

'Student C is field dependent.'

Therefore: 'Students A, B, and C will be poor language learners.'

Or: 'Students A, B, and C should not participate in language learning.'

First of all, our knowledge is not definitive enough to make any such statements or predictions with confidence. But even if it were, using the analyses of learner factors in this way would be grossly unfair. What our present knowledge can do is sensitize teachers and students to differences in predispositions with which different language learners will approach language learning. It could also be used for initial placement of students in learning groups, but not for selection or elimination.

Applying strategies and techniques

Although a definitive list of language learning strategies has not emerged, the strategies described in Part I and Part II, chapter 4, section 3 and Appendix 1, appear sufficiently plausible and useful to allow certain generalizations. Regardless of learner differences, in our view the following emerge as essential for successful second language learning:

(1) The learner must be active in his approach to learning and practice.

(2) The learner must come to grips with the language as a system.

(3) The learner must use the language in real communication.

(4) The learner must monitor his interlanguage.

(5) The learner must come to terms with the affective demands of language learning.

Since we cannot claim to have found an exhaustive and non-redundant list of strategies and techniques, the various attempts that have been made to develop such an inventory can in our view be useful to teachers and students. They can form the basis of an awareness of major language learning strategies and specific learning techniques. The interviews with experienced adult learners and with students in elementary and high schools indicate that many (not all) learners are capable of analyzing their learning experiences. The interviews suggested that it would be useful for teachers and students to talk about ways of language learning.

We do not believe that long lectures on strategies and techniques, or even lengthy discussions on the subject, would be particularly profitable. But hints from the teacher or periodical brief exchanges with students about different ways of learning would change classroom language learning from a fairly mechanical routine into a more deliberate cooperative undertaking. Different approaches to learning could be planned and tried out in a more conscious way than has been customary. We therefore recommend a cautious teaching how-to-learn approach.

One finding of the Adult Interview Study which has particularly impressed the research team was the active and directing role which the adult interviewees had taken in making their language learning successful. In contrast, the Main Classroom Study did not reveal a great number of personal strategies among classroom learners. It is commonly agreed that learners should be actively involved. But in classroom language learning the use of carefully prepared course materials and the great number of question-and-answer exercises, exclusively directed by the teacher, somehow disguise the fact that the learner should play a part in making decisions and be allowed to exercise personal choice. Recent efforts at individualization are in the right direction, but generally they do not go far enough. The present study suggests that too close, step-by-step direction of language classes may not always produce the desired effect because the learner has too little chance of developing his own learning strategies.

The student's view of teaching

The present study has only given certain suggestions of the complexity of the interplay between teaching and learning in language classes. It has confirmed through student interviews that class teaching provides different learning environments for good and poor students. It has also shown that some students have a preference for highly structured language programs and for being constantly corrected, while others prefer to be left alone, to be allowed to try out the second language when they feel so inclined, and to make mistakes in it. Some want more mother tongue explanations, others fewer. While it would not be possible, under conditions of class teaching, to cater to all these individual variations, it would probably be helpful for students to become aware of their own ways of learning and their particular preferences or difficulties. Recent studies by Hosenfeld (1976) have shed light on the different ways in which learners interpret the learning tasks in the language class. Teachers, for their part, should become more sensitized to individual learning preferences and differences in the way students respond to different teaching techniques.

Applications to teacher education

It follows from these observations that the findings of this study have relevance for the education of language teachers. First of all, it seems to us important for future language teachers to engage in a process of self-analysis. As experienced language learners themselves, their own linguistic 'autobiography' should provide them with insights into their own characteristics and learning experiences and their implications for teaching. If an outline similar to the interview schedule developed in the Adult Interview Study is applied to a class of future language teachers, it should yield differences in background, personality, aptitude, and attitudes. It should also bring to light varieties of teaching–learning experiences among the student teachers and the gradual development of success as well as failure in second language acquisition. Such self-awareness could be a valuable part of training in guiding the learning of students in language classes.

Complementary to this stock-taking of their own language learning, student teachers could gain insight by working with individual students with learning difficulties and compiling case studies. The various kinds of case studies we have described in the Adult Interview Study and the Main Classroom Study indicate different aspects to consider.

   Student teachers who in the course of their training had made a detailed analysis of their own linguistic auobiography and compared it with their fellow students', and who had had some training in case study methods in working with a single student, would approach class teaching with an understanding of the learner and learning which would stand them in good stead.

APPENDICES

I. Rubin's List of Strategies

(1) The good language learner is a willing and accurate guesser.

(2) The good language learner has a strong drive to communicate, or to learn from communication. He is willing to do many things to get his message across.

(3) The good language learner is often not inhibited. He is willing to appear foolish if reasonable communication results. He is willing to make mistakes in order to learn and to communicate. He is willing to live with a certain amount of vagueness.

(4) In addition to focussing on communication, the good language learner is prepared to attend to form. The good language learner is constantly looking for patterns in the language.

(5) The good language learner practises.

(6) The good language learner monitors his own and the speech of others. That is, he is constantly attending to how well his speech is being received and whether his performance meets the standards he has learned.

(7) The good language learner attends to meaning. He knows that in order to understand the message, it is not sufficient to pay attention to the grammar of the language or to the surface form of speech.

Note

1. This list was adapted from 'What the "Good Language Learner" Can Teach Us', *TESOL Quarterly,* 1975, 9, 41–50.

II. Questionnaire for Interviews with Adult Second Language Learners

Part I

I would like to talk to you about your own personal language learning experience, when and how you learned a second (or third) language, in what sequence, etc.

Your name will be kept confidential, and there is *no* testing involved.

If you don't mind, however, I'd like to tape our conversation as an aid to memory for myself.

May I now ask you a few general questions for our research records?

Respondent:

NAME: AGE GROUP:

ADDRESS: 18 and under:
                                                      19 – 25:
                                                      26 – 35:
                                                      36 – 50:
PHONE: 51 – 65:
                                                      over 65:

EDUCATIONAL BACKGROUND:

   High School (or equivalent):

   Beyond High School:

   Highest Qualification:

Present or previous occupation:

Present:

Previous:

I'd like to ask you some facts about yourself and your language learning experience from your childhood to the present time.

(1)   Where were you born?

(2)   Where did you spend your childhood?

(3)   What languages were spoken in your home?

(3.1) What do you regard as your native language?

(4)   What languages were spoken in your neighborhood?

(5)   Which was the first foreign language you learned. . . ?

(6)   When did you start and how long did your learn. . . ?

(7)   Where and under what circumstances did you learn. . . ?

Possible subquestions:

(a) When you learned . . . (at school/at home, etc.), what did you study, mainly grammar, for example?
(b) What kind of text-books did you use?
(c) Did the teacher speak in the foreign language most of the time?
(d) Did you have to speak to speak a lot yourself or did you mainly read and/or translate?
(e) Do you remember what kind of homework you had to do?
(f) Do you remember what you had to practise, what was really difficult for you?
(g) Did you have any contact outside the classroom/your home with speakers of that language?
(h) Did you have the chance to listen to the radio or see films in the foreign language/in class or outside?

(8)   Which other languages have you studied or tried to study?

(9)   Which of these languages have you maintained to the present?

(10) Could you tell me how well you know these languages *now* or when you were *at your best*?

Would you look at this card, please.

If you had to describe your knowledge of . . . , which of these statements would be most appropriate? [see Table 1.]

Interviewer: Ask about the different stages of language learning:
      elementary
      intermediate
      advanced

You can indicate if your knowledge is slightly above or below these levels.
(For interviewer: *circle language,* if reference to past knowledge is made.)

	Below Elementary	Elementary Proficiency	Working Knowledge	Advanced
Understanding				
Speaking				
Reading				
Writing				

Sequence (start with best language):
   (1)
   (2)
   (3)
   (4)
   (5)

Overall proficiency in . . .

(11) Are you satisfied with your achievement in . . . (the different languages)
or would you like to know more?

   Satisfied: *More:*   *Other:*

   Language: Language:

(12) Some people say they have a gift for languages, others say they haven't.
Would you regard yourself as *strong* or *weak* in languages?

   Strong: *Weak:*   *Medium:*

   (1) Do you think that you have a good ear for languages?

   Yes   No   *Other:*

   (2) Do you have a good memory?

   Yes   No   *Other:*

   (3) Do you like to take the language apart and analyze it?

   Yes   No

   (Do you like to figure out the language on your own or would you
   rather have the teacher tell you rules, etc.)

(13) *If applicable:*

Considering your level in (your success/failure in learning . . .), would you say this was due to the *teacher/s* (thanks to the . . ./ the teacher's fault.

the *teacher*

or did it have something to do with the *school or the environment*

or would you say that you developed some special *study habits*

or that you may have *some particular personal characteristics* that helped/hindered you in learning . . .

Part II

I would now like to ask you a few more specific questions concerning language learning. Some of the questions may not apply to you. Don't feel obliged to answer.

I.   Imagine that you had the opportunity and time to learn another language now. What would you be inclined to say at the thought of learning a new language?

(1) I hate the thought of it.   1

(2) It scares me.   2

(3) I don't mind doing it.   3

(4) I would look forward to doing it.   4

(5) I am very excited at the idea of it.   5

If answer (1):

If you had to do it nevertheless, which language would you choose?

For what reasons would you choose . . . ?

What would you expect to get out of it in the long run?

Subquestions:

Would your final goal be to . . .

Speak and understand the spoken language?

Read and write the language?

Speak, understand and read?

Speak, understand, read and write?

Other:

II.   Let's now consider how you would actually go about learning . . .

      What would you like to do *first* of all?

      (1) Travel to the country and simply immerse yourself in the
           language?   1
      (2) Travel to the country and take a language course there?   2
      (3) Buy a course and study by yourself? What kind of course?   3
      (4) Go to a teacher or a language school for private lessons?   4
      (5) Join a language class?   5
      (6) A combination of these? Specify: 6
      (7) Other: 7

      Can you suggest a reason for your choice?

II.1. If time were no consideration, would you prefer to learn the language
       in a concentrated effort (e.g. an intensive course for 4 weeks)?

       or gradually (e.g. 2 hours a week + homework) over a longer period
       of time?

       Intensive:

       Gradually:

       Combination:

III.   Some people think that learning a language is different at the elemen-
       tary, intermediate and advanced stages.

       Would you agree or disagree with this? And could you tell me why?

III.1. Beginning now with the *early* stages of language learning, what would
       you *mainly* like to do at that level?

       I'll give you some examples. Please tell me which of these you regard
       as *most* important. But feel free to disregard them or add your own
       ideas.

       (1) I'd mainly like to learn to *understand the spoken language.*   1
       (2) I'd mainly like to learn to *read.*   2
       (3) I'd mainly like to learn the *pronunciation.*   3
       (4) I'd mainly like to learn simple *conversational phrases.*   4
       (5) I'd mainly like to learn how to *write* the languages.   5
       (6) I'd mainly like to get an overview of the *grammar.*   6
       (7) I'd mainly like to learn about the *cultural background.*   7
       (8) I would like a combination of these. Could you please
            specify?   8
       (9) Other: 9

III.2. At the elementary stages would you prefer to be *firmly guided* by the teacher or a course,

or would you rather be left to your own devices and learn the language in your own way?

(By 'firm guidance' I mean, for example, doing language drills with the teacher or following a text-book and doing prescribed grammar exercises regularly.

In contrast to that you might prefer to work mainly on your own, at your own speed, selecting your own learning material, etc.)

Guided: *Own devices:*   *Combination:*

IV. Some of the ways of learning a language seem to involve you as a learner more *actively* (for example, in some cases you are made to speak right from the start).

Others allow you to be more *passive* (for example, you just listen to the teacher or you read widely).

Generally speaking, would you prefer to be relatively passive or rather active in the early stages of language learning?

Active: *Passive:*

V. You have mentioned what you would like to learn at the early stages of language learning. Can you think of anything you would particularly like to learn or emphasize at an intermediate or advanced level?

Intermediate: *Advanced:*

VI. Some people say that you *cannot* make a conscious effort in learning a foreign language. They hate to study grammar; they say you must simply allow the language to sink in gradually.

Others argue that language learning is a *conscious and systematic* process. You set about it by studying, practising, by constantly asking for explanations and rules. In short, by actively thinking about it.

Which of these ideas would more represent yuour point of view?

Unconscious: *Conscious:*

VII. Some people find that in learning a new language you must completely forget your native language. Others say you cannot and should not. To what extent do you find that comparing your native language with the foreign language helps you in learning a new language?

(1) To what extent do you find translations useful?

(2) Would you prefer to use a bilingual dictionary or rather a dictionary that offers explanations in the foreign language?

VIII. Do you feel that one can actually learn to *think* in the foreign language?

Yes: *No:*

(1) If yes: How do you think one might achieve that?

(2) How important do you think it is?

Very: *Not so much:*

IX. If you have learned a third or fourth language, to what extent did you find that your learning was influenced by your previous language learning experience?

(Interviewer: Wait for reaction and then summarize)

In general, would you say that knowing another foreign language helped you or hindered you in learning a new language?

Helped: *Hindered:*

X. So far, we have talked about what you'd like to learn, how you would go about doing it and how your native language might influence your learning other languages.

Considering all this, would you say that you have developed any language study habits (gimmicks, tricks, ways, techniques) that you would find useful in learning the new language?

(1) in learning the *sound system*
e.g. reading aloud to yourself (in front of a mirror), repeating words silently to yourself after the teacher, etc.

(2) in learning the *grammar*
e.g. memorizing rules through humorous rhymes, etc. forming, hunches about regularities and rules and then applying them etc.

(3) in learning *vocabulary*/words
e.g. by repetition, by finding relations between words, writing down words, etc.

(4) in developing *listening comprehension*
e.g. by listening to records, to the radio, etc.

(5) in learning to *talk*
e.g. through contact with native speakers, by insisting on constant correction or by imagining dialogues in your mind or by talking to yourself, etc.

(6) in learning to *read*
   e.g. by reading popular magazines or books on your own

(7) in learning how to express yourself in *written form*
   e.g. by writing to pen-pal

XI. My final question now concerns your *feelings* about your language learning experience.

Many language learners feel very negative about their learning experiences.

(1) They say they feel
   (a) discouraged
   (b) frustrated
   (c) impatient
   or (d) confused by the difficulties of the language learning task.

Have you experienced any of these feelings?

Could you tell me more about your feeling of . . . ?

(2) Other language learners say that the new language feels (e) absurd to them, and that they feel (f) ridiculous expressing themselves in the foreign language.

Did you ever feel that way?

(3) Some people feel very (g) inhibited and (h) helpless when they actually *use* the language.

Is this experience familiar to you? Could you elaborate?

In general, as (if) you shared (some of) these feelings, what did you do to overcome them?

(Interviewer: This question could be asked after each particular experience, if appropriate.)

Bibliography

Bailey, N., Madden, C. and Krashen, S. Is there a 'natural sequence' in second language learning? *Language Learning*, 1974, 24, 235–243.

Brown, H. D. Affective variables in second language acquisition, *Language Learning*, 1973, 23, 231–244.

Brown, H. D. (ed.) Papers in Second Language Acquisition. Ann Arbor, Michigan: Special issue of *Language Learning*, 4, 1976.

Budner, S. Intolerance of ambiguity as a personality variable. *Journal of Personality*, 1962, 39, 29–50.

Buhler, R. A. *Computing System for File Manipulation and Statistical Analysis of Social Science Data.* Princeton, N.J.: Princeton University, 1971.

Burstall, C., Jamieson, M., Cohen, S. and Hargreaves, M. *Primary French in the Balance.* Slough, Bucks.: National Foundation for Educational Research, 1970.

Carroll, J. B. Research problems concerning the teaching of foreign or second languages to younger children. In H. H. Stern, *Foreign Languages in Primary Education.* London: Oxford University Press, 1967, 94–109.

Carroll J. B. *The Teaching of French as a Foreign Language in Eight Countries.* New York: John Wiley, 1975.

Carroll, J. B. and Sapon, S. M. *Modern Language Aptitude Test (MLAT).* New York: The Psychological Corporation, 1959.

Carroll, J. B. and Sapon, S. M. *Modern Language Aptitude Test-Elementary* (EMLAT). New York: The Psychological Corporation, 1967.

Clark, J. L. D. *Foreign Language Testing: Theory and Practice.* Philadelphia: Center for Curriculum Development Inc., 1972.

Corder, S. P. The significance of learners' errors. *International Review of Applied Linguistics*, 1967, 5, 161–170.

De Fazio, V. Field articulation differences in language abilities. *Journal of Personal and Social Psychology*, 1973, 25, 351–356.

Dulay, H. and Burt, M. Natural sequence in child second language acquisition. *Language Learning*, 1974, 24, 137–153.

Dyer, F. N. The Stroop phenomenon and its use in the study of perceptual, cognitive and response processes. *Memory and Cognition*, 1973, 1, 106–120.

Eysenck, H. J. and Eysenck, S. B. *Manual for the Eysenck Personality Inventory.* Educational and Industrial Testing Service, San Diego, 1963.

Fröhlich, M. Case studies of second language learning. Unpublished M.A. thesis, University of Toronto, 1976.

Gardner, R. C. and Smythe, P. C. Motivation and second language acquisition. *Canadian Modern Language Review*, 1975a, 31, 218–234.

Gardner, R. C. and Smythe, P. C. *Language Research Group National Test Battery, Form A.* London: University of Western Ontario, 1975.

Gardner, R. C. Motivational variables in second language learning. In G. Taggart (ed.) *Attitude and Aptitude in Second Language Learning.* Proceedings of Fifth Symposium, Toronto: Canadian Association of Applied Linguistics, 1975.

Gardner, R. C. and Smythe, P. C. *Language Research Group National Test Battery, Form A.* London: University of Western Ontario, 1975.

Goodman, D. R. Cognitive style factors in linguistic performance with ambiguous sentences. Unpublished master's thesis, York University, 1971.

Gudschivsky, S. C. *How to Learn an Unwritten Language.* New York: Holt, Rinehart and Winston, 1967.

Guiroa, A. Z., Brannon, R. C. L. and Dull, C. Y. Empathy and second language learning. *Language Learning,* 1972, 22, 111–130.

Hakuta, K. Prefabricated patterns and the emergence of structure in second language acquisition. *Language Learning,* 1974, 24, 287–297.

Hatch, E. and Wagner-Gough, Z. Explaining sequence and variation in second language acquisition. *Language Learning,* special issue, 1976, 4, 39–57.

Hidden Figures Test-V. Princeton: Educational Testing Service, 1962.

Hogan, R. Development of an empathy scale. *Journal of Consulting and Clinical Psychology,* 1969, 33, 307–316.

Hosenfeld, C. Learning about learning: Discovering our students' strategies. *Foreign Language Annals,* 9, 117–129.

Jackson, D. N., Messick, S. and Myers, C. T. Evaluation of group and individual forms of the embedded figures measure of field independence. *Educational and Psychological Measurement,* 1964, 24, 177–192.

Jacobovits, L. A. *Foreign Language Learning: A Psycholinguistic Analysis of the Issues.* Rowley, Mass.: Newbury House, 1970.

Jensen, A. R. and Rohwer, W. D. The Stroop color-word test: A review. *Acta Psychologica,* 1966, 25, 36–93.

Krashen, S. D. Formal and informal linguistic environments in language acquisition and language learning. *TESOL Quarterly,* 1976, 10, 157–168.

Krashen, S. D. and Seliger, H. W. The essential contribution of formal instruction in adult second language learning. *TESOL Quarterly,* 1975, 9 (2), 173–183.

Larson, D. N. and Smalley, W. A. *Becoming Bilingual – A Guide to Language Learning.* New Canaan, Conn.: Practical Anthropology, 1972.

Macnamara, J. How can we measure the extent of a person's bilingual proficiency? In L. G. Kelly (ed.) *Description and Measurement of Bilingualism: An International Seminar.* Toronto: University of Toronto Press, 1969, 80–119.

Macnamara, J. Nurseries, streets and classrooms: Some comparisons and deductions. *Modern Language Journal,* 1973, 57, 250–254.

Mehrabian, A. The development and validation of measures of affiliative tendency and sensitivity to rejection. *Educational and Psychological Measurement,* 1970, 30, 417–428.

Messick, S., and Fritzky, F. J. Dimensions of analytic attitude in cognition and personality. *Journal of Personality,* 1963, 31, 346–370.

Naiman, N. The use of elicited imitation in second language acquisition research. *Working Papers on Bilingualism,* 1974, 2, 1–37.

Nida, E. A. *Learning a Foreign Language: A Handbook Prepared Especially for Missionaries.* New York: Friendship Press, Council of the Churches of Christ, 1957.

Oller, J. W. and Richards, J. C. (eds) *Focus on the Learner: Pragmatic Perspectives for the Language Teacher.* Rowley, Mass.: Newbury House, 1973.

Ministry of Education, Ontario. *Report of the Ministerial Committee on the Teaching of French.* Toronto: University of Education, Ontario, 1974. (The Gillin Report).

Pettigrew, T. F. The measurement and correlates of category width as a cognitive variable. *Journal of Personality,* 1958, 26, 532–544.

Pimsleur, P. *Pimsleur Language Aptitude Battery.* New York: Harcourt, Brace and World Inc., 1966.

Pimsleur, P., Sundland, D. and McIntyre, R. *Underachievement in Foreign Language Learning.* New York: MLA Materials Center, 1966.

Pritchard, D. F. An investigation into the relationship of personality traits and ability in modern languages. *British Journal of Educational Psychology,* 1952, 22, 157–158.

Reibel, D. A. Language learning strategies for the adult. In P. Pimsleur and T. Quinn (eds) *Psychology of Second Language Learning.* Cambridge, Mass.: Cambridge University Press, 1971, 87–96.

Richards, J. C. (ed.) *Error Analysis: Perspectives on Second Language Acquisition.* London: Longman, 1974.

Rosenthal, R., and Jakobson, L. *Pygmalion in the Classroom: Teacher Expectation and Pupils' Intellectual Development.* New York: Holt, Rinehart and Winston, 1968.

Rubin, J. What the 'good language learner' can teach us. *TESOL Quarterly,* 1975, 9, 41–51.

Sampson, G. P., and Richards, J. C. Learner language systems. *Language Sciences,* 1973, 26, 18–25.

Schumann, J. H. Affective factors and the problem of age in second language acquisition. *Language Learning,* 1975, 25, 209–236.

Schumann, J. H. Second language acquisition research: Getting a more global look at the learner. *Language Learning,* special issue, 1976, 4, 15–28.

Selinker, L. Interlanguage. *International Review of Applied Linguistics,* 1972, 10, 209–231.

Selinker, L. Swain, M. and Dumas, G. The interlanguage hypothesis extended to children. *Language Learning,* 1975, 25, 139–152.

Stern, H. H. *Perspectives on Second Language Teaching.* Toronto: Ontario Institute for Studies in Education, 1970.

Stern, H. H. Psycholinguistics and second language teaching. In J. W. Oller Jr. and J. C. Richards (eds) *Focus on the Learner: Pragmatic Perspectives for the Language Teacher.* Rowley, Mass.: Newbury House, 1973, 16–28.

Stern. H. H. What can we learn from the good language learner? *Canadian Modern Language Review,* 1975, 31, 304–318.
Paper was later slightly revised and published in the *Canadian Modern Language Review,* 1975, 31, 304–318.

Stern, H. H. Optimal age: Myth or reality? *Canadian Modern Language Review,* 1976, 32 (3), 283–294.

Stern, H. H. Swian, M., McLean, L. D., Friedman, R. J. Harley, B. and Lapkin, S. *Three Approaches to Teaching French.* Toronto: Ministry of Education, Ontario, 1976.

Stern, H. H. and Weinrib, A., Foreign languages for younger children: Trends and assessment. *Language Teaching and Linguistics: Abstracts,* 1977, 10, 5–25.

Swain, M. French immersion programs across Canada. *Canadian Modern Language Review,* 1974, 31, 304–318.

Swain, M. Dumas, G. and Naiman, N. Alternatives to spontaneous speech: Elicted translation and imitation as indicators of second language competence. *Working Papers on Bilingualism,* 1974, 3, 68–79.

Swain, M. Changes in errors: Random or systematic. *Proceedings of the Fourth International Congress of Applied Linguistics.* Vol. 2. Stuttgart: Hochschulverlag, 1976.

Van Ek, J. A. *The Threshold Level in a European Unit/Credit System for Modern Language Learning by Adults.* Strasbourg: Council of Europe, 1975.

Wesche, M. B. The good adult language learner: A study of learning strategies and personality factors in an intensive course. Unpublished doctoral dissertation, University of Toronto, 1975.

White, B. W. Visual and auditory closure. *Journal of Experimental Psychology,* 1954, 48, 234–240.

Wilkins, D. A. *An Investigation into the Linguistic and Situational Content of the Common Core in a Unit/Credit System.* Strasbourg: Council of Europe, 1972.

Witkin, H. A., Dyk, R., Faterson, H. F., Goodenough, D. R. and Karp, S. A. *Psychological Differentiation.* New York: John Wiley and Sons, 1962.

Witkin, H. A., Oltman, Philip K., Raskin, E. and Karp, S. A. *A Manual for the Embedded Figures Tests.* Palo Alto, California: Consulting Psychologists Press, 1971.